Colonial and Postcolonial LITERATURE

Discourses, Disruptions and Intersections

Colonial and Postcolonial LITERATURE

Discourses, Disruptions and Intersections

Editor
Joydev Maity

AUTHORSPRESS

Worldwide Circulation through Authorspress Global Network
First Published in 2021
by
Authorspress
Q-2A Hauz Khas Enclave, New Delhi-110 016 (India)
Phone: (0) 9818049852
E-mail: authorspressgroup@gmail.com
Website: www.authorspressbooks.com

Colonial and Postcolonial Literature:
Discourses, Disruptions and Intersections
ISBN 978-93-90891-83-2

Printed in India at Thomson Press (India) Limited

Preface: Post-Intersectional-Coloniality

Listen ye all, let me tell you a story. It is a story about six blind men and an elephant. One day six blind men went to an elephant. The first man approached the "broad and sturdy side" of the elephant and touched it. After touching it, he felt that the elephant is like a wall. The second man approached and touched the tusk of the elephant. After touching it, he felt like he is touching a spear. The third approached the elephant and touched its trunk. After touching its trunk, he felt that the elephant is like a snake. The fourth approached the elephant, touched its foot and felt that the animal is like a tree. The fifth touched the ear and believed that the elephant is like a fan. The sixth touched the tail of the elephant and concluded that the elephant is like a rope (Interculture TV, 2017). In this way, each and every man analysed and interpreted the elephant in their respective manner and all of them were right in their own way. Their interpretations vary because they have perceived the elephant from six different perceptions.

This anecdote argues that our ways of perceiving the world depends on "*who* we are and *from where* we speak" (Dussel 16). In other words, while producing knowledges, it is important for us to acknowledge each other's social, cultural racial, political, economic, geographical and topographical positionalities. But, the "imaginary of the modern/colonial world-system" (Grosfoguel 203) has been treating the planet as a massive laboratory for performing different forms of epistemological and ontolgical experiments, through sterilising the existential diversity of the indigenous communities, through strategically imprisoning them within the binaries of superior/inferior, good/bad, high/low, authentic/inauthentic, human/inhuman, etc., and through establishing a "God's eye" (Moya 80) view of the world. This edited volume titled *Colonial and Postcolonial Literature: Discourses, Disruptions and Intersections*, makes an effort to interrogate the god's eye view of knowledge and propose an "interpretative horizon" of knowledge systems (Alcoff 45). According to Linda Alcoff, interpretative horizon is a "substantive perspectival location from which the interpreter looks out at the world, a perspective that is always present but that is open and dynamic, with a temporal as well as physical dimension, moving into the future and into new spaces as the subject moves" (Alcoff 53).

In a similar manner, this edited volume makes a commendable effort to establish diverse, open and dynamic perspectives by engaging with themes like epistemicides and linguicides as seen in the chapter "The Loss of Native Language" by Fedya Daas; the loss of individual and collective identity in the chapter "Postcolonial Caribbean Rootlessness and Identity Quandary" by Bame Tomnyuy; the experiences of insecurity, guilt and fear of the European colonisers as portrayed from a psychoanalytical dimension in the chapter "Guilt and Fear in Anglo-Indian Tales" by Abhijit Maity; the "colonial/modern gender system" (Lugones 188) as observed in the chapter "A Postcolonial Feminist Critique" by Rafraf Shakil and Mehak Fayaz; the issues of sexual subjugation and gendered dehumanisation in "The Predicament of the 'White Cockroach'" by Animesh Biswas; the condition of women in Bengal by Angana Bose; the tensions of diasporic identity and caste hierarchies in postcolonial India in "Disseminating Diasporic Discourse" by Kalyan Pattanayak; the challenges of reviving 'storytelling' as a methodological tool to dismantle the universalised systems of colonial knowledge production in "Representing the Oppression of Indigenous Women through Storytelling" by Mohonlal; the objectification of women as 'apt marriage materials' and patriarchal adjectivisation of women as good/bad, descent /indecent, cultured/uncultured, etc. in "Modern need for Reinforcing Identities" by P.K. Smitha; the different forms of socio-cultural confusions and identity crisis that are triggered by the experiences of migration and racism in "Assessing the Issues of Migration, Racism and Cultural Bereavement" by Shraddha Dhal; the authentication, systematisation and internalisation of "Euro-North American-centered world view" (Ndlovu 84) by physiologically traumatising the colonised and pushing them into a chaotic state of epistemological and ontological impotency in "The Need for Decolonising Trauma" by Abhilasha Phukan; communal and gendered violence during the partition of India in the "Depiction of Wounded Women in Partition Stories" by Shivani Sharma; the colonially reconfigured violence of the caste system in postcolonial India in "Causes and Fallouts of Caste System" by Jalendra Phukan; the traditional patriarchal subjugation of women in 19th century Bengal and the interventions of the European colonisers (mostly British, Scottish and Irish) to empower the women in resisting traditional patriarchy in the chapter "A Journey from Ignorance to Knowledge" by Manik Mondol; the transition of the "color line" (Du Bois 71) of racism into the "epistemic line" (Ndlovu-Gatsheni, 2018: 17) racism in the form of caste-based hierarchies as portrayed by Amitav Das in the chapter "Quest for Identity Assurance"; the influence of the colonial heteronormative narratives in sketching magical characters and shaping events of wizardry in "Re-reading J.K. Rowling's *Harry Potter*" by Giangthuiliu Gonmei; the semiotics of racism in the chapter "Krishna, the Shyamsundar" by Priya Samni; the 'benevolent coloniser' and the 'noble savage' in *Robinson Crusoe* by Shreyosee Chattopadhyay; subalternity and post-subalternity in the chapters "Postcolonial Literature and Subaltern Cultural Context" by J.S. Anantha and "The Subaltern in Sara Suleri's *Meatless Days*" by Nilim Mohan;

the hidden undertones of European white-centric racism through fetishism towards fair skins as argued by Manisha Mishra in the chapter "Postcolonial Hangover"; the pain of physical agonies as unleashed by the invisible forces of colonialism/capitalism in the postcolonial era in the chapter "No World is Without Pain" by Amandeep Rana; the "orientalist gaze" (Said cited in Steenhuisen, 2013) of the European colonisers towards the colonised in "Tintin in Nepal" by Manidip Chakraborty; linguistic otherisation in "Postcolonial African Literature and Writing in the Language of Other" by Yacine Belguendouz; the ways in which individual identities are "signposted in everyday environment" (Steyn, Tsekwa and McEwen 269) and pushed within inactive and suffocating existential spaces through "cartographical, "landscaped" (ibid. 267) languages as elaborated by Mouna Benhaddou in "Investigating Issues of Identity Politics and Space Negotiation"; the reading of histories and shaping historiographies from the margins (Chakraborty, 2000) in "An English Bahujan Colonial Narrative" by Manashi Singh; the reconfigurations and expansion of the already existing caste-based hierarchies of precolonial India during the European colonial era in Mridul C Mrinal's "Presentation of Caste in Colonial Narratives"; and the epistemological and ontological "infertility" (Canclini 110) of hybridity in "Hybridity in Colonial India" by Swagata Bhattacharya.

Through a wide range of themes, this vast collection of chapters shows how the physically visible colonial empires have systemically and epistemically metamorphosed into invisible empires. In an interview with Duncan Omanga, Sabelo J. Ndlovu-Gatsheni observes: "If you remove colonialism physically without epistemically, it will not disappear" (2020). Through invading the tenets of the metaphysical colonial empire, the diverse arguments in the chapters make a consistent effort to interrogate the "Europeanisation of the world" (Headley 55). The process of planetary Europeanisation has been possible through "racialisation of human population, enslavement and colonisation" (Ndlovu-Gatsheni, 2014: 184). The process continues into the contemporary era as the deeply embedded existential ideologies of European colonisation are consistently pipelined into our habitual lifestyles in the forms of body languages, verbal expressions, food habits, fashion, linguistic engagements, etc. Therefore, it is necessary to move beyond the colonially structured dichotomy of colonial/postcolonial and analyse the invisible empires of coloniality within a complex and uncategorised space of 'post-(intersectionalising) coloniality'. The phenomenon of 'post-intersectional-coloniality' is a habitual dehierarchical exercise of "epistemic awakening" (Wiredu 81) that invites individuals and communities to address the challenges of colonial/Eurocentric apparitions of knowledge production in the contemporary era, by venturing beyond the restricted compartments of academic disciplines and pushing into the intersectional spaces of everyday life.

To elaborate further, usually, within the academic institutions the notions of coloniality and postcoloniality are addressed in a very limited manner and the 'right to address' remains in the hands of the socially, economically, politically, racially, culturally, geographically and topographically privileged sections of the society, whose habitual thoughts and actions are widely steered by the colonial/Eurocentric apparitions of existence. The phenomenological exercise of 'post-intersectional-coloniality', on the one side, disrupts, de-borderises and de-institutionalises such hierarchical and compartmentalised spaces of thinking and doing, and on the other side, irrespective of one's social, political, cultural, economical, racial, geographical, topographical and gendered affiliations, opens up gateways and invites individuals, to collaborate, co-create and revive intersectional spaces of "Indigenous 'decolonial knowledge-making'" (Nakata et.al. 130). Within the phenomenon of 'post-intersectional-coloniality', the collaborative and co-creative exercises of indigenous decolonial knowledge-making are underlined with the practice of what Melissa Steyn identifies as "critical diversity literacy" (379). According to Steyn, critical diversity literacy understands "human reality as a multilayered and multiperspectival, shifting, ambivalent and open to yet unknown possibilities" (380). The various textual and contextual themes that have been discussed by the authors in this edited volume invite the readers to engage with two major aspects of critical diversity literacy. They are:

a) *Social Literacy:* The practice of social literacy generates awareness about the emerging social imaginaries of the 21st century (Steyn 380) like media, information, health, science, emotional experiences and more. Though the different social, cultural, racial, geographical, topographical and gendered aspects, as elaborated in this volume, are set in different zones of space and time, yet it will allow the readers to actively participate in the readings with respect to their individual and collective socio-cultural awareness. Hopefully, the readers will be able to curate non-linear, de-hierarchical, and diverse spaces of understandings by interpreting the chapters from their respective contexts. As one will read through these short essay-styled chapters, one will be able to understand that they deviate from the usual patterns of heavily impregnated theoretically jargonised writings, and engage with various forms of experiential socio-cultural narratives that are diversely relatable in the contemporary era.

b) *Critical Literacy:* The practice of critical literacy motivates the individuals to analyse and interpret the habitual existential experiences through "embracing" and "celebrating" (Steyn 380) differences. It is crucial to acknowledge differences because "[d]ifferences of all sorts, including cultural differences (as long as the culture have money and can consume) are celebrated since they simply allow communities of practice to be infused with diverse knowledge and skills..." (Gee 184). The spontaneous storytelling manner of the chapters in this edited volume, will allow the readers to avoid the trap of pre-conceived, half-baked, 'blind-eyed' and superficial interpretations of knowledge's, and nurture a 'critical eye' towards each and every aspect of habitual existence.

Prior to accepting or rejecting any form of ideology, it is necessary to interrogate each and every premise of knowledge production. The 'act of questioning' should not be owned by certain socially, culturally and racially privileged classes of people; should not be glorified as a special individual and/or collective attribute; and should not be a monopoly of the institutional spaces like classrooms and meeting rooms any more. Rather, as argued by the chapters in this volume, it should be firmly embedded as a usual practice in everyday life.

Overall, Joydev Maity's edited volume, *Colonial and Postcolonial Literature: Discourses, Disruptions and Intersections*, approaches the commonly addressed phenomena of colonialism and postcolonialism in a unique, multidimensional and intersectional manner. Altogether, this volume not only makes an effort to systemically, epistemically and ontologically invade and bulldoze the still existing complexes of colonial (visible and invisible) narratives, but also makes an effort to build a "multiplex world" (Acharya, 2014), where diverse constellations of knowledge systems exist and evolve in a de-hierarchical, deterritorialised and intersectional fashion.

Works Cited

"Reflexivity in Perception." YouTube. Uploaded by Interculture TV, 9 Feb. 2017, https://www.youtube.com/watch?v=VcHT10xICKg.

Acharya, Amitav. "From the Unipolar Moment to a Multiplex World." *YaleGlobal Online*. MacMillan Center. 3 Jul. 2014. Web. 13 Apr. 2021. https://yaleglobal.yale.edu/content/unipolar-moment-multiplex-world.

Alcoff, Linda Martin. *Visible Identities: Race, Gender, and the Self.* New York: Oxford University Press, 2005. Print.

Canclini, Nestor Garcia. *Hybrid Cultures: Strategies for Entering and Leaving Modernity.* Minneapolis: University of Minnesota Press, 1995. Print.

Chakraborty, Dipesh. *Provincialising Europe: Postcolonial Thought and Historical Difference.* Princeton: Princeton University Press, 2000. Print.

Du Bois, William E.B. *The Souls of Black Folk.* New York: Dover Publications, 1903. Print.

Dussel, Enrique. "From Critical Theory to the Philosophy of Liberation: Some Themes for Dialogue." *Transmodernity* 1.2 (2011): 16-43. Print.

Gee, James. "The New Literacy Studies: From "Socially Situated" to Work of the Social." *Situated Literacies: Theorising Reading and Writing in Context*. Ed. David Barton. London & New York: Routledge, 2005. 177-193. Print.

Grosfoguel, Ramon. "Colonial Difference, Geopolitics of Knowledge, and Global Coloniality in the Modern/Colonial Capitalist World System." *Review* 25.2 (2002): 203-224. Print.

Headley, John M. *The Europeanisation of the World: On the Origins of Human Rights and Democracy*. Princeton: Princeton University Press, 2008. Print.

Lugones, Maria. *Pilgrimages/Peregrinajes: Theorising Coalition against Multiple Oppressions.* Lanham, Maryland: Rowman and Littlefield, 2003. Print.

Moya, Paula M.L. "Who We Are and From Where We Speak." *Transmodernity* 1.2 (2011): 79-84. Print.

Nakata, Martin N., Victoria Nakata, Sarah Keech and Reuben Bolt. "Decolonial goals and pedagogies for Indigenous studies." *Decolonisation: Indigeneity, Education & Society* 1.1. (2012): 120-140.

Ndlovu, Morgan. "Why Indigenous Knowledges in the 21st Century? A Decolonial Turn." *Yesterday & Today* 11 (2014): 84-98. Print.

Ndlovu-Gatsheni, Sabelo J. "Decolonisation, Decoloniality and the Future of African Studies: A Conversation with Dr. Sabelo J. Ndlovu-Gatsheni." *Items: Insights from the Social Sciences* 14 Jan. 2020. Web. 13 Apr. 2021. https://items.ssrc.org/from-our-programs/decolonization-decoloniality-and-the-future-of-african-studies-a-conversation-with-dr-sabelo-ndlovu-gatsheni/.

Ndlovu-Gatsheni, Sabelo J. "Global Coloniality and the Challenges of Creating African Futures." *Strategic Review for Southern Africa* 36.2 (2014): 181-202. Print.

Ndlovu-Gatsheni, Sabelo J. "The Dynamics of Epistemological Decolonisation and in the 21st Century: Towards Epistemic Freedom." *Strategic Review for Southern Africa* 40.1 (2018): 16-45. Print.

Said, Edward. "The Orientalist Gaze: A Conversation with Edward Said and With Myself." *Steenhuisen's Musings* 21 Oct. 2013. Web. 13 Apr. 2021. https://blogs. commons. georgetown.edu/steenhul/2013/10/21/the-orientalist-gaze-a-conversation-with-edward-said-and-with-myself/.

Steyn, Melissa, Jennie Tsekwa and Haley McEwen. ""Whole Masses of unchartered territory": Metaphors, Internal Spatiality, and Racialised Relationships in Post-Apartheid South Africa." *Critical Philosophy and Race* 5.2 (2017): 267-295. Print.

Steyn, Melissa. "Critical diversity literacy: Essentials for the twenty-first century." *Routledge International Handbook of Diversity Studies*. Ed. Steven Vertovec. London & New York: Routledge, 2014. 379-389. Print.

Wiredu, Kwasi. *Conceptual decolonisation in African philosophy: Four essays*. Ibadan: Hope Publications, 1995. Print.

Date: 13-04-2021

Dr. Sayan Dey
Postdoctoral Fellow
Wits Centre for Diversity Studies
University of Witwatersrand

Introduction

To understand colonial and postcolonial literature, we must get a glimpse of the terms colonialism and postcolonialism first. The process of colonialism suggests colonizing a country, to rule and dominate over a country by another country from every aspect like political, social, cultural or religious. The prefix 'post' in postcolonialsim implies the end of a process, hence, the end of the colonialism in this regard. Keeping such concept in mind, colonial literature can be described as literature written during the colonial period, usually by the colonisers. Postcolonial literature, on the other hand, can be described as literature written after the colonial period, usually written by the writers from colonised country. However, the time frame of colonialism and postcolonialsim is often unintelligible, and such process also varies from country to country. So it will be wise to judge any literary work as colonial or postcolonial by its approach and themes, rather than by any time frame.

Colonial literature generally approves the process of colonisation and depicts it in a way that as if the process is for the amelioration of the colonised. Postcolonial literature, on the other hand, exposes the trauma and absurdity of this vile process. A foremost colonial work like Joseph Conrad's *Heart of Darkness* portrays Africa as a dark continent and its people as savage and even cannibals. Such depiction was highly criticised by the African Chinua Achebe in his ground breaking postcolonial work *Things Fall Apart*. Most of the literary works, dealing with colonial themes, like the colonisation process itself, are based on some stereotypes, some assumption regarding the colonised countries and their people. Stereotypes like the people of East are inferior and they need the control of the West are very much common in most of the colonial works. The famous postcolonial critic Edward Said takes a dig at such stereotypes in his epoch-making work *Orientalism*, published in 1978. Spivak's *Can the Subaltern Speak* is also an important contribution in this aspect.

With the passage of time, interpretation of colonial and postcolonial literature has gained a unique status, so also their composition. Thus, it is interesting to note that even Shakespeare's *Othello* or *Antony and Cleopatra* are being interpreted from colonial and postcolonial point of view, although there were no such concept of colonialism and postcolonialism at the time of their composition. This book, *Colonial and Postcolonial Literature: Discourses, Disruptions and Intersections*, which is a collection of scholarly articles on such literary works, brings a unique and revolutionary interpretation of some famous works of these fields. Besides interpreting major works of colonial and postcolonial fields, the book also scrutinises the contexts under which such literatures were composed. Although readers have never lost their interests in colonial and postcolonial literature, this book, I believe, will invite them to fall in love with such literary works in a new way.

April, 2021
Purba Medinipur (W.B.), India

Joydev Maity
joydevmaity1993@gmail.com

Contents

1

Asylum, USA: Assessing the Issues of Migration, Racism, Cultural Bereavement & Identity Reconfiguration

Shraddha Dhal

The term 'Postcolonial' is used for a historical phase that corresponds to the aftermath of European colonisation. The period is witness to the effects of colonialism on languages, cultures and communities in the post-independence era. The ineradicable mark of the European colonisation on the contemporary world has not only resulted in a process of unification as well as diversification but also has caused the most controversial global concerns like economic instability, ethnic rivalries, cultural violation, migration and dislocation, expatriation and hybrid nations formation along with cross culturalism and ethnic inclusiveness. This sets a question of 'identity' as one of its prime deliberations. The people belonging to the pro colonised paradigm quander in the hunt for a consolidated 'identity' while in the process of doing so find themselves consumed by insecurity and self-doubt. This concern of postcolonial dimension of the quest for identity has been widely addressed by one of the leading Indian Parsi writers in English, Boman Desai in *Asylum, USA*. The present paper endeavors to illustrate how migration and cultural conflicts impacts the immigrants' sense of insecurity which alters their distinctive identity by leaving a permanent deep subterranean chasm in their lives and their persistent efforts to bridge up this gap of identity with reference to the Parsi community in *Asylum, USA*.

Boman Desai, who is born and grew up in Mumbai, is an Indian expatriate himself as he shuttles back and forth between two major cities of the world and their reflections – Bombay and Chicago. His writings are mostly evocative of some predictability in terms of approach, certain consistency in form of narratives, technique, and choice of subject matters – reminiscence of the past, migration, nostalgia, transculturalism, longingness for identity, alienation, and the theme of marriage – all of which mostly revolve around the Parsi Zoroastrian community. He is certainly more inclined towards emphatically affirming his 'Parsiness' through his works. Desai has the powerful skill to blend his memories of India and that of his community with its transitional reality in the novels written by him. His writings are reflective of his erudition, knowledge of art, trendy feminism, and most significantly they are symbolic of a spellbinding self portrait of Desai himself. Stuck between the Indian and American cultures, he finds himself neither belonging to any of the places. In an interview, Desai admits: "No, I do feel a bit out of place. My Hindi is rusty, I can't stand the heat. So I try and schedule my visit when it's not too hot. But I don't feel completely at home in the United States either, being an Indian in America sets you apart, even after many years" (Chaudhury, Shoma. "In Gratitude"). His experience of dual identities often makes him "a flicker here a flicker there". The constant cultural conflicts that he experiences along with his migration make him what Rushdie terms as a "translated man" who has to "deal in broken mirrors, some of whose fragments have been irretrievably lost" (Rushdie 11). Hence, Desai's alienation which is triggered by his dislocation and cultural hybridity propels him to create narratives carrying an innate sense of reality. Homi Bhaba in his essay "The Postcolonial and the Postmodern: The Question of Agency" states:

> Culture becomes as much an uncomfortable, disturbing practice of survival and supplementarity – between art and politics, past and present, the public and the private – as its resplendent being is a moment of pleasure, enlightenment or liberation. It is from such narrative positions that the postcolonial prerogative seeks to affirm and extend a new collaborative dimension, both within the margins of the nation-space and across boundaries between nations and peoples. (Bhabha 193)

The hallmark of Desai's writings is the depiction of his dual experience of migration that discovers the interactions in the Parsi community in India's disturbed historical milieu, validating the local and embracing the syncretic nature of Post-colonial experiences. They explore the relationships among self, place and identity revolving around his community. The very conspicuous postcolonial traits of loneliness, longing nostalgia, homelessness and social estrangement are found in most of Desai's fiction and *Asylum, USA* is no different. The novel revolves around the protagonist Noshir Daruwalla's journey of the quest for identity which achieves self-awareness and contemplation in course of adaption and acculturation in abroad. The 23 years Bombay-based Noshir, under the rage of his father's overwhelming desire of having a "Son in America" and earning a foreign degree, goes to America to study Engineering and to settle in the country of freedom. Like most Parsis, he too believes that India does not have much opportunity for young generations. His hard efforts to bear his educational cost while negotiating the diasporic condition in Chicago enable him to eke out in the metropolitan city. Being in the land of freedom and opportunities, Noshir was as Desai writes set free "to enjoy everything…beholden to no one, responsible only to himself" (Desai 46).

Much influenced by the American way of life, he follows the money-spinning popular culture of the states and marries a homosexual American girl named Barbara to get a green card and become an authorised permanent resident of America. Even he pays off Barbara for this act of fraudulence. He broods,

"Everything was permitted because I had given myself permission. What a world!" (37). His transformed self which is a result of his immediate environment starts feeling an affinity towards the culture of freedom. When his parents visit him in Chicago, he explicitly discloses his love for Chicago. When his mother barges in, "Nonsense, Bombay will always be your home" whereas for Noshir, it does not make much difference. Chicago has become the place of his dream where he finds comfort and most importantly freedom. He develops more affinity towards the hedonistic pleasures and materialistic comforts of America and enjoys the list of non-serious carnal relationships he shares with his girlfriends. His marriage with Barbara is also flagger basting.

Unlike conventional marriages, their's is based on a mutually beneficial relationship in which partners can come in and move out once their need is fulfilled. Barbara makes him available to other young women as she says "you know husband, you can bring girls home if you want to." (41) Eventually, he gets sexually intimate with a number of girls giving up on the sacred inviolability of marriage. He even feels proud for his long list of lovers. Easily going with so many relationships at a time is what reflects a spiritual and emotional vacuum in oneself.

The kind of superficial relationship which is being shared between Noshir and Barbara not only dehumanises the sacred bond of marriage but also leads towards a permanent reluctance to commitment and responsibility. Noshir's concept of 'self-identity' undergoes significant changes with the kind of facetious attitude he carries with himself – the result is pervasive sense of personal emptiness, grief and loneliness, discontentment and despondence. Eventually when he is dumped by Lisa, one of the girls in his list, he found it really difficult to cope with.

He realises:

> There was a hole in her she didn't know how to fill, and the same hole in me....There was a hole in me, yes, but more than a hole, a vacuum, a suction, a black hole, and the night provided the illusion that I could fill the hole with Sheila. (140-141)

Even when Blythe, one of his girlfriends, wants him to take control over their relationship, he fails. She finds him insecure, uninvolved, and therefore thinks "he's an exile from his homeland, estranged from family, the hole in himself bigger than Jupiter he needed to fill" (123). She finds the similar 'hole' in herself too, pointing at the homelessness and rootlessness of migrants who may have the same "hole bigger than Jupiter" in the quest of a definite identity. Even Noshir eventually realises that his frivolous relationships were an "illusion: insecure people rushing into intimacy to give themselves the appearance of worldliness, kidding themselves someone cared about them" (260). The 'insecurity' that a young modern man like Noshir carries that has been heightened as a result of his migration is emblematic of the displacement of the doubly diasporic experience of the members of the Parsi Zoroastrians community. They are none less than nomadic Jews in search of a place which they can call as their 'homeland'. In fact, their condition is much more difficult than the Jews as the Jews had finally returned to Israel, their place of final settlement whereas the Parsis did not have any such specific place to return to. They are scattered all over the world and India, their host country gave them the status of "second class citizens" (Mistry 55).

Not only has that Noshir undergone a huge identity configuration in the process of having so many nonserious relationships, but also he experiences a reckless reckoning around racism. Racism which is so deeply embedded in the American minds, always creates an inequality in color, caste and status. Noshir hopes that the educated liberal future generation would "Respect man, not his racism" and "there is hope" – hope for a better and brighter civilisation. While talking about racism, Desai tries to pinpoint at the Parsi Zoroastrians' penchant for the white skin tone and strong inclination towards western way of life. Their relatively fairer skin as compared to the Indians always makes them feel proud. They do not, however, enjoy the status of being recognised as Indian. Their proclivity for everything western along with their skin tone makes them feel superior specially while siding with the British even though the British never consider them as their likes. Desai, in doing so, laughs at the idiocy of his community. He puts it through the voice of Noshir:

> At the moment of truth the joke was on us, on all of us Indians who laughed with the English at the expense of other Indians, we were laughing at ourselves, victimisers and victims at once, because while we might have laughed with the English at the babus, the natives, we could never be the English, only sad English wannabes. (Desai 89)

Desai highlights the ludicrousness of his own people, who despite living with their co-existent inhabitants, despite their assimilation and acculturation with the Indian milieu, do not feel like one of them. Rather, they feel more anxious and vulnerable under the strain of the dominant cultures. The secessionist party-politics that always questions and unnerves the position of the ethnic minorities in India results in impertinence and insecurity among members of the minorities. When Noshir gives Barbara a description of India, he says,

> India is "such a difficult country to live in.
> Why difficult?
> So much heat, so much chaos, so much insecurity, such an inferiority complex I think sometimes.
> Why an inferiority complex?
> It's a question of history. For too many years, too many centuries, if you weren't British in India you were less than British. (17-18).

Such a bash and discomfort directs most of the ethno-minorities to migrate to the land of dream and opportunities. However, even though like Desai's characters, most of the Parsis do migrate to the western countries, they neither feel a sense of belongingness towards the host country nor do they remain deeply connected to the country they originally belong to. Hence, a struggle between community identity and dissolution of boundaries is what comes out as a result of their hybridity. On one hand, they are regarded as Indian as per their national affiliation, language, and history, but on the other, they are often identified with the South Asians ethnic groups who add to the tanned color of the American stew, thereby contributing one more ingredient to the 'Salad bowl' of the western multicultural society. The varied American culture nevertheless pushes them to the margin again resulting in the continuation of the re-search of 'home'. Whether its Rusi in *The Memory of Elephants* or Farida in *Women Madly in Love* or Noshir in *Asylum*, none of them could feel loved and contended while trying to settle in an alien land. They, however, do not even have much inclination left towards Bombay like Desai. They are only appreciative of the 'comfort' of the materialistic life and the 'luxury' of the modern American way of living.

Desai's characters give a sense of an autobiographical touch. The voice is their's while the words are Desai's. Needless to mention, Desai himself is an eyewitness to the gradual debasement of western value system during his stay in the States. Hence, this "Absent-present portrayal of self" is frequently seen in his works. The western culture is marked by shameless materialism, opportunism, ephemerality of love and lust. Values are substituted with hypocrisy, betrayal, pretension, coldness, double standard, and loneliness that dehumanise self-esteem.

The Parsis have always been haunted some sense of loss, alienation and insecurity concerning their position and identity among the dominant cultures. One can see even when the names of the streets in India are changed in the process of withdrawing from the colony, it gives them the insecurity of effacing their identity which may get sealed off. Hence, migration to the west in search of greener pasture and better opportunity. Almost all of Desai's characters from Homi, Rusi and Adi in *The Memory of Elephants* to Noshir in *Asylum, USA* migrate to the USA in the quest for better future perspectives and eventually all landed up becoming wandering souls in an alien land. This raises a real concern for the next generation Parsis if they can reconstitute their identity in their second diaspora or would slowly fade away in the melting pot of the multicultural and multi-ethnical United States.

Desai successfully portrays the cynical American culture of the 60s along with its socio-cultural gaps which he considers as "a difficult time" (147) where "everything was permitted" (37) and Noshir, like most of his Parsi protagonists, is a product of his immediate society whose perception is regulated by what they see and feel. One can observe that at the beginning of the novel, Noshir has a strong affinity for the American ethos while toward the end, he understand the cultural differences between the two countries and realises the 'hollowness' he has been carrying which is "as big as Jupiter". As he returns to Bombay after his five years stay in the States, he confesses,

> Bombay again. How it had changed, but it hadn't. I had, and my perceptions. There's a book here but this isn't it. I grinned meeting my parents again, shook my father's

> hand, bore my mother's embrace: after five years I could manage no more. In me there was a hole big as Jupiter; between my father and me a chasm wide as space – which is again another book, and again this isn't. (167).

Noshir's emotional cognition seems to be inadequate throughout the novel. He realises his true self only when he is hurt. In course of time, he actualises the significance of the traditional values and commitments, the absence of which creates what Desai terms as "the Disneyland syndrome" (114). Noshir's emotional vacuum is no less than Desai's own as Desai himself believes that traditional norms serve as the panacea for all problems as to him, "the values remain constant" and "are at their most valuable when at their least fashionable" (115). One can, above all, see that even though Desai is migrated to the western world, his affinity for the Zoroastrian culture and values is still intact. The character of Noshir represents all the members of Parsi community, who moves to the foreign land leaving behind their 'homeland', undergoes 'cultural shock', compromising 'identity' in order to 'adapt' to the land of their exile. Double migration troubles them and disconnects them from either land.

Desai has beautifully fused together history, culture, values and a sense of autobiographical touch. His presentation of the American social intercourse and cultural approach on the marginalised group is emblematic of 'otherisation' of his own community. The varying plots of his narratives with a tempering of wit, humour and irony are what make his works more engrossing. He through the lens of his writings, like his fellow Parsi writers, provides the entire community with 'a perpetual asylum' in the minds and hearts of the readers.

Works Cited

Chaudhury, Shoma. "In Gratitude". Interview Of Boman Desai On "Who's Who" @Tehelka.Com

Rushdie, Salman. *Imaginary Homelands: Essays And Criticism.* Granta Books, 1991, p. 11.

Bhabha, Homi K. "The Postcolonial and The Postmodern: The Question Of Agency." *The Cultural Studies Reader.* Edited By Simon During, 2nd Ed., Routledge, 2001, p. 193.

Desai, Boman. *Asylum, USA* Harpercollins Publishers, 2000.

Mistry, Rohinton. *Such A Long Journey.* Faber, 2006, p. 55.

2

Hybridity in Colonial India and the First Bangla Novel

Swagata Bhattacharya

In her 'Introduction' to *Early Novels in India*, Meenakshi Mukherjee says, "The emergence of the novel in India coincided with a new and unprecedented interest in history and historiography in the 19th century." (Mukherjee 2002, xvii). At present, we all generally agree that the first Bangla novel is *Durgeshnandini* (1865) by Bankimchandra Chattopadhyay. (1838-1894). However, what is to be noted here is that *Durgeshnandini* was not regarded a novel at the time of its publication because it did not deal with contemporary issues. Mukherjee further says that, "The canon legitimised by literary historians was constructed on the unarticulated premise that there was a universal paradigm of novel writing,…and the appellation 'novel' bestowed only on those long narratives which best adapted this European form to incorporate local material." (2002, viii). In his *History of Bengali Literature* Sukumar Sen says that the characteristics of the western novels were-(I) wholly or partially imaginative stories (ii) narration of realistic events (iii) portrayal of contemporary characters and (iv) not small in length. Out of these four, Bankim retained only the first one in his first Bangla novel – i.e. his story was partially imaginative.

In India the evolution of the novel was linked to the development of prose, the rise of the English-educated middle-class, and the social reformations of the nineteenth century. Kshetra Gupta points out that before Bankimchandra, there had been three distinct trends in Bangla narrative fiction. The first was the satiric 'naksha' which exposed social anamolies and bitterly ridiculed them, for e.g. Bhabanicharan Bandopadhyay's *Nababababubilash* (1825) & *Nababibibilash,* Pyarichand Mitra's *Alaler Gharer Dulal* (1857) and Hutom's *Hutom Pyachar Naksha* (1862). The second Trend was that of religious and didactic narratives like Catherine Hannah Mullens' *Phulmani O Karunar Bibaran*, (1852) Lalbehari Dey's *Chandramukhir Upakhyan* (1857) or Madhusudan Mukhopadhyay's *Sushilar Upakhyan* (1860), and thirdly, there was another trend of writing narratives taking their plots from the itihasa or the puranas, like Krishnakamal Bhattacharya's *Durakankher Brithabhraman*(1856) or Bhudev

Mukhopadhyay's *Oitihasik Upanyas* (1862) All these narratives had the seeds of novel, but the appellation was not bestowed upon them

When the thoroughly western-educated Bankimchandra Chattopadhyay wrote his first novel, it was in English titled *Rajmohan's Wife* and was a purely social novel. Published in 1864 in *The Indian Field Weekly* ed. by Kishorichand Mitra, it was in tandem with the fashion of his age. As Meenakshi Mukherjee says, "Replicating the 'realism' of British Victorian fiction seemed to be one of the professed intentions of the early (Indian) novelists, and various contests and prizes announced by the British administrators for Indian language narratives documenting 'native' life also emphasised the mimetic element." (viii-ix) But, *Rajmohan's Wife,* the social 'Indian realist' novel was not at all well-received. This leads Ksetra Gupta to comment that Bankimchandra did not go back to social novels upto seven years after his first publication. His first Bangla social novel *Bishabriksha* came up in 1873, only after he has succeeded in firmly creating a class of his readers who were fed on a new genre called historical novel.

The term 'historical novel' or 'oitihasik upanyas' may at first sight appear contradictory. By history we mean true facts, and the word 'upanyas' denotes an imaginative story. This word has been derived from Kalidas' *Abhijnanasakuntalam*, where, when Sakuntala revealed her identity in King Dushyanta's court, the king said, "Kimidam upanyastam", i.e. you are recounting an imaginary story. If we pay attention to the use of the term 'history' in Indian, or more specifically Bangla literature, we will find that history has been used to denote both traditionally accepted tales and completely imaginary stories. For example, the stories of William Carey's *Itihasamala* were by no means historical tales yet named *Itihasamala.* Again, *Tutikahini* and *Persian Tales* have been translated into Bangla as *Tota Itihasa* and *Parasya Itihasa* respectively. Starting from Bharatchandra to Radhamohan Sen, 'itihasa' or history in Bangla literature has denoted imaginary stories or 'moulik galpo'. We also have the tradition of Kavikankan Mukundaram, Bharatchandra or Manikram often referring to their poems as 'itihasa'. This 'itihasa', then, differed widely from the sense in which the word is used today. History as a discipline came to India as a result of British colonialism. It was only after the distinction was made clear between history and upanyas in the nineteenth century that the 'oitihasik upanyas' came into being. This genre retained the story-telling capacity of the earlier narratives, and merely added historical facts to make them more appealing to their readers. The historical novel has been very popular in Bangla literature right from the moment of its inception.

But why did Bankim choose history as his subject? The Orientalists had generated a deep interest in the Indian past. From his biography we know that Bankim had a deep and profound interest in history. Haraprasad Shastri says, "At college Bankim Chandra was a voracious reader of history, and he always longed to be a distinguished historian." (Bagal, 1360) (v) Bankim longed to read India's history which was not available at his time. He had also started writing about history in the pages of *Bangadarshan* but could not continue for long. Out of his twelve novels (excluding *Radharani* and *Jugalanguriya*), nine have a historical setting or backdrop.

In his *The Historical Novel* (1955), Lukács says that the advent of the "genuinely" historical novel at the beginning of the 19th century is to be read in terms of two developments, or processes. First, the development of a specific genre in a specific medium i.e. the development of the historical novel's unique stylistic and narrative elements. Secondly, the development of a representative, organic artwork capable of capturing the fractures, contradictions, and problems of the particular productive mode of its time (1963 55). Acharya Jadunath Sircar had commented on historical novels by saying that history and novel are not one and the same thing, historical novel belongs to the category of literature, and not history…the modern readers can know the past only in fragments from historical accounts, the several gaps thus left are filled up by the historical novels.

Thus history and novel both emerged in Bangla at the same time. It was not only due to Bankim's personal interest in history. It had a greater socio-political implication. In the nineteenth century it was necessary in the face of colonialism to tell the colonisers that the Indians have a history of themselves, and to instill among the Indians a patriotic feeling and feeling of unity. What later became a discourse on Hindu nationalism in *Anandamath* had already started with *Durgeshnandini.* Here Osman says, Pathans are not Bengalis, they are not subservient to anyone. This is actually Bankim's mockery of the contemporary Bengali race. As historian Bipan Chandra has pointed out that, "When Bankimchandra first appeared, educated Bengalis used to think of their race as an inferior one. They used to bow their heads when compared themselves with Europeans…Bankimchandra begun to counter-act this self-abasement of the Bengali psyche." (Chatterjee 1994, 80) By showing this Pathan-Mughal rivalry Bankim wanted to emphasise on the fact that rivalry among the races has led to the decline of India; the need for unity among the different races of India, Osman's indomitable spirit and Birendrasingha's courageous efforts – all have a contemporary relevance. When Jadunath Sircar asks, "How much of real history is in Bankim's Durgeshnandini? The majority is taken from the accounts of the highly imaginative sahib historian called Captain Alexander Dow" (Bagal 1360 xxxi-xxxii), we know its true. Dow and Stuart's *History of Bengal* had provided the historical basis. But Shantinath K. Desai has rightly pointed out that Bankim "chose the historical romance and not the historical novel as his genre. He was interested in the present. The romance part of his historical novels was an exploration of the values needed for the renaissance of the present." (Chatterjee 1994, 509) As Uma Chakravarthi says in her essay 'Whatever Happened to the Vedic Dasi' that, "History …came to occupy a key position in the cultural conflict between the ruling power and the colonised subjects." (35) Hence it was necessary for the nineteenth century novelist to resort to history and create a glorious past. Bankimchandra himself had not considered *Durgeshnandini* a historical novel. In fact, he had remarked after finishing *Rajsingha* that he had written his first historical novel. But in the third chapter of *Durgeshnandini* we find the narrator saying "this chapter is related to history, if the readers are too impatient they might abandon the chapter, but the author's advice is that impatience is not good." (Bhattacharya 1996, 15) This clearly indicates that history is necessary for the understanding of the novel. But more importantly it made the novel appear less absurd and more inspiring. Thus *Durgeshnandini* is a historical novel in its embryonic form.

With this comes the hybrid nature of Bankimchandra's fiction. By hybridity is generally meant the fusion of cultural forms, often as a result of inequalities of commercial or political power. (Hawthorn 2003, 2-3) Homi Bhabha defines hybridity as the sign of the productivity of colonial power. Due to his interaction with the colonial system of education Bankim is forced to bring in changes in the indigenous narrative forms. Bankimchandra, educated in Western ideas and ideals, brings in the western novelistic form. The novel is divided into two 'khanda's or parts – Part I in 'Gada Mandaran' and Part II in 'Katlu Khan's Palace'. This division was completely new in indigenous narrative structure. The triangular love-story, presence of dominating, active and defiant female characters like Bimala and Ayesha, and murder in the novel were distinct novelties. There is an eternal debate among critics whether Scott's *Ivanhoe* had influenced Bankim. Bankim had denied reading *Ivanhoe* before he composed *Durgeshnandini*. But definitely the phenomenon of the rise of the individual and free spirit of nineteenth century Europe had influenced him. Again, undoubtedly he has been influenced by Bhudev Mukhopadhyay's *Oitihasik Upanyas* (1862), and particularly by the story 'Anguriya Binimay', the love-story between Shivaji and Roshinara, Aurangzeb's daughter. This has been taken from J.L. Caunter's *The Marhatta Chief*. Sukumar Sen specifically points out that Ayesha is modeled on Roshinara, Jagatsingha on Shivaji and Abhiram Swami on Ramdas Swami. Both Bhudev and Bankim have given significance to the ring because of the Indian tradition of using the ring as a token (may be because of the influence of *Sakuntala)*. With this is the use of the supernatural, an almost constant feature in Bankim's works. His personal belief in astrology has also been reflected often dramatically in his novels, along with the setting of the forests, and his preference for darkness. All these had been the influences of the earlier Perso-Arabic tales. *Durgeshnandini* opens in a deserted area at night. Sukumar Sen tries to explain – Bankim had adhered to the structure of the western novel while resorting to the accepted tales like *Vidyasundar* or *Arabya Upanyasa*. The Asmani-Viddyadiggaj episode and especially the latter's somewhat crude sense of humour was in keeping with the traditional narratives. This was also due to the better acceptance on the part of his readers.

Actually, with his *Durgeshnandini*, Bankimchandra had created a class of Bengali readers who were of a hybrid type. They were all western-educated, middle-class males who yearned for the incorporation of Western ideas and ideals into their indigenous narratives, but weren't too sure of its impact. This class of Bengali 'bhadralok's was non-existent before, they are a result of colonialism, a product of hybrid culture. In trying to cater to their needs, Bankimchandra had to resort to the use of a hybrid language, deriving both from Sanskritic tradition as well as the Perso-Arabic tradition, and tried to create a separate Bangla literary standard of its own. The choice of words is also noteworthy – 'shuddha' Bangla mostly derived from Sanskrit is used in the first part and Perso-Arabic words in the second part.

The novel as a genre came to India due to western contact, and thus became a hybrid space where form and content did not always match. For example we find Kandukuri Veerasalingam's *Rajasekhara Charita* (1878) being influenced by Oliver Goldsmith's *The Vicar of Wakefield* but at the same time using the indigenous title 'charita'. Bakhtin defines hybridity as two utterances and belief systems within a single speaker/writer. Bankimchandra's need to go to the past has been present in Walter Scott also. Like Scott's historical novels which were linked with contemporary history, Bankimchandra's historical novels were not merely historical, i.e. for knowing the past only. They had a greater political purpose. It is not just an escape route going back to the Bengali era 997, which was approximately 1600/1700 AD; he was trying to reconstruct the history of Bengal, and arouse the drooping spirits and confidence of the colonised Bengalis by narrating to them the chivalrous adventures of the Rajput prince Jagatsingha. In serving this purpose Bankimchandra uses the Western fictional form. The 'nyas' in the word 'upanyas', indicates the style or technique. Bankimchandra's text, then, is an assimilation of the Sanskritic, Perso-Arabic as well as English trends. The presence of many voices and many beliefs have led Bankimchandra to form his own writing, taking history as setting to set forth a tradition of its own, and subvert the colonial site of authority. The colonisers had wanted to give the Indians a history of their own, Bankimchandra has given his readers a history – both political and literary.

Works Cited

Bagal, Jogeshchandra ed. *Bankim Rachanabali* Vol.1. Calcutta: Sahitya Sansad, Asvin 1360.

Bhattacharya, Mrityunjay ed. *Bankim Rachanabalii.* Calcutta: Narayan Pustakalay, 1996.

Chakravarthi, Uma "Whatever Happened to the Vedic Dasi? Orientalism, Nationalism and a Script for the Past" in Kumkum Sangari & Sudesh Vaid eds. *Recasting Women: Essays in Indian Colonial History.* New Delhi: Kali for Women, 1989.

Chatterjee, Bhabatosh ed. *Bankimchandra Chatterjee: Essays in Perspective.* New Delhi: Sahitya Akademi, 1994.

Hawthorn, Jeremy. *A Glossary of Contemporary Literary Theory* 4th ed. London: Hodder Education, 2000.

Lukács, Gyorgy. *The Historical Novel.* New York: Marlin Press, 1963.

Mukherjee, Meenakshi. *Early Novels in India.* New Delhi: Sahitya Akademi, 2002.

3

Causes and Fallouts of Caste-system: A Postcolonial Outlook of Bama's *Karukku*

Jalendra Phukan

Introduction

The writings of Dalit writers have been very influential in representing the social reality of Dalit lives. Their voices play a vital role in molding the minds of people. Writers from different backgrounds have tried to represent caste, gender and religion in the form of literature. Some of the writers have represented caste while some have focused on the class issues. Religion has also been one of the crucial topics reflected in Indian literature. Firstly, the literature of Dalits or 'Dalit Literature' occupies a significant place that reflects caste and religion. It is a direct encounter with subjects like caste, gender, class, and religion. Moreover, it is literature about the pain and suffering of Dalits from ages under the hands of the upper castes. Autobiographical writings such as *Joothan* by Om Prakash Valmiki and *The Weave of My Life* by Urmila Pawar portray the stories of painful sufferings. These writings reflect the caste and religious issues of lower castes communities. There are many other influential Dalit writers like Datta Bhagat, Daya Pawar, Namdeo Dhasal, Sharan Kumar Limbale, etc. who have represented the atrocities on lower castes communities under the suppression of upper castes. Secondly, mainstream Indian writers like Mulk Raj Anand, Raja Rao, and R.K. Narayanan had portrayed the realities of lower castes societies. Though they are not directly grouped under the class of Dalit writers, their writings have very painstakingly reflected the issues relating to the Caste-System. Anand's novels *Untouchable* and *Coolie* depict the dark reality of the Indian Caste-System. Similarly, the novels of Narayanan raise the issues of caste in Hindu traditions. Rao's novel *Kanthapura* reflects the oppression of lower castes people by the privileged Brahmin castes in rural India. Arundhati Roy is a living writer who has depicted the caste relations and social discrimination in Indian societies. Her novel *The God of Small Things* turns the Indian Caste-System upside down. Apart from these writers, many other regional writers had written on the caste and religious issues of India.

The name Bama occupies a significant place in Dalit literature especially when we talk about Dalit women writers. Like all others, she is a major proponent of modern Dalit literature. Bama was born and brought up in the state of Tamil Nadu. She hails from a Dalit Christian family. From the very early days of her life, she experienced exploitation of the Dalits at the hands of upper caste peoples.

In the text *Karukku*, Bama has very painfully exposed the hardship and exploitation of Dalit women. She rewrites her past and shapes it into a revolution against the oppressors. Bama attempts to bring a kind of Dalit consciousness among the readers. The word 'karukku' is a pun having double meanings. It refers to palmyra leaves which have serrated edges on both sides as double-edged swords. Secondly, in Tamil 'karu' means embryo or seed which signifies freshness or newness. Hence, in a way, she reflects the sufferings of a Dalit woman and raises her voice against the caste-centered society. On the other side, she creates awareness in society and proposes a new start in the lives of Dalits with equal rights and opportunities. She expresses the sad and grim realities of her life right from the very infant age. The exposition of her struggle for education and establishment is very significant in this novel. In every walk of her difficult life, she dares to stand boldly to tackle the circumstances. From her childhood to school life, from higher studies to becoming a nun, and finally selection in a service, everywhere, all her life she has always been exploited. But her boldness and will power made her stand tall among the others to advocate for their rights.

Discussion

Caste-System is well known in India and it is the root cause of inequality in Indian society. At present, there are many causes which help in keeping the caste system alive. The causes and consequences of the caste system are well depicted in the text *Karukku*. In the text *Karukku*, though caste is not portrayed similar as it is mentioned in the Vedas, but still many similarities exist. Owing to the passage of time, many turns have taken place in the lives of Shudras. The mention of caste is found in the Vedas, which are considered one of the earliest works of human civilisation. The description of three major castes namely Brahma, Kshatra, and Visha are found in the Rig Veda. In the later hymns of the same book, there is the mention of the fourth caste called shudra. The fifth class is Untouchables which is sometimes considered lower than the Shudras and sometimes as those groups, who are lowest in order within the shudra caste. *Karukku* is mainly about the lives of women belonging to this caste called Shudras or Untouchables. Each caste has its occupation according to birth and belief. Similarly, the text, *Karukku*, reflects on the occupation of the Dalits which is related to their birth. According to the Hindu religious texts, it is widely believed that these castes originated from the body of God Brahma, who is believed as the creator of the world in the Hindu religion. The Shudras and the Untouchables are lowest in the line of the caste-system. They are believed to have been born from the bottom of Brahma's feet. Therefore, their work is related to menial jobs like labourers, sweepers, cleaners, etc. Bama has significantly depicted the lives of Dalit women from various perspectives. But, in the Post-colonial period, they have no longer remained Hindus, colonial forces have subjugated them under the Christian religion. The social position of a person is ranked according to their hereditary caste where one was born, not by his qualifications or status of wealth. They start positioning themselves high or low based on their castes. The status of a person remains unchanged from the time of birth until the time of death. In the select novel, the Dalit women characters are victimised by the upper castes people. They are pushed to the peripheral levels of society. In his autobiography *Joothan*, Om Prakash Valmiki mentions that, "One can somehow get past poverty and deprivation, but it is impossible to get past caste" (21).

Having a stereotypical thought in upper castes people over the lower castes population is a common phenomenon in society. It is one of the most significant reasons for the existence of caste differences. In such a phenomenon, though a group of people work or live together they keep on segregating their fellow members in the name of caste superiority. This phenomenon has been observed and it is recurrent in *Karukku*. The characters start making groups by choosing their sub-caste or tribe people. This kind of groupings further results in disunity among the fellow members. The select novel reflects on the groupings of the upper caste students while leaving the Dalit students to remain aside. Caste endogamy or marriage within the same caste group is another important factor that leads to casteism. Such kinds of practice in a society make people more caste centered. People living in such type of society believe that marrying another caste woman may bring danger to their genetics. This could endanger future generations.

In the present century, globalisation and migration of people may also be considered one of the causes in the formation of caste-based societies. People migrate from one place to another in search of work and start searching for people belonging to their caste seeking security and help. Such helpings bring a sense of caste-based mentality into their minds. In the text *Karukku*, it has been observed that Bama is victimised by the senior nuns. At first, she is appointed to teach in a village school, but then again she is transferred to Jammu. The Provincial and the senior nuns manage to keep someone from their community in place of Bama. They preferred to take care of nuns belonging to their own community rather than Bama. Modern means of transportation and communication also help in developing caste feelings among the people of similar castes. Because of improvements in transportation and communication people of similar castes living in different geographical locations can unite through meetings and organisations. Moreover, it allows them to attend in their ceremonial and caste-based functions. Such possibilities promote the sense of caste unity by breaking geographical barriers.

Lack of education is one of the major issues of caste sensitivity. A man without knowledge remains narrow-minded. People cannot develop a secular mindset without getting proper education which brings caste-based ideology into their thoughts. The scarcity of educational institutions is well depicted in *Karukku*. Most of the rural places in India are in lack of proper schools for imparting quality education. Though the governments have taken many steps to educate the people, they have failed to bring changes in the opinions of men.

Religious dogmas and blind beliefs have always been important parts of life in Indian society. Most of the people in India do believe in such practices. Due to irrationality and blind faith they keep on practicing their caste-based traditional rituals. These types of rituals strengthen the faith in one's religion by neglecting other religions with a sense of inferiority. People of higher castes groups maintain a kind of distance from the lower castes people in their day to day life. A kind of physical and psychological space is always maintained by the upper castes people. Such spaces restrict these people to work together or live together in the walk of everyday life. Hence, caste identity is maintained everywhere in the form of religious culture. These eventually separate the populations in the name of caste type groups.

Caste-based society has created tensions among the populations. This system separates society into many small sections. Because of these divisions of people into segments, it results in continuous disputes among the communities. The spread of regular conflicts create differences in their opinions. Such disputes are very often seen in the select text of Bama. Differences among the communities lead to tensions and clashes which further stand as a barrier in national growth. It is rightly said that democracy is 'by the people' and 'for the people'. But, a nation where caste system prevails, democracy would not function well for the welfare of people. In the text *Karukku*, Bama mentions how the police officials are offered with food and wine to torture the poor Dalits. Castiest ideology of a party brings political fragmentation and makes the government unprogressive. The disunity within the political parties gives birth to too many small and regional parties. Communal violence has become an important tool used in elections. It is very horribly depicted in *Karukku*. Corruption is yet another consequence of the caste system. A government formed with the majority of leaders from the same caste gives preferences to own caste. Directly or indirectly such a government body fails in providing equal status to all. In various appointments and service positions, caste-based preferences play a major consideration rather than merit and capabilities. In the select novel, Bama is exploited by the upper caste authorities on several occasions for their interests. Caste-based society has always created a threat to the minor castes in a state. These minor castes with weaker economical background become subject of dominance in the hands of upper castes. It will be an injustice to say that caste-system and religious laws have only affected the lower classes. In many ways, this system has also affected the upper caste people according to time and conditions. Since, there are various religious rules laid down within the upper castes. Such strict laws and rules have always been a matter of tension among the upper-class people. By reading the religious and historical texts it can be easily assumed that prevailing rules were initiated by male members. Hence, most of the rules were made in the interest of men. The women in the select texts suffer from various types of social and religious rules. Neglecting women's interest aside in the early period had been the most tragic flaw in the history of human civilisation. Women of any caste, either it may be from an upper or lower caste, have to follow the rules made by men. The caste system in India is intertwined with full of such religious and patriarchal rules. These laws have been playing a crucial role in the domination of women in the hands of men. As depicted in *Karukku*, women belonging to lower castes are discriminated through the laws of untouchability and pollution. They are being targeted in the name of purity and loyalty. Almost all the laws are found to have a pro-patriarchal nature. As a result, women in all walks of life remain like puppets under the commands of men. There are many laws laid for women in the Hindu caste-system. But in contrast to those laws, not a single law has been introduced for men with respect to women. Many traditional ceremonies are being performed by women in the name of their husbands. A ritual like Vatt Savitri is very popular among upper castes women displaying their loyalty towards husbands. Karwachaut is yet another ritual performed by women wishing long life for their husbands. Such rituals have always resulted in gender inequality in society. In the select text, it has been noticed that the notions of purity and impurity have pushed women towards extreme torture. Further analysis of Bama's text *Karukku* and *Sangati* bring us to notice how a woman is considered impure when she willingly marries with some other caste person. She is no longer allowed to revisit her parental home. Today, it is horrible to hear about Caste-System in history books. Though it is not practiced actively at present, low castes people of today are bound with caste laws to follow in their lives. In *Karukku*, Bama has attempted to portray all those agonies of lower caste women. They are directed to follow the caste rules strictly. Moreover, Dalits are considered impure and restricted from a parallel society. Such irrational laws have created aloofness in their lives. In contrast to the upper caste lives they exploited and suppressed every day at the hands of upper caste people.

Conclusion

The consequences of caste-system are very dismal in India. From the very period of its origin, it has always brought pain and agony into humanity. In every age of history, it has left some dark shadows creating mischief in human society. The select text in studies reflects some similar impacts of the caste-system. Through caste-system only certain sections of people are benefited from society. The majority of groups are bound to remain insecure and dependent on upper castes people. From a very lower caste person to an upper caste person, it affects everyone from an individual to larger society as a whole. This system brings dehumanising results in the lives of the people in a nation. The novel *Karukku* projects on such dehumanising consequences in Dalit societies. Caste-based ideology institutes inequality among the populations in society. Further, it largely fails in providing justice and equality concerning every caste groups. Institutions and organisations based on castes have always been a threat to social order. Such institutions propagate caste-based unity and bring disharmony within a state. In the select text, Bama portrays the caste-based discriminations in the social and educational institutions. Groupings of people in this process have alarmed a threat in the maintenance of peace and harmony. Caste-system compels people to stay within the boundary of own culture. Such a system restricts people to develop a multi-cultural society. In the selected text, it has been noticed that people of upper castes do not visit the lower castes villages. They do not even participate in the social and traditional events. It develops an orthodox and conservative mindset in a person from the very beginning of childhood. In this new India, people must think logically to eradicate the practice of caste-system from our society.

Works Cited

Abhrams, H. M and Geoffrey Galt Harpham. *A Glosary of Literary Terms.* New Delhi: Cengage Learning, 2012.

Agnes, Flavia. Law and Gender Inequality. New Delhi: OUP 2001.

Ambedkar, B.R. *The Untouchables.* Kalpaz Publications: Delhi. 2017.

.... *The Annihilation of Caste.* Rupa Publications Pvt. Ltd: New Delhi. 2018.

Anand, Mulk Raj. *Coolie.* New Delhi: Penguin India, 2001.

.... *Untouchable.* London: Bodley Head, 1970.

Ashcroft, Bill, Gareth Griffiths and Helen Tiffin, *The Empire Writes Back.* London and New York: Routledge, 2008.

Bama, *Karukku*, Macmillan India Limited, Chennai, 2000.

......., *Sangati* (Events), New Delhi: OUP 2009.

.... *Dalit Literature.* Trans. M. Vijayalakshmi. Indian Literature XLIII.5 (1999): 97-98.

Barry Peter, *Beginning Theory.* New Delhi: Viva Books, 2013.

Bhande, Usha. *Writing Resistance.* Indian Institute of Advance Study: Shimla. 2006.

Butler, Judith. *Gender Trouble.* London and New York : Routledge. 2007.

Chandrakala, Priyadarsini and Sunitha. *Women Rights and Gender Justice.* New Delhi: Regal Publications. 2015.

Dangle, Arjun. "*Dalit Literature. Past, Present and Future*" in Arjun Dangle ed., *Poisoned Bread*: Translations from Modern Marathi Dalit Literature. Delhi: Orient Longman, 1992. pp. 234-266.

Doniger and Smith. *The Laws of Manu.* Penguin Classics. 2000.

Eagleton, Terry, *Marxism and Literary Criticism.* New Delhi: Atlantic, 2000.

Fanon, Frantz. *The Wretched of Earth.* Penguin Classics. London. 2001.

Guha, Ranjit. *Subaltern Studies I & VI: Writing on South Asian History and Society.* New Delhi: OUP. 2010.

Gupta. Vijay Kumar. *Gender Discrimination and Human Rights.* New Delhi: MDPublications. 2008.

Jogdand, P.G. *Dalit Women.* Gyan Publishing House: New Delhi. 2013.

Khan, A.R. *The Constitution of India.* G.K Publications: New Delhi. 2018.

Kothari, Rajni. *Caste in Indian Politics.* New Delhi: Orient BlackSwan. 2010.

Limbale, Sharan Kumar. *Towards an Aesthetics of Dalit Literature: History, Controversies and Considerations.* Trans. Alok Mukherjee. New Delhi: Orient Longman, 2004.

4

Postcolonial African Literature and Writing in the Language of the Other: The Algerian Postcolonial Novel as an Example

Yacine Mohamed Belguendouz

The post-colonial theory is based on two fundamental elements: the study of Western literatures and cultures in terms of egocentricism and superiority, and the study of literatures and cultures of the Third World that is undeniably making a stand on European imperialism. These literatures began to vividly counterattack the empire in an attempt to regain their places in the world, to get back to the spotlight unrightfully taken by Europe. In light of this colonial culture, there was a need for the emergence of a literature aimed mainly at confronting the ideological discourse of the West, and working at giving the stand to those casted away. This eventually shaped what became known later as Post-Colonial Writings or Post-Colonial Literature.

Post-colonial Literature

If the concern of colonial literatures was to justify and support European imperialism, the post-colonial literatures represent the act of demolishing, dismantling and opposing the previously mentioned colonial discourse. Post-colonial literature is a combination of opposition and imitation, as it merges revolution and peace. This duality is the very essence of its strategy, style, and themes in a way not always easily perceived by critics (Asante-Darko 2). Therefore, the emergence of a particular type of post-colonial novels written by colonised hands was inevitable, it had to come as an opposition and contrast literary work within the imperialist culture, such as the novels (Najma) by Kateb Yacine, which is a parallel creation to Albert Camu's (The Stranger), and (Season of Migration to the North) by Tayeb Salih versus (Heart of Darkness) by Joseph Conrad... Thus, the authors expand the field of the term post-colonialism in some post-colonial texts such as 'The Empire Writes Back', to include all literary productions in English by those societies that were subject to colonisation.... the African, Australian, Canadian, Caribbean, Indian, Malaysian, Maltese, New Zealand, Pakistani, Singapore, Pacific Island states and Sri

Lanka literatures..; are all post-colonial literatures (Shohat 2). These literatures were called earlier "Commonwealth Literatures" in Europe, Britain, America, Australia, Canada, the Caribbean and all the countries that were subordinate to the British Empire.

The Colonial Language

The most important sphere of colonial domination was the mental space of the enslaved, that is to say, control made through language. Because economic and political control cannot be effective if not accompanied by cultural one. This is what happened in most of the occupied countries, where the colonial language replaced the native and national languages, it even defined primary education. This resulted in a split of the children's consciousness from their natural and social surroundings, as the colonial language became the measure of intelligence and culture, a criterion for success in education and the means to reach the colonial elite. The colonial child began to see the world through the languages, cultures and history of Europe, while the Margins were seen from the Center and described with adjectives of backwardness and ignorance. These figures cannot be easily erased from a child's psyche. When speaking of the spread of European culture as it replaced local traditions, the Algerian novelist Kateb Yacine says: "Despite my success in school and in absorbing French culture, I felt that I was gradually moving away from my mother, my country, and my language.

However, teaching a foreign language cannot be at the expense of the student's culture. The culture associated with the language is only for helping learning the language. This cannot mean as well that we have to demolish what we gained from the colonial era, but rather that we must convert it in a useful way. However, it is necessary to refer to the negative side of the situation, what is called the hidden effects of the colonisation, because by using the language of the coloniser, we also follow his example of thinking, as if we were bound by the same values. This negative impact can only be eradicated by going back to the national culture.

In this regard, some analysts believe that *Francophonie* means, in one way or another, the production and promotion of standard models of decay in Algeria in particularly and in Africa generally. Otherwise, how do we explain that all French-speaking countries, even those that use French as an official language, are countries living in a state of economic, social and cultural regression, and whether the French language was able to lift these countries out of underdevelopment and poverty in a broad sense? In spite of everything, Francophonie is a political movement that aims to make France the center around which the economic movement revolves in those French speaking countries, in other words, placing these countries in the spot of economic and cultural dependence on them.

What we should point out here is that even the French language itself is trying to preserve and protect its identity and status, when it felt persecuted in its own home due to globalisation and the flourishing of the English language, the French authorities have enacted laws to mainstream the use of the French language, denounce the spread of English and deplore the invasion of the American culture. We can also site an example on the Asian continent, where the local national languages have maintained a distinguished place in cultural communication, as they are used in various areas of life, literature and media mainly and exclusively use it. In spite of the circulation of foreign languages among the scientific, intellectual and technocratic elite, it is rare for colonial languages to be used with non-foreigners there.

For instance, Vietnam presents a fascinating image of patriotism and protectiveness over its identity, as Hanoi regained in record time its national language, also South Korea is one of the most technologically advanced countries out there, it wiped the intruding words and terms from the Japanese language, and all transactions – from the most modern laboratories to the press are in the Korean language. It only uses Western languages to communicate with foreigners.

Whereas in the African continent, the colonial language still dominates the cultural arena even after the independence of these former colonised countries, thinkers and researchers in literature and science who use local languages in their writings, a few copies are printed for them and their production is unknown outside their countries. For example, in Algeria, those who write and publish in Arabic do not usually print more than three thousand copies, which is the same number that is distributed in a municipality of Europe whose population does not exceed 25 thousand people. This brings us to the issue of the African literature written in foreign colonial languages.

African Literature in the Language of the other (the coloniser's language)

African literature emerged with the emergence of liberation movements in the continent, as most of its countries gained independence since the 1960s. It is a melting pot that includes in its entirety a variety of literature in different languages and dialects, written and oral, and embraces several folk tales, proverbs, wisdom, myths, symbols, poems and novels. The Kenyan writer Ngugi Wa Thiong'o argues that if literature has to be written, then it will become apparent how inappropriate the word is to define "the verbal embodiment of the creative spirit of people." Referring to the position of oral literature in East Africa, Ngugi explains that East Africa, like the rest of the entire continent, is rich in lyric poems, poetry and stories dating back to ancient times (Pydah 118).

African literature is seldom concerned with art for the sake of art, nor is it concerned with the expression of selfish feelings or individual aesthetic emotions, or personal creations... But it is practiced in a narrow framework only as an expression of a culture and a social structure: it is a very committed literature with a feature that is often clearly educational. Even the most entertaining and pleasurable texts are not without an esoteric background that can only be understood by a few people, and not without a social function that goes beyond their entertaining value (Alexandre 149).

African literature depicts the reality of Africa in all its dimensions; this includes not only the conflict with the former colonial powers, but also conflicts within the African continent. African literature is divided into literature written in colonial languages and one in the African languages. Although the majority of the African writings are in colonial languages, it is worth mentioning that the number of African authors who are choosing to write in their mother language is constantly increasing (Dijk MA 16). Thus, the issue of African literature written in foreign languages such as French is raised in Algeria, for example: Is literature written in French by Algerian writers to be considered a national literature or is it a foreign one?

This cultural phenomenon is interesting for it is a new one that's not known in the cultural history of the Arab people. But it is an attribute of countries liberated from colonisation or from colonial dependency. Naturally, the issue of the association of form to content, and the one of thought to language, and the connection of the French imaginary with the Algerian one arises sharply this question.

In this regard, some divide French literature in North Africa into two parts: indigenous literature and colonial literature, while others see it as meaningless to talk about dividing the writers of the Maghreb into French and non-French. The core of their division lies in their innovations, some fought the colonisers and others justified their crimes. The first literature was able to set the first bases of the Maghreb national literature, while the second literature movement departed with the departure of the coloniser. Moreover, some post-colonial novels were written before the achievement of the political independence, as the Algerian novel written in French emerged in the early 1950s from the ruins of the colonial novel, which had a monopoly on the Algerian fictional space.

Algerian Postcolonial Novel

Speaking of the colonial novel, Albert Camus wrote about Algeria, but in the vein of a lot of French writers, he could not enter into the depths of its children's souls, he did not penetrate their hearts, he could not feel their pain nor sympathise with their wounds, but was satisfied with describing the beautiful nature of Algeria and describing its customs, traditions and popular rituals. Algeria was a backboard for their writings. As for the aspirations of the Algerian people towards freedom and independence, only those who emerged from the depths of the Algerian land, the true sons of Algeria were able to capture it.

The Algerian literature is filled with examples, such as Mouloud Faraoun, Mouloud Maamari and Mohamed Deeb...Even if these writers took it upon themselves to expose the woes of the French occupation, it is clear and tangible that the colonial language displaced the mother tongue, and we still bear witness to the effects of this to this day. Nevertheless, African literature written in French is a hybrid literature that fought both old and new tyrants through its foreign language. It also played an important role in the foundation of new national identities and cultures for North African countries. This literature reflected the aspiration of those who were occupied once, to read their own history, to know their past, their civilisation, their capabilities and the surrounding world, it expressed their desire to overcome the difficulties and obstacles left behind by the occupation. This literature also looked at the past and extracted the useful lessons for its future, understood the present, responded to its events, and drew a picture of its present with all its complexities.

It must be said that most of the Arab writers dealt with the topic of "Self and the Other", meaning the East and the West, or more specifically the Arabs versus Europe, they went then, to addressing the Maghreb social reality. Nationalism was at its strongest in the post-independence period. Then, literature began to deal with social issues, and writers advocated democratic systems and progressive transitions.

As for the special case of the French language, it is understood that Western culture penetrated through it to Maghreb society, and helped shape the Maghreb model for culture and literature. It also gave new horizons for Maghreb literary relations with other French-speaking regions in Africa and elsewhere, and enriched the possibility of getting out into the world and entering the global literary process as well as the linguistic arena of the French-speaking countries in general. And, of course, it was the language that opened the way to reaching the largest possible number of readers, especially outside the Maghreb lands. Arab writers who wrote in French have great merit in forming new Arab literature in the region of the Maghreb; it has grown since then more and more. Literature written in the French language in the countries of the Maghreb still pays off and it hasn't melted yet, despite the *Arabisation* policy and the measures taken by governments of North Africa aimed to erase the effects of the French occupation, and unite the people to have one language, one culture and education everywhere.

Despite its French language, the true message of this literature is to express the Algerian personality, it is an Algerian literature written in a foreign language but expressing an authentic Algerian culture. Literary nationality, as the Algerian novelist Malek Haddad says, is not a creation of geography, but of history. The Algerian writer is the one who chose to link his destiny to that of the nation in order to reflect its hopes and dreams and its will to live free, dear and independent.

This literature that has emerged over two historical eras – the age of occupation and the era of national rebirth... had played a hard role in the resistance for national independence in order to take out national independence and to fight for the people's right to independent spiritual and cultural development, It also fought with a weapon taken from those who robbed it of this right, as Kateb Yacine put it, the French language was "a gun ripped out of the hands of the occupiers." This literature became a bridge joining up together a foreign culture and a borderline that does not segregate people or civilisations, nor does it lead to clash and confrontation between them, but it rather brings them closer together and combines them into: a wonderful mixture in which East and West are mixed. Algerian writers who write in French have added a qualitative addition to French literature, as they created new climates in the sensitivity of the French language; they made it embrace new topics that would not have existed without these innovative writers.

Conclusion

It was essential for the emergence of post-colonial literature seeking to destroy the prevailing theory that the white civilisation of Europe invaded the colored world to connect it to civilisation and raise it to the level of the high race, and thanks to this literature we understood the effects of the coloniser, and we discovered another history that we did not see to that extent, for it was amputated or corrupted, as if it was an untouchable history, written by historians belonging to the "race of the superior. This literature is mostly written in the Coloniser's language, which dominates the local languages, especially African and Algerian literatures. In any case, this is a national literature at the heart, even if its mold is foreign, expressing African and Algerian identities and cultures, a bridge for a meeting with foreign culture, it also has a great impact on the formulation of new Arab literature in the Maghreb.

Works Cited

Asante-Darko, Kwaku, *Language And Culture In African Postcolonial Literature*, Volume 2 Issue 1, Purdue University Press, National University Of Lesotho, 2000.

Shohat, Ella, *Notes On The Post-Colonial, Social Text, No. 31/32, Third World And Post-Colonial Issues*, Duke University Press, 1992.

Pydah, Meena, "The Language Of Discord In The Novels Of Ngugi Wa Thiong'o", *International Journal Of English, Language, Literature And Humanities*, Vol. 1 Issue 4, 2014.

Alexandre, Pierre, *Langues Et Language En Afrique Noire*, Payot, Paris, 1967.

Dijk MA, Marthe, *The Translation Problems Of African Literature, MA English Language And Culture Master's Programme Translation Studies*, Utrecht University, Germany.

5

No World is Without Pain: Highlighting Unavoidable Physical Agony in R.K. Narayan's Fictional World

Amandeep Rana

Everyone in this world is subject to the difficulties of life and the frailties of the flesh. We, as human beings, cannot help asking the question: Why does God permit human suffering? Why do people die of cancer and other such diseases? Why are there earthquakes that destroy entire cities? Why do some people have to work so hard to live? Man, down the ages, has tried to find the cause of human suffering; however, there has not been any satisfactory answer to it. Suffering has been one of the most difficult subjects to understand in this world. Human suffering happens every day, everywhere, in many types and ways all around us. It is an affectively unpleasant experience. Broadly, there are two types of suffering – suffering of the body and suffering of the mind. Suffering of the body is called physical suffering. It is sometimes used as a synonym for pain. Pain is an unpleasant bodily experience which gives physical suffering. Physical suffering may include pain or injury to the body from weapons, poison or burns etc. Such experience may also arise from inadequate food and clothing. The pain of disease, which can strike the young and the old alike, is unbearable. Physical suffering can result in fear, anger, agitation etc. It can also arise from psychological suffering. If we suffer psychologically, we also experience physical suffering, for example, if we suffer psychologically from loss of job or death of some relative, our health is also affected by the same.

Narayan has dealt with the theme of suffering in his novels and short-stories. There are characters who suffer terribly in the course of their lives. His characters suffer both physically and mentally. However, he has not dealt with the physical suffering of his characters intentionally. The intensity of mental or psychological and spiritual sufferings in his novels is far greater than that of physical suffering. He does not present the physical suffering of his characters in the manner of Mulk Raj Anand. Unlike Anand, who is interested in the poverty stricken Indian world, most of Narayan's characters come from middle class upper-caste urban families. Thus, it is obvious that his characters do not suffer from hunger. Although he seems to present us a very bleak portrayal of Malgudi where life is hard and human happiness is very little, yet physical suffering of his characters is so natural that the reader fails to find his characters suffering physically.

Narayan's first novel *Swami and Friends* is episodic in its structure. The story of the novel presents various episodes in the life of Swaminathan, a schoolboy. Swaminathan is mere a child when the novel opens. In the course of the novel, he confronts a number of experiences. As a consequence, he suffers terribly and there is a perceptive growth in his character. In fact, what he observes and how he reacts to it, constitutes the stuff of the novel. Narayan, through Swaminathan and his friends, has been "able to trace the curve of ideals... of young as their sensitive minds and hearts encounter oppression, injustice and exploitation at various levels" (Goyal 1-2). Corporal punishment results in physical suffering. Such punishment, many a time, becomes the cause of physical suffering of young children. Swaminathan has to suffer pain when Vedanayagam, one of his school-teachers, beats him. Here Narayan writes: "He felt a terrible pain in the soft flesh above his left elbow. The teacher was pinching him with one hand, and with the other, crossing out all the sums" (4).

In certain cases, children suffer at the hands of their elders. Swami's is always a naughty mind, and, consequently, he becomes the victim of physical punishment in the school. He is deaf to the questions of the Headmaster. He is indignant and his response to his teacher is rather derogatory. This invites the Headmaster to bring down his stick on his back. Despite having broken the panes, he refrains from the confession of his guilt. He is unmoved in the face of punishment: "Don't beat me, sir. It pains" (106). Narayan's treatment of this theme of the suffering of children is in stark contrast to that of Mulk Raj Anand. Anand, in his novel *Untouchable*, presents different dimensions of this theme. In this novel, Lakha, the father of the hero, rebukes his sons but does not beat them. Physical suffering of children, in his novels *Untouchable* and *Coolie*, is the result of poverty and class discrimination. Narayan, on the other hand, is not a writer of a single section of society, but rather covers the entire gamut of Malgudi society. About this difference, Dnyate writes:

> Anand's *Coolie*, a study of teenager, may make a striking contrast with Narayan's *Swami and Friends*. Munoo, the coolie, is inseparably linked with his creator's keen awareness of the existing class discrimination and the horrifying poverty in a section of the society in India. Suffice is to say that if the social concern has been regarded as Anand's forte, it may never be called Narayan's cup of coffee. (47)

During pre-independence, Indians suffered physically at the hands of British rulers. Those, who struggled and raised their voice against foreign tyranny, were mercilessly beaten with *lathis*. Existential sufferings correspond to the struggles for one's existence. A large number of novels written before Indian independence, deal with the physical suffering of Indians. There were several Indians who were physically tortured by the British rulers. They were treated merely as animals and slaves, and inflicted physical punishment upon them for their rising against the

British *Raj*. Narayan, in his novels, does not deal much with political activities. In an interview, he says: "The British were imperialists, and we didn't like that, but I'm not interested in politics" (Croft 31). The British ruled over India for a long period of two hundred years and as such Narayan could not remain completely blind to it. Hence, we find references to the oppression of Indians and the Indian struggle for freedom in some of his novels. *Swami and Friends* presents the pre-independence struggle of Indians. When agitating people move in a procession to peacefully protest against the government, the policemen charge them with *lathis*. Several people die and many others get injured. Swaminathan, along with many other students, also takes part in the procession shouting *Bharat Mata Ki Jai* and *Gandhi Ki Jai*. He is also beaten mercilessly by the policemen. The *lathi* blows cause him much physical pain. Narayan writes: "Now as he turned there was a pang about his hips. And then he felt as if a load has been hung from his thighs. And again as he thought of it, he felt a very monotonous pain in the head" (103).

In *The Dark Room*, the cause of the physical suffering of Babu, a school-going boy, is fever. Due to his illness, he is unwilling to go to school. Savitri, his mother, is aware of his physical suffering due to illness and draws Ramani's attention to it. But Ramani, Babu's father, does not want the boy to stay at home and bluntly tells Savitri to mind her own business. Babu dresses up and leaves for the school, though he is not feeling well. The acuteness of his physical suffering is perceptible when Savitri asks Ramani: "Can't you see how ill the boy is" (2)?

Like *Swami and Friends*, corporal punishment causes physical suffering to Babu also. On the *Navratri* festival, Babu and his friend put up some new bulbs for the dolls. But the light goes off when Babu switches it on. At this, Babu's father loses his temper and slaps him, ignoring the pleadings of his mother, unwittingly. Babu, in fact, is blind to his fault. Thus, the punishment meted out to him compounds his suffering. The poignancy of situation becomes pronounced when he cries: "I didn't know... I didn't know it was wrong to add those lights" (48). Human life is a journey from childhood to old age. This span is punctuated by joys and suffering. In old age, people lose their physical strength and energy. The resistance of body against the diseases also decreases with the advancement of age. It does not happen universally, but in majority of cases it does. The result is sickness, fever, bodily pains or aches and a loss in capacity to work. In *The English Teacher*, the old man, who wishes to give his house on rent to Krishna, is a partially blind old man. He is a victim of paralysis. He expresses his grief to Krishna: "I am semi-blind. Till three months ago, I could see clearly, but it came on suddenly. And I can't talk without faltering; that's what paralysis has done for me" (25). These lines clearly bring out the pathos of old age and the intensity of physical suffering that one may have to undergo in old age. Physical suffering in the old age is also described by Narayan in *Mr. Sampath* where he refers to paralysis stricken father of Ravi. The attack of paralysis makes the old man incapable of earning for his family and consequently, the responsibility comes upon the shoulders of Ravi, the elder child of the family. Thus, the old man's physical suffering and his subsequent incapability to work make the condition of the family miserable. The worst condition of Ravi's household is described by Narayan in the words of Ravi's little sister who asks for a loan of ten rupees from Srinivas: "We have had no rice for two days and we have been trying to eat something else" (118).

Susila, Krishna's wife (ET), suffers from physical ailment which, subsequently, results in her death. Krishna's grandfather-in-law offers him some money to buy a house for them. Both Susila and Krishna inspect a number of houses in Malgudi. During their inspection of a house in Lawley Extension, Susila gets bitten by a fly. After their return from Lawley Extension, the wife is taken seriously ill, as the author explains: "Three days, four, five and six days passed and still she did not leave her bed. It was difficult for her to swallow any food or medicine" (68). Gradually, her physical condition deteriorates. Illness causes severe physical pain to her. She cries in pain. There is no improvement in her health despite all efforts. Krishna explains her pathetic condition: "It was becoming difficult to make Susila swallow the pills. It agitated her poor heart so much that she felt suffocated and perspiration left her prostrate" (75).

In *The Vendor of Sweets*, the life of Jagan's wife is agonising as she also suffers from physical ailment. Like Susila, she also dies of her illness. Neither the doctor nor the nature-cure therapy of Jagan could help her. She is a victim of brain-tumour, an incurable disease, as the doctor says: "No doctor could do more, a very rare type of brain tumour, if one knew why it came, one would also know how to get rid of it" (36). In fact, she is already having terrible headache and is also fed up with the nature-cure theory of Jagan. At the initial stage of her headache, Jagan remains completely indifferent and persuades her to follow his theory instead of taking medicine. He does not like her appearance with a towel knotted around her head and her disheveled hair. She suffers from inexplicable headache as she laments: "Oh, this headache is not half as unbearable as your talk. You would sooner see me dead, I suppose" (21).

In *The Bachelor of Arts*, fever becomes the cause of physical suffering of Chandran. Chandran, whose mind is already disturbed by the news of marriage of the girl he loves, is caught by fever. His fever, in fact, is the consequence of his intense psychological suffering in love. It is an off-spring of his tensions and his failure in love. In frustration, he leaves home and ultimately decides to embrace the role of an ascetic as a revenge upon the society which does not allow him to marry the girl of his choice. In his so-called, self-imposed *Sanyasa,* he undergoes several physical and psychological experiences. Thus, the problems caused by love in his life not only tear him within, but also add to his physical suffering: "His cheekbones stood out; the dust of the highways was on him; his limbs had become horny; his complexion had turned from brown to a dark tan. His looks said nothing; they did not even seem to conceal a mystery; they looked dead. His lips rarely smiled" (108).

Physical exertion or heavy work-load also results in one's physical suffering. Overwork leads to physical disorder. This is what happens to Mohan (BA), who works as a reporter, does not get enough time to rest and it seems to him that reporting has swallowed him up: "Everything, I took up this work as a stop-gap till I should get a footing in the literary world. And now what has happened? Reporting has swallowed me up" (153). Similarly, in *Mr. Sampath*, Srinivas, the editor of a newspaper, also suffers because of overwork. He remains busy with his work all the time and does not get sufficient time to maintain his health and family. He himself is very much conscious of his extra physical exertion and his inability to escape it. He tells himself: "There is perhaps some technique of existence which I have not understood. If I get at it I shall perhaps be able to manage things better. Am I such an idiot that I cannot manage these things better" (36)?

Physical suffering is a recurrent theme in *A Tiger for Malgudi*. Narayan describes in detail the personal suffering of the tiger arising from physical pain. Here, the novelist shows an interest in painful plight of the animals for which none other but human beings are responsible. People use all available methods to tame the wild animals. For this, they not only beat them but also keep them without food. The very opening of the novel is expressive of what happens to Raja, the tiger. He tells: "If you could read my thoughts, you would be welcome to come in and listen to the story of my life. At least, you could slip your arm through the bars and touch me and I'll hold out my forepaws to greet you, after retracting my claws, of course" (12).

Driven by selfish ends, people do not hesitate to kill wild animals. The tigress and her cubs have been shot dead by the villagers. The tiger is full of fury but he finds himself helpless in front of human beings, even though he is the lord of the jungle. The number of pet animals in the village is decreasing day by day. The villagers attribute it to the devil's act. But, when they realise that the tiger is responsible for the decrease in their flocks, they attack the tiger. They hit the tiger with arrows and stones. They torture him with smoking and red-coloured flaming torches viciously. The crowd is inclined to murder him and consequently, the tiger feels frightened. Undoubtedly, the tiger has encountered human beings so many times, but he has never seen them so revengeful earlier in his life. The tiger is surprised at such behaviour of human beings as he narrates the event:

> They came rushing down in great force holding up flaming torches, hatchets, crowbars and staves. I was about to dash out with my prize, but in the confusion that ensued, I lost sight of the door. I had never seen humans in such a frenzy of shouting. I never knew that human beings could be so devilish. (27)

The physical pain is also the cause of the tiger's suffering. When the tiger is caught, the Captain and his men try to tame him. Hariprasanna describes it thus: "While the tiger is busy trying to take revenge on the villagers for having killed its kin, it gets trapped by the Captain of Grand Malgudi Circus to be trained to perform various feats" (128). The tiger feels helpless. His plight is miserable as he loses his strength due to acute hunger. The tortures on him continue and the intensity of his physical suffering increases as the story moves. His natural instincts are killed. He is forced to have milk in the company of a goat. But he revolts and attacks the goat. He kills it before the Captain and his men take him under control. In order to teach him a lesson, they decide to punish him. They keep him thirsty and hungry for a couple of days or more. He is helpless as he cries: "They gave me neither food nor water for three days on end, Captain's usual method of chastening one's temper. I wished I could have explained that what I had done was due to robust health and hunger and in no way to be described as distemper" (75).

In this novel, the Captain's greedy and avaricious nature culminates into thorough paced cruelty to Raja. He becomes the worst sufferer after his sale by the Captain to a film-company. They neither allow Raja rest nor show any kindness. In this regard, Ramana observes: "Captain tortured the tiger into performing unnatural and impossible tricks for the film" (63). The Captain drives him to despair by compelling him to stand on his legs even though the tiger is completely tired out. The Captain uses his chair and whip to train Raja. The following lines speak of his painful physical agony:

> He was never satisfied and wanted me to repeat, improve, further improve and repeat, my Captain blindly carrying out his orders, whipping hitting and yelling. This went on day after day. They neither gave me rest nor showed kindness – Captain was loosing grip over himself and his self-respect. (111)

In old age, man is incapacitated physically. He feels loss of energy to a very large extent. In *The English Teacher*, the old age of Krishna's father makes life impossible for him. Due to his physical suffering in the old age, the father cannot live alone for a single day, and consequently, Krishna's mother is unable to stay with Krishna for a long time in the city. After the death of Susila, Krishna needs the presence of his mother to look after his little daughter. But, the mother is helpless because she has to look after her husband who is the victim of some senile diseases in his old age. So, she has to return to the village. Krishna does not compel her, as he knows that his father has "become utterly helpless, nearly starved, and could not look after himself even for an hour if she was away. He did not know where his clothes were, when to go in for dinner, or what to ask for at dinner" (97). His symptoms show that he suffers from Alzheimer, a disease in which one loses memory and muscular control.

In a like manner, Narayan throws light on the physical suffering of animals in the old age. In *A Tiger for Malgudi*, the saint calls the tiger and tells him: "Raja, old age has come on you" (174). In fact, the tiger is also aware of his physical incapacity as such. Raja is weak and prefers to go without food than undergoing the strain of chasing animals. He cannot run fast to catch anything and spends most of his time in a corner hidden behind the shrub. He is not even able to hear the voice of his master when the latter summons him. In the old age, the fear of starvation and of attack from hunters and other strong wild animals, make him suffer as he confesses:

> My claws sometimes struck and most of my teeth had fallen. It was difficult for me to tear or chew. My movements were becoming so slow and clumsy that I was often outwitted; and when I succeeded in cornering some animal, I could not kill it successfully. I took a long time to consume it. The result was that in due course, I was underfeeding myself and my skin fell in folds. (173-174)

Rash decisions contribute to man's tragedy. Decisions taken in hurry lead to one's physical suffering. In *Swami and Friends*, Swaminathan has already left his school. He is also facing some problems in the new school. He does not find enough time to practice for the match because of heavy homework. He tries to get permission from the Head Master, but in vain. In frustration, he decides not to go home after the school because he thinks that his father will not allow him to stay at home and play. He realises that it is no longer possible for him to stay in Malgudi. He, therefore, runs away from home and from Malgudi. Soon he is tired, hungry and terrified for he is all alone on the road and it is also getting dark. Here, he remembers the comforts at home. At present, a fierce hunger "raged within him. His thighs were heavy and there was pain around his hips. When hunger became unbearable, he plucked and ate fruits" (155-156).

In *The Dark Room*, the sufferer is woman protagonist. Savitri, the heroine of the novel, like Swaminathan, leaves home in frustration. She also attempts suicide, however, is rescued from water by a henpecked lock-repairer and umbrella-mender, Mari. Her suicidal venture and her rescue lead to her suffering. She is a lady with self-respect. So, she cannot live on food given by others. She decides to work and earn her own food. She asks Mari and his wife to find some job for her. Very soon, she gets it in a temple. But at night, she feels lonely and the temple seems to her a more horrible place. Narayan has thrown a light on her physical suffering in the temple due to her fear. She is all alone with only a dim-oil lamp. The trapping and paraphernalia add to her otherwise miserable plight. She is horror stricken as her grief grows into utter helplessness: "Everything terrified her. The whole air was oppressive; the surrounding objects assumed monstrous shapes in the solitary hours. As the hour advanced and the stillness grew deeper her fears also increased" (189).

Raju, the protagonist in *The Guide*, is also a victim of physical suffering. After his release from jail, Velan mistakes him for a saint. The younger brother of Velan declares in the village that Raju, the *Swami*, does not want food, as he undertakes fast – an act of self-purification, until it rains in the village. The villagers consider him a great man. Each day, he stands in knee-deep water muttering prayers. He wants to end the ordeal, but there is no way out. His urge to escape the ordeal of fasting is very strong. When surrounded by a large number of villagers, his suffering is both poignant and touching: "Get out all of you, and leave me alone. I am not the man to save you. No prayer on earth can save you if you are doomed. Why do you bother me with all this fasting and austerity" (235)? He is compelled to undertake the fast to ensure rains. At least the villagers believe so. It is during the course of his fast that he undergoes terrible physical suffering. William Walsh contends: "Raju is horrified at the fix he is in. He hoards his remaining scraps of food, but there isn't enough for more than a day or two" (128). In due course, life becomes difficult for Raju. Due to his deteriorating health, he is unable to keep a continuous flow of talk. The doctors begin to watch him. His kidneys are damaged, and the doctors give him small doses of saline and glucose. The government also issues a telegram to save his life. His physical suffering, at this stage of his life, is very acute. It is not due to illness, as it is in the case of Susila, rather it is due to lack of sufficient strength in the absence of appropriate food. Towards the end of the story, he gets up and goes down the steps of the river. But, he pants with the effort. His fast has enfeebled him physically: "It was difficult to hold Raju on his feet, as he had a tendency to flop down" (247).

The physical suffering of Raja, the tiger is entirely different from that of all other sufferers in Narayan's novels under study. Raja's physical suffering is highly symbolic. He suffers without any fault of his own. No doubt, many of Narayan's other characters also suffer without their own fault, but the physical suffering of Raja is the most poignant. His suffering seems to be the fruit of his evil deeds in previous lives because we do not find him doing any causeless evil or harm in his present life. He is a sufferer from the very beginning of the story and remains so till the last page of the book. In fact, in this novel, Narayan seems to convey a message to us that our physical suffering is the result of our past *Karma* or actions. In no other novel Narayan seems to be so didactic. However, in *The English Teacher*, Susila, Krishna's wife, dies a premature death and her physical suffering due to ailment and her eventual untimely death can also be seen as the result of her past *Karma*. Narayan has not provided enough reason behind her illness, and the biting by a simple fly, leads to her ceaseless physical suffering and subsequent death. Same is the case with the wife of Jagan in *The Vendor of Sweets*. Narayan has not thrown much light on her character and what all we get is that she suffered and died of brain-tumour, an incurable disease. What the novelist has focused here is that the Nature-Cure therapy of her husband does not work for her and she dies mainly because of the lack of proper treatment. The life, thus, does not seem favourable to her and all her physical suffering due to tumour and her subsequent death can be related to her past *Karma*.

The physical suffering of Chandran when he assumes the role of an ascetic is rather self-imposed and hardly seems to be the result of past *Karma*. Same is the case of Raju, the guide, whose suffering, however, is not self-imposed but is imposed on him by others. There is no denying the fact that Raju is destined to suffer in latter part of his life and no action or deed by him or even by others can save him from physical suffering. The physical suffering of Swaminathan and Babu is quite natural and obvious as we find several such examples of physical suffering of the children at the hands of elders. In our day to day life, we see many children suffering physically because of their naughty and mischievous behaviour. Similarly, the suffering of old people, in some novels such as *The English Teacher* and *Mr. Sampath* has highlighted by Narayan, is also natural. In our daily routine life, we encounter many such old people who are incapacitated physically by one disease or the other.

We, thus, observe that Narayan has not so much involved himself in the description of physical suffering of his characters. In most of his novels, he has just presented the view of routine life of common people of Malgudi who suffer physically in their day-to-day life.

Works Cited

Croft, Susan E. "Interview with R. K. Narayan." *R. K. Narayan: A Critical Spectrum*. Meerut: Shalabh, 1983. 25-33.

Dnyate, Ramesh. *The Novels of R. K. Narayan: A Typological Study of Characters*. New Delhi: Prestige, 2000.

Goyal, S. Bhagwat. "Thematic Patterns in the Early Novels of R. K. Narayan." *R. K. Narayan: A Critical Spectrum*. Shalabh: Meerut, 1983. 1-24.

Hariprasanna, A. *The World of Malgudi: A Study of R. K. Narayan's Novels*. New Delhi: Prestige, 1994.

Narayan, R. K. *A Tiger for Malgudi*. Mysore: Indian Thought Publications, 1983.

.... *Mr. Sampath*. Madras: Indian Thought Publications, 2000.

.... *Swami and Friends*. Chennai: Indian Thought Publications, 2003.

.... *The Bachelor of Arts*. Chennai: Indian Thought Publications, 2003.

.... *The Dark Room*. Mysore: Indian Thought Publications, 2000.

.... *The English Teacher*. Madras: Indian Thought Publications, 2004.

.... *The Guide*. Mysore: Indian Thought Publications, 2000.

.... *The Vendor of Sweets*. Mysore: Indian Thought Publications, 2002.

Ramana, P. S. *Message in Design: A Study of R. K. Narayan's Fiction*. New Delhi: Harman, 1993.

Walsh, William. R. K. *Narayan: A Critical Appreciation*. New Delhi: Allied, 1995.

6

Guilt and Fear in Anglo-Indian Tales: A Psychoanalytic Study of Rudyard Kipling's 'The Story of Din Muhammad' and Alice Perrin's 'Chunia, Ayah'[1]

Abhijit Maity

The relationship between the East and the West, between the colonisers and the colonised, between *we* and *they* dichotomy, is a complicated discussion in Post-colonial studies. While the colonisers encountered the colonised subjects, they became instantly aware of two important things: on the one hand, they had the opportunities to enjoy satisfaction less liberally than their subjects, and on the other, that they failed to understand much of the sentiments of the colonised subjects which virtually distanced them. Both of the above facts are psychologically linked with two apparently disconnected feelings: the desire to be like the Other and fear of the Other. This leads to the assertion that any kind of discussion about the East-West relationship welcomes psychoanalytic view to avail new channel of interpretation. In this paper, I take up two short stories written during the colonial period by two Anglo-Indian writers, and try to point out particularly how the feelings of guilt and fear in the colonisers is reflected in these texts.

The question why I stated in the title of my paper 'guilt and fear', and not fear and anxiety, is vital one here. There is a subtle objective difference between fear and anxiety in psychoanalytic theory. Freudian theory states, "anxiety is related to a state with no direct allusion to an object, while in fear the person's attention is precisely focussed on the object" (Mijolla, 563). In the colonial context, fear of the colonised Other is prominent in the colonisers' psyche, though the long-lasting fear led many colonisers to anxiety disorders and as a result, the British administration in India had to build up mental asylums like "the central asylum at Bhowanipur in Calcutta," or "European Mental Hospital in Ranchi" (Bandyopadhyay 58). However, one thing is clear that the colonisers in India encountered many mysterious and traumatic

1 Part of this article was published in *The Quest*.

experiences while ruling the masses, and their writings confirm that they had many focused disturbances with those fearful experiences.

Among the two contemporary Anglo-Indian writers, Rudyard Kipling is a renowned, popular and successful writer, and the other one is neglected and forgotten. By a comparative study of these two texts, I shall show how the feeling of guilt and fear plays an important role within the psychodynamics of the colonisers in context of the British-Indian relationship. For a better understanding of how the colonisers had to face intimidating situations, I am referring to Sullivan's observation: "The metaphor of empire as "family" was part of a colonial construct of British imperialism in India that saw Queen Victoria as "ma/baap" (Mother/Father), the native as untrained child, and the empire as drawing room – a refined and civilised space where appropriate rules of conduct would ensure permanent occupancy" (3). The colonising Self was always in fear of both the permanency of the Empire as well as the mysteriously unknowable qualities of the land. In addition to that there grew a sense of guilt because they had to dominate or control, and thereby, perpetrate violence upon the colonised Other. So when one is inflicting violence on the object of desire, the Self must have to suffer from a sense of guilt.

The feeling of guilt and remorse is overtly expressed in 'The Story of Muhammad Din'. Rudyard Kipling (1865-1936) originally published the story as 'Mahommed Din' in *Civil and Military Gazette* on 8 September, 1886 and also reprinted it in the *United Services College Chronicle*. The story centres the death of a little boy, who is the son of *Khitmutgar* or butler Imam Din. Imam Din worked as a sort of a servant in the narrator's house. One day, while Imam Din was cleaning a room, he found an old unused polo-ball, which he apologetically begged the narrator for his little son. On the next day, when the narrator returned from office, earlier than usual, he first met the boy, who was loitering stealthily in the dining room. But the sudden appearance of the Sahib startled the boy, who slipped off instantly. The thought process of the two subjects – the boy and the Sahib – is very different here: the narrator took the matter easily and did not mind anything except a little curiosity in the child's behaviour; on the other hand, the little one and also the father were frightened that the Sahib might have taken the matter seriously and was angry on them. This thought in the little one would affect him later in the story in a terrible manner.

Within ten seconds the father started sobbing despairingly and admonished the crime: "This boy', said Imam Din judicially, 'is a *budmash* – a big *budmash*. He will, without doubt, go to the *jail-khana* for his behaviour'" (Kipling 223). But the narrator's sympathetic attitude to the boy, which is again another site of exposure of Kipling's self-reflexivity, made him more acquainted and familiar with the boy than ever before. After that, the narrator and the boy exchanged greetings regularly: "'...Talaam, Tahib' from his side and 'Salaam Muhammad Din' from mine" (223). This is how there grew a close relationship between them. The boy used to play in the narrator's garden within a small space. The accident that happened within that enclosed space into the garden can be seen as a microcosmic version of the colonial enterprise. The entire incident is described:

> One day I stumbled upon some of his handiwork far down the grounds. He had half buried the polo-ball in dust, and stuck six shrivelled old marigold flowers in a circle round it. Outside that circle again was a rude squire, traced out in bits of red brick alternating with fragments of broken china; the whole bounded by a little bank of dust....
>
> Heaven knows that I had no intention of touching the child's work then or later; but, that evening, a stroll through the garden brought me unawares full on it; so that I trampled, before I knew, marigold heads, dust-bank, and fragments of broken soap-dish into confusion past all hope of mending (224).

The narrator *unconsciously* breaks apart the entire set up of the child's enclosed *playing-house* (Italic mine) and its materials. The problem is why at all the narrator, consciously or unconsciously, steps out to enter into the place or space where he is never naturally expected to. He leisurely walks over, which is absolutely a non-normative act, into a child's terrain. The grown up narrator's entering into the formed or deformed, acceptable or unacceptable terrain of that boy and breaking the small bits of creations can metaphorically be seen as a disapproval or denial of – on the part of the coloniser – letting any attempt of building safe-house for the colonised subject. In other words, the child representing the builder/creator of a small "handiwork" symbolising a house – the metaphor of nation – appears as a threat to the coloniser from inside. And the narrator's fatal desire to dominate the colonised Other unconsciously made him perform the political duty of a powerful/dutiful coloniser. As if the colonised subject is building his own rightful place within the colonised space, which is politically unacceptable to the empire builder. Here the coloniser's immediate action is to disrupt any kind of anti-Imperial activities performed by the colonised subjects. The incidents hereafter would lead the narrator to a deep sense of remorse.

The boy was lied that the narrator's trampling over his small beautiful creations is the expression of the latter's anger on him; and thereby, the narrator while returning from the office is greeted as "Tallam Sahib" by the boy with a "tearful and apologetic face" (224). For a few months, the boy kept him busy in creating another "magnificent palaces from stale flowers thrown away by the bearer, smooth water worn-pebbles, bits of broken glass, and feathers pulled". The narrator always kept his eyes on the child's activities and waited to see the new creation, but that "palace was never completed". Inquired by the narrator, one day, Imam Din informed that the little one is "suffering slightly from fever and needed quinine" (225). Few days later, the narrator stood awestricken to see "the Mussulman burying-ground" and Imam Din "carrying in his arms, wrapped in a white cloth, all that was left of little Muhammad Din". Somehow the narrator's sense of guilt and remorse, which also qualifies with Kipling's own, is revolved and heightened around the unresolved mis/understanding between him and the boy. That the narrator never disapproves the boy's presence and, his activities remained unacknowledged by and unknown to the latter. This accelerates much pain in the narrator's mind while the latter died. The affection of the narrator to the boy caused him much displeasure and painful remorse. Inger K. BrØgger in his paper at the Kent Conference in 2007 explores a different meaning to the story:

> 'The Story of Muhammad Din' (1886) epitomises the colonial experiences of the British. The story opens with a question 'Who is the happy man?' And the answer is immediately provided: 'He that sees, in his own house at home, little children crowned with dust, leaping and falling and crying'. But the narrator in 'The Story of Muhammad Din' is not very happy, he not really 'in his own house at home', for he is an Anglo-Indian, literally a hybrid and an invader in a foreign land, and the little child crowned with dust that is leaping, falling and crying is not his own child, but that of his native servant. Throughout the story the opening question hovers in the background and sets a tone of unease (BrØgger).

About Kipling's sympathy for the child in the story, Thomas Pinney in *Kipling's India* (1986) interprets that the story bears Kipling's message to the colonisers in India that they should take care of the servants, their families and children in particular. The unhappiness as stated by BrØgger or remorseful guilt, in my opinion, comes out from the psychological attachment or closeness with someone we lose, and to say more precisely, when that someone becomes a part of one's own Self.

The sense of fear and guilt is aggravated if it's been connected with a sense of disgust and detestation. The colonial mission in some way or other practically destroys the natural course of living for the colonisers also. Psychologically, the people exiled in India to serve the empire had to suffer not less than the people they had been ruling. Much of the suffering was caused by fear. This kind of fear and surprise is epitomised through the story 'Chunia, Ayah' by Alice Perrin. The name Alice Perrin is almost a new name in postcolonial studies. Alice Perrin was not only the contemporary of Kipling but to a large extent had biographical affinities with the latter. She was born in India in 1867 and like Kipling, she was sent to England for further education. Alice was the daughter of John Innes Robinson, the Major General of the Bengal Cavalry, and Bertha Beidermann Robinson. In 1886, at the age of nineteen, Alice returned to India with her recently married husband Mr. Charles Perrin, who was by profession an engineer working in the India Public Works Department. Now, she had the similar opportunity to know India from the perspective of a young writer as it had been to Kipling. Alice published her first collection of stories *East of Suez* in 1901, and then on, she got to publish over seventeen complete novels like *The Spell of the Jungle* (1902), *The Anglo Indians* (1912), *The Happy Hunting Ground* (1914), *The Woman in the Bazaar* (1914), *Star of India* (1919), and *Other Sheep* (1932) was her last published novel. Still, in the academia as well among public space her writings remain little read and less discussed. Alice and her narratives are neglected not by her own people only but also by many others.

Here, I shall show how closely Alice Perrin experiences the British-Indian encounter and how fear was a recurrent theme in her writings. 'Chunia, Ayah', published in her first short stories collection *East of Suez*, revolves around the experience of an unnamed speaker who unfolds the horrible incidents of her life to the narrator. The speaker, while visiting to a friend named Mary to look after the twenty months daughter Dot, met an ayah, whose name was Chunia. Her first encounter with the Indian ayah was awkwardly intimidating, "I remarked that the ayah looked bad-tempered" (Perrin 165). Later in the story she said, "I am sure the ayah is a brute....I never saw anything so dreadful as the look she gave you just now" (166). One day, she had received a letter from her friend's husband that Dot was dead and the body could not be found anywhere, and she was requested to keep the ayah in her house as a faithful servant. The strange things started to happen since the day Chunia ayah came to the speaker's house. Everything seemed to be horribly dreadful and unbelievably mysterious to the speaker who saw and heard the most fearful thing in her life, "...Chunia kneeling in front of the outer door imploring somebody to "go away" at the top of her voice" (169). With an utter bewilderment she found that in her dressing room she had sheltered an insane native, who ruthlessly killed and had thrown away the little girl. The ayah did this because Dot's mother once struck her with shoe, and "a devil entered into my heart" (170).

The speaker stated at the beginning of the story that she does not believe in ghostly matters. Then how could the speaker, apart from the insane Chunia, hear the shrilling cry of a child in her house? A kind of fearfulness and estrangement had been registered in her psyche when she first encountered the ayah, and that resultantly led her to form in her mind a devilish attribution to the character or activities of Chunia. When she was going to decide whether to keep Chunia in her house, she stated, "I forgot my old antipathy to her" (168), but from psychoanalytic point of view, her intimidation remained repressed in her unconscious mind, and would later be incited and aggravated as she came close to the ayah. The fear that the speaker already had is reinstalled when she had to live with the fearful other. She had already framed her mind about the Indian ayah as the cruel subject – a dreadful other and, thereby, having the opposite qualities of the Self. Alice Perrin had to victimize the ayah as the murderer of the lost child. Otherwise, the less responsive parents failing to look after their little daughter would be an insult on the part of the colonisers.

Works cited

Bandyopadhyay, Debashis. "The Past Unearthed: New Reading of Ruskin Bond's Supernatural Tales". *Children's Literature Association Quarterly* vol. 30, No. 1, 2005, pp. 53-71.

BØgger, Inger K. "Little Children Crowned with Dust: A Reading of Rudyard Kipling's "The Story of Muhammad Din". *Kipling as an International Writer*, 21 October. www.kiplingsociety.co.uk/rg_kent_abstracts.htm#brogger.

Kipling, Rudyard. *Plain Tales from the Hills*. Penguin Classics, 2011.

Mijolla, Alain de. *International Dictionary of Psychoanalysis*. Macmillan Reference USA: An Imprint of Thomson Gale, 2005. *Google Books*.

Perrin, Alice. *East of Suez: Stories of Love, Betrayal & Hauntings from the Raj*. Speaking Tiger, 2016.

Sullivan, Zorheh T. *Narratives of Empire: The Fiction of Rudyard Kipling*. Cambridge University Press, 1993.

7

Tintin in Nepal: A Brief Encounter between the Coloniser and the Colonised

Manidip Chakraborty

The fact that *Tintin in Tibet* (published in 1960 as the twentieth volume of the comic series *The Adventures of Tintin*) has secured its position among the canon of Popular Literature in the UGC approved under-graduate curriculum of English Literature students, alongside the works of Lewis Carroll, Agatha Christie, and J. K. Rowling, bears multiple implications. First, the medium of comic strip must have garnered its due dignity after having been considered for over a century as an inferior art form meant only for children. Second, the Tintin book (originally written in French) opens up the scope for translation studies for the students from an early age. Finally, the selection of this particular book from the Tintin stable is immensely important. Since the story is based on Tintin, the global icon's journey to Delhi (the capital of India), then to Kathmandu (the capital of Nepal), and then to the less-known territories of Tibet (currently a part of China) to find his supposedly dead Chinese friend Chang, it is evident that the book covers a good deal of encounters between the West and the Orient. A text appearing only a decade after India's independence, *Tintin in Tibet* talks a lot about the racial and linguistic issues. The present article attempts to selectively explore the nature of encounters between Tintin (accompanied by Captain Haddock) and the various native (i.e. Indian Sub continental) characters during the course of the story, and try to trace the colonial issues the book covers within its limited scope.

Herge, "an extraordinarily well informed armchair traveller", heavily relied on his "painstaking research" and "constantly swelling archive files" (Farr 8); to get all the information right regarding the sojourn of the hero into what largely used to be virgin territories to the majority of Western readers. *Tintin in Tibet* is not the first book of Herge depicting Tintin's journey to the Far East. Chronologically speaking, *Cigars of the Pharaoh* (1934) is the first book that lets Tintin set his foot on the Far East; in this case, India. It is however in *The Blue Lotus* (1936) that Herge, as many critics unanimously hold, has presented the Far East (i.e. India, China and Japan) in a more convincing, unbiased and definitely well-researched way. The story, unlike some of Herge's previous portrayals of the Orient (including *Tintin in the Congo*, 1931), does not intend to project the Orient in general as the breeding ground of all that is magical and beyond rational discourse. The same endeavour continues after nearly two decades in *Tintin in Tibet*, but in a far more refined and markedly apolitical way. But the Tintin stories had already become a global phenomenon in the early 1960s and at least the English translation was circulating in some parts of the Indian Subcontinent. Herge thus had to take special care of the details regarding the places and persons Tintin would meet during his search for his lost friend. Though accuracy has been the most distinguishing forte of Herge's art, this time, after the crumbling of the British Empire in the Indian Subcontinent, he had to be really cautious not to let in the typical Western preconceived ideas regarding the Orient in general.

Cigars of the Pharaoh had heavily relied on such preconceived ideas and anecdotes regarding the Orient, and much of the locale of the story remains anonymous, or rather uncharted. Perhaps this is why Herge decided to redraw the entire book and publish the coloured version in 1955, perhaps to admit his current role as an artist highly acclaimed for accuracy based on research. It is therefore safe to say that *Tintin in Tibet* is the first book that documents that historic moment when Tintin ceremoniously sets his foot in India, as the plane lands in Delhi airport. The experiences that Tintin and the Captain have during their short stay in Delhi are revealing in many ways (beginning from the last panel of Page 6 to the end of Page 9). Herge here uses some commonplaces regarding the typical 'Indian' ways which are irrefutably true indeed – the local guides swarming around the foreigners, 'sacred' cows blocking the road, Sikh taxi drivers rushing through the crowded, danger-infested roads, and of course the hospitable staff of Air India. There is nothing ignominious or caricaturish in this presentation. No extra colour has been added to serve the imagination of people from the West (a charge which was frequently brought against Herge in his early career as he wrote books like *Tintin in the Congo*, or *Land of Black Gold*). And at the same time, the carefully drawn images of India have made sure that no objection should arise from any sect of the country. Herge, however, decides to go deep into the colonial issues as Tintin and the Captain travel to Nepal, before they go on for their expedition to the unknown lands of Tibet.

At Kathmandu, Captain Haddock, as one might expect, is furious when he is hit by a harmless-looking native, carrying fruits and vegetables on baskets hanging from a pole (see the last panel of Page 10). (Tibet 10) This is the kind of role a native is meant to play in a markedly European text. In the previous sequence we have seen the Captain expressing his utter disgust (see his facial expressions) to find a native man, well-versed in the European language, and visibly authoritative, as the airport manager (See the first ten panels of Page 10). This 'collision' on the road might be seen as an interesting encounter between the West and the East; 'interesting' because the Captain, a proud representative of the supreme (or, may be decadent and happily biased) values of the West, never gets the chance to cover his true face with the mask of the benign white westerner. In the first panel of Page 11, he scoffs at the docile native with marked authority: "Wake up, you milk-maid, and look where you're going!" (Tibet 11) Doesn't this convey the West's typical pride in the discourse of Enlightenment which it claims to have begot and represented?

No doubt offensive, but this is what makes the Captain who he is. But this 'wake up' call is more than invigorating, and in the next moment he finds his own words prophetic as well as ironical. In the very next panel he gets hit by another native, this time a timid-looking coolie (Tibet 11). The Captain is now absolutely furious and he calls them (here 'them' refers to all those imbeciles from the East) a "gang of Bashi-bazouks" (Tibet 11). Innovative as ever in his selection of phrases, the Captain now makes use of a phrase with Turkish origin which literally means "one whose head is turned, damaged head, crazy-head", roughly "leaderless" or "disorderly" (Wikipedia). The retaliation comes unexpectedly, and no-less violently: "*Kyon ji? Dekhte nahin samne kya hain*?" (Tibet 11) This literally means: Hey you, can't you see what is ahead? This is followed by some curses. Praised universally for his accuracy, Herge does not even attempt to translate this for his Western readers, and retains the Hindi script intact.

The previous native carrying the pole on his shoulders seemed somewhat perplexed, if not intimidated, due to his lack of knowledge of the coloniser's language. The porter however (with a typical postcolonial attitude) expresses no sense of awe towards a 'superior' language and retorts in what then happened to be the 'National' language of the newly independent India (although the locale happens to be Nepal, separated from India just a decade before). Once again the Captain's facial expressions are more than revealing – he is stunned by the unexpected lash that he never saw coming. Tintin briskly concludes: "What's the matter, Captain? Met your match at last?" The typical feeling of disbelief, still prevailing in Europe even decades after the dismantling of the empire, is evident here. Tintin, with his globally known 'liberal' approach, seems to be in knowledge of the colonial history in the Indian Subcontinent. Perhaps his coming from Belgium, a Francophone country, is one of the reasons why he appears untouched by the idea of Western supremacy in a land which has only recently been a British colony.

The avid readers of the Tintin-verse have always been more than indulgent towards the Captain, who possesses a seemingly never-ending list of vices. He has often been understood as the alter-ego of Tintin, or rather the 'Other' Tintin. From a psychological perspective, then, he might be understood as the one representing all the hidden or subdued aspirations of Tintin. During his heated exchanges with the natives (be it in Nepal, or in India, or in Peru, or in different Arab countries), almost invariably Tintin is seen as a silent observer. He never participates in the verbal exchanges the Captain takes part in, either to aid him or to restrain him. Is this some sort of passive approval of the Captain's condescending attitude? There is no way one can firmly deny this hypothesis, since all one gets from Tintin is a joking, even patronising remark: "What's the matter, Captain? Met your match at last?"

As a postscript, it might be added that the whole effect of the colonised now being able to speak back to the coloniser is spoilt after a few pages when the same porter, now in a far more servile attitude, stands before the Captain and says (now in a broken version of the coloniser's language): "Sherpa Tharkey send me Sahib. He says: everything ready. I am porter Sahib." (Tibet 15) Perhaps with the intention of appeasing the ego of his Western captive readers, Herge thus lets Captain Haddock have the last laugh, who utters in a sinister way: "Then we shall have fun!" (Tibet 15) It is interesting to see that the readers do not get a glimpse of the Captain's face here (see the second panel of Page 15), and one fails to see his exact reaction as he gets his moral triumph in the battle of power. The porter resorting back to the English language is another sign of his admittance of the Western superiority.

Then again, one must not forget that the Francophone Captain and Tintin should not share the same attitude towards the natives of the Indian Subcontinent as their British brethrens. The French colony of India (formally the *Établissements français dans l'Inde*) had been limited to a few small territories of the Coromandel Coast and Malabar Coast of the Indian peninsula and of Bengal. The French East-India Company was eventually overpowered by its British counterpart in the long-term run in the Indian Subcontinent as a colonial power. As a result, the simple logic of the coloniser encountering the colonised does not apply to the Captain-Porter scenario. But then comes in the prospect of the larger East-West dichotomy which forces both parties to inadvertently conform to the age-old hegemony. Tintin, the 'good' sahib has been placed by the side of the Captain, the 'not-so-good' sahib.

The recognition comes near the end of the story when the Grand Abbot of the Tibetan monastery heaps all praises on Tintin: "...what you have achieved, few would have dared to undertake. Blessings upon you, Great Heart, for the strength of your friendship, for your courage, and for your steadfastness." (Tibet 61) Captain Haddock, on the other hand, receives accolades of a slightly different nature: "You too, Rumbling Thunder – blessings upon you, for in spite of all, you have the faith that moves mountains." (Tibet 61) Ironically, the 'faith' that the Abbot speaks of has always been restricted to his bond of friendship with Tintin, and not to anything beyond rational. His rejoinder, if heard or understood by the Abbot, might prove to be quite ignominious: "Moves [the mountains]? I'd sooner flatten them!" His belittling comments must be aimed towards the Western readership that is largely accustomed to viewing the Eastern mysticism through the glasses of disbelief or mockery. But Tintin, being the global icon he is, must not make fun of the Tibetan rites and customs. The recognition (of superiority?) on the part of the Orient has just been received. He therefore, like always, stays silent. It is the visual aspect of the comic book medium that adds to the scope of discussing the facial expressions and reactions of the characters in different situations. And this is exactly what lets the reader assume different ideas regarding the psychology of different characters, without the verbal intervention of the author.

The Orient has always been presented as a floating reality which is difficult to be pinned down with the device of the typical Western rational approach. But Tintin, the perpetually young idealistic reporter-cum-detective-cum-explorer, finds almost burdened with the task of decoding the myths surrounding the East (that the Orientals are 'gullible', 'devoid of energy and initiative', 'much given to fulsome flattery, intrigue, cunning and unkindness to animals', 'inveterate liars', 'lethargic and suspicious' and in everything 'oppose the clarity, directness, and nobility of the Anglo-Saxon race') (Said 38-39), and thereby setting right the society and culture that is out of joint. This self-imposed project of Enlightenment, hidden beneath a vein of sympathy and (perhaps genuine) concern for the people of the Orient, reveals the cultural imperialism embedded in the character of Tintin. The acrimonious (or rather sharply political) nature of his past encounters with the East has been toned down in *Tintin in Tibet*, no doubt, but traces can still be found in the frequent outbursts of the Captain as well as the self-imposed silence of Tintin. As a postcolonial text, therefore, *Tintin in Tibet* can be studied as a treasure trove in discussing the changing nature of the relationship between the West and the Far East.

Works Cited

Apostolides, Jean-Marie. Trans. Jocelyn Hoy. *The Metamorphoses of Tintin: or Tintin for Adults.* Stanford, California: Stanford University Press, 2010.

Assouline, Pierre. Trans. Charles Ruas. *Herge: The Man Who Created Tintin.* New York: Oxford University Press, 2011.

Farr, Michael. *Tintin: The Complete Companion.* London: Egmont UK Ltd, 2011.

Grenby, M.O. *Children's Literature.* Edinburgh: Edinburgh University Press Ltd, 2008.

Hergé. Trans. Leslie Lonsdale-Cooper, and Michael Turner. *Cigars of the Pharaoh.* London: Egmont UK Ltd., 2012.

.... *Land of Black Gold.* London: Egmont UK Ltd., 2012.

.... *The Blue Lotus.* London: Egmont UK Ltd., 2012.

.... *Tintin in the Congo.* London: Egmont UK Ltd., 2012.

. *Tintin in Tibet.* London: Egmont UK Ltd., 2012.

<https://en.wikipedia.org/wiki/Bashi-bazouk>

Hunt, Peter Hunt, ed. *Understanding Children's Literature: Second Edition.* New York: Routledge, 2005.

Lofficier, Jean-Marc, and Randy Lofficier. *Tintin.* London: Oldcastle Books, 2011.

McCarthy, Tom. *Tintin and the Secret of Literature.* London: Granta Books, 2011.

Mountford, Tim. *The Graphic Mythology of Tintin – a Primer.* eBookIt.com, 2013.

Peeters, Benoit. Trans. Tina A. Kover. *Herge, Son of Tintin.* Baltimore Maryland: Johns Hopkins University Press, 2012.

Said, Edward W. *Orientalism: Western Conceptions of the Orient*. Gurgaon: Penguin Random House India, 2001, 2016.

Sanders, Joe Sutliff, ed. *The Comics of Herge: When the Lines Are not so Clear*. University Press of Mississippi, 2016.

Thompson, Harry. *Tintin: Herge and His Creation*. London: John Murray Publishers, 2011.

Tuten, Frederic. *Tintin in the New World: A Romance*. Baltimore Maryland: Black Classic Press, 1993, 2005.

Westfahl, Gary. *Science Fiction, Children's Literature and Popular Culture: Coming of Age in Fantasyland*. London: Greenwood Press, 2000.

8

Robinson Crusoe: Re-reading the Text through a Postcolonial Lenses

Shreyosee Chattopadhyay

Robinson Crusoe is a well celebrated and renowned novel by Daniel Defoe, first published in 1719; this text carries a sense of a travelogue narrated by a character named Robinson Kreutznaer or Robinson Crusoe. This literary text of Daniel Defoe was greatly perceived in the literary world and is often credited as marking the beginning of realistic fiction as a literary genre, it is also considered to be the first English novel. Apart from all its success and celebration, there is one particular thing that drew several modern critics as well as me towards a thorough analysis of the text that is the subtle connotations of the racism and the stereotypical equation of the coloniser and the colonised that has been layered throughout the text.

The very moment we stumble upon the text of *Robinson Crusoe* with the lenses of post-colonial studies, we are posed with the character sketches of Friday and Crusoe that the text consists with and the nature of the relationship that exists between these aforementioned characters, where we find several underlying elements of the text which establishes the character of Crusoe as a prototype of the English coloniser or as Brett C Mcinelly states that in this text Crusoe is an allegory or figure of colonialism. My paper is concerned with how a traveller, trapped in the faces of danger emerges out as an orientalist scholar by enforcing the power structure which enables him to deny all the agencies of his oriental subject including his native language and culture, through this process of prolonged epistemic violence. To connote precisely, epistemic violence is a form of oppression that is exerted through knowledge and language, however it does have a complex theoretical trajectory. The idea of *episteme* can be originally located in the writings of Michael Foucault especially in "*History of Madness*" and *"The Order of Things"* but it is Gayatri Chakravarti Spivak who originated the idea of epistemic violence in her famous essay *'Can the Subaltern Speak'* to reflect how the imperial powers are propagating this tool of epistemic violence on the marginalised by a conscious destruction of their beliefs traditional and cultures to gain power over the marginalised.

The very first chapter where we encounter Friday is the chapter named "A Dream Realised", here we find Crusoe engaging in a tussle with the "savages" (Crusoe 324) and he eventually discovers and saves a man whom he would later rename as "Friday". In this chapter, what posed me with a sense of discomfort was the description of the native man as in Friday's activities provided by Crusoe. Crusoe talks about how Friday scraped a hole in sand or how he was trying to communicate with signs, the entire narration carries a sense of dehumanisation of the person described. Thus, one cannot help but locate the elements of the oriental gaze present in the text and as Ronald Inden points out the elements of oriental gaze present in a text, essentially emphasises the image of European rationality and poses the native lands as "dreamlike irrationality" (Ghose 24) which is hinted at the title of the chapter itself. This idea of European rationality is described as a pivotal element to induce the inferiority complex amongst the colonised people which produces a mass consent towards adopting the language and culture of the coloniser which gradually results in the loss of native culture and language. As previously mentioned Crusoe fights against the savages and discovers the native man renamed as Friday, as a result Friday almost immediately recognises the supremacy of Robinson and establishes the theme of the coloniser as the rescuer of the uncivilised colonised in the text. Friday is further imposed with this idea of supremacy with the signifiers of the civilisation that Crusoe contains an essence of such as his modern weapons like guns, his clothes and etcetera as mentioned in the text, "when he came to him, he stood like one amazed, looking at him, turning him first on one side, then on the other; looked at the wound the bullet had made" (Crusoe 326). We find the similar theme pointed out by Sudhansu Kumar Dash aptly in his essay named, "Politics of Cultural Dehumanisation: A Study of The Post-Colonial Lives", he argues how colonialism was posed as the extension of civilisation which necessarily justified the self-ascribed superiority (racial and cultural) of the European or the western world over the non-western world where these self-ascribed superiors imperials propagated their ideologies to affect the intellectual and moral reformation of the coloured people of the lesser cultures of the world to save them from their uncivilised native cultures or language, similarly, in the text we find Crusoe trying to teach Friday his European habits which Crusoe considers to be the nature of a civilised person. Hence, Crusoe tries to educate Friday with the teachings of religion, changes his food habits and makes him learn the English language, being completely oblivious or ignorant of the fact that Friday could have his own native language, thus creating a hegemonic order exactly as an English coloniser expects it to be. Franz Fanon in his *Black Skin, White Masks* talks about this idea of white supremacy where the white race's supremacy provokes the colonisers or the non-white people to adopting the culture of the racist rulers; this not only wipes off the native culture but also creates hybrid identities as mentioned by Homi Bhabha.

This particular chapter also deals with several important aspects of epistemic violence that the character of Friday, a symbol of all the colonised people, was subjected to. The readers are encountered with the fact that every time Crusoe mentions about Friday, he utters several phrases like "my man Friday" (Crusoe 329) which entails a sense of ownership. In fact, it is interesting that to emphasise this ownership Crusoe eventually names the native man as "Friday" while being arrogantly oblivious to the possibility that this man could have had his own name which signified his native culture and also meeting the native man, Crusoe almost immediately concludes him to be an uneducated or uncivilised being without even considering the possibility of the fact that maybe in the man's native culture the utterance of a language means nothing, it is only signs that they induce to communicate. However, several modern scholars have pointed out how this episode of "naming" the native man remains as one of the powerful ways of establishing one's superiority over another. According to them it is the postcolonial idea of "naming is claiming" trope that text indulges with, that is Crusoe enables a complete ownership over the native identity as he provides him a name, a new identity made by him. This theme of ownership is connoted in several instances present in the text, such as when the readers encounter Crusoe uttering phrases like "my man Friday" (Crusoe 329) or when are directly hinted at how Crusoe is teaching Friday to call him "master", Crusoe states, "I likewise taught him to say Master" (Crusoe 328) and this quite obviously signifies the sense of entitlement that he nurtures towards Friday. The interesting factor to be noticed here is that the process of reinforcement of power occurs twice here, once through Crusoe denying the existence of Friday's native ways of communication and the other extreme being that Crusoe is not only imposing the coloniser's language on the native but he is necessarily identifying him through certain signifiers which would dehumanise him and pose Crusoe as the almighty, all powerful imperialist.

This master-slave relation which results in a gradual oppression towards native culture and language exemplifies the dynamics of colonialism analysed by Frantz Fanon in his essays. According to Fanon, the nature of unequal relationship between the oppressor and the oppressed is typically the most dominant element of colonialism. The colonial world which circles around the native is Manichean (in Fanon's words) in that the coloniser declares a self-composed supremacy which he propagates to the mass, that it is him who is the one to write history, and maintains an oblivion to any historical existence or any pre-colonial social achievement of the colonised. In the text, similarly Friday is made to believe that he is an exemplary savage and it is Crusoe who can teach him the words of civilisation to rescue him from this web of savagery. He instantly recognises the supremacy of Robinson as his rescuer as he instantly falls into the trappings of civilisation as Mcinelly would call it, which restricts him to question his master's teachings or the assumed superiority of Robinson's civilisation over his own which results in the obvious destruction of his own native culture, rituals and habits.

This gradual process of propagating supremacy and denying the agency of the colonised people and a conscious oblivion towards the native culture which has been portrayed through the text is a microscopic view of all the countries which indulge themselves in barbaric exertion of power to enforce their reign over the entire world which has not only lead to this enormous destruction of native culture but it has also caused mass murders, wars, poverty, famine and so much more and it is also important to note that Daniel Defoe was severely criticized by Chinua Achebe for endorsing several problematic elements of colonialism in the text, and as postcolonial scholars it is necessary to analyse a text with the lenses of discourse to further understand the problems concerning ethnic supremacy that resided in the society through ages.

Works Cited

Dash, Sudhansu. "Politics of Cultural Dehumanisation: A Study of the Postcolonial Lives." *Academia.edu*,www.academia.edu/12639270/Politics_of_Cultural_Dehumanization_A_Study_of_the_Post_Colonial_lives.

Defoe, Daniel. "A Dream Realised". *Robinson Crusoe.*

Fanon, Frantz. *Black Skin, White Masks*. Penguin Classics, 2020.

Ghose, Indira. *Women Travellers in Colonial India: the Power of the Female Gaze*. Oxford University Press, 2000.

Mambrol, Nasrullah. "Homi Bhabha's Concept of Hybridity." *Literary Theory and Criticism*, 2 July 2020, literariness.org/2016/04/08/homi-bhabhas-concept-of-hybridity/.

Mcinelly, Brett C. "Expanding Empires, Expanding Selves: Colonialism, The Novel, and 'Robinson Crusoe.' pp. 1-21.

Riach, Graham K. *An Analysis of Gayatri Chakravorty Spivak's Can the Subaltern Speak?* Routledge, 2017.

9

A Journey from Ignorance to Knowledge: Tale of Resilience and Perseverance in Rassundari Devi's *Amar Jibon*

Manik Mandal

Since the creation of the earth and human being, our society has been groping through a journey from ignorance to knowledge. Humans have been experiencing a kind of transition in the process of modernisation. In this context, my focus will be on the empowerment of 19th Century Bengali women who were considered earlier as the object of subjugation, subordination and dominance. It was the time when women had no right to go outside the territory of the four walls. Their lives were modeled upon the patriarchal society. In this article, my focus will be on how Rassundari Devi (1809-1899) in her autobiography *Amar Jibon* has challenged the patriarchal norms through her leading of life through resilience and perseverance. Her passionate dream was to form a new self of her own through educating herself. It will focus on how a woman with her own determination taught herself to read and write. A journey started from her childhood then through the advent of her marriage to her married life and later on. It portrays the dissatisfaction, fear and frustration of Rassundari Devi being born a woman in such society.

Indian Education has a long history from ancient times when children were taught in Gurukuls. The education system of India even was celebrated for its learning all over civilised Asia and Europe. The motto of education was open to all and it was seen as one of the methods to achieve *Moksha*, spreading knowledge wiping out ignorance among people. Though there was discrimination of education due to the basis of *varna* and caste, but the system of predominantly male centric. Women were not allowed to take part in the field of education and other social works. Their world was limited within the family itself taking care of their males, children, family members and household chores. Only there were few instances where women came with their leading role and that has been found in Sangam Literature, the ancient Tamil Literature and is the earliest known literature of South Asia.

If we came in the modern time when India was under British rule, we have instances of missionaries teaching in the pattern of British Public Schools system. After that a drastic change has started in the system of Indian education. They did plenty of reformation in the education system. As a result the Indian people entered public administration and professional state bureaucracy. But still, women were not allowed to take part in all these. In this regard I quote Arpita Mukhopadhyay's remark on liberal feminism: "Men wielded power and authority in the Church, in the state and within families. Women had no legal or political rights and had restricted access to higher education" (Mukhopadhyay 4).

I am completely agreeing with Mukhopadhyay placing her views in respect of India being the conservative society, it did not allow their women to come out of their domicile. The males even did not share their views, decisions, and perspectives with their wives. They never thought of seeking any kind of discussion with their daughters or wives considering it to be womanly as Okonkwo have felt in Chinua Achebe's *Things Fall Apart.* The same condition was all over India at that time irrespective of caste, class and society. Here, my focus is ascertained with the social as well as education system of Bengal. Likewise all over India, in Bengal too the pre dominance of males in education was very much observable. There were very little traces of female education during the pre-independence of India. Only a few women showed their interest to educate themselves but the objective of this was very much narrow in shape. They did so to read only religious texts and to communicate with their males asking their needs and following instructions. Gradually, people realised the necessity of women education to cope up with their illiterate wives. But to serve these mere purposes will not play a full-fledged role in empowering women. There require a self-awareness among the women. If they do not feel what they need then there will be no such external power to provide a space of their own. In the words of Immanuel Kant, these people require to enlighten themselves leaving behind their immaturity. If they become successful in doing such then there will be no such power to keep them behind within the concretised four walls. A similar kind of delineation has been found in Rassundari Devi's *Amar Jibon.* It is considered to be the first published autobiography in Bengali Language. Here, she highlights how bleak the Bengal society used to be for women in the 19th Century. It is a kind of manifesto of all the women not only in Bengal but also all over India.

The book was first published in 1876 when her husband died. It contained sixteen compositions delineating typical Bengal society and her life along with the people around her. Then in 1897, she published the second part of it containing fifteen compositions which recount her philosophy about life, decay, destruction and the end of life. Each and every line of this book creates a kind of sensation for all the women living in this postmodern era. The struggle what Rassundari had done is a kind of nightmares to all. We have given an immense credit to Mary Wollstonecraft for being the proponent of women empowerment and their liberty. But in my opinion Rassundari Devi is also no far behind. We cannot deny how Rassundari fought against her society where she had nothing in favour of her. Her *Amar Jibon* is the testimonial of women living in the corner of any society where women still not have provided their basic rights. They are terminated, subjugated, oppressed and alienated within their family as well is in the society. These women need to make them well aware about the journey of Rassundari undergoing from her ignorance to knowledge through the wings of educating herself. Her book was praised abundantly by one of the greatest playwrights of Bengal, Jyotirindranath Tagore, "the wonderful train of events and its simple sweetness of expression" (Wikipedia). Dinesh Chandra Sen, another stalwart of Bengali literature also praised Rassundari and her prose writing as an 'epitome of simple prose compositions of the bygone era' (Wikipedia).

Rassundari Devi was born in a rural zamindari family of Bengal. Her father died when she was very young. Due to this she was raised by her widowed mother. She had to sacrifice a lot to lead her family. But she had an immeasurable amount of faith in divinity and she believed God will protect them. From her, Rassundari had developed a strong devotion to God. God is the only one to these socially isolated people and even to the people leading diverse sexual identity as mentioned by Dr. Manabi Bandyopadhyay, the first transgender principal of India in an interview. She never found an opportunity of formal education as women had no right of education. We have to accept the bitter truth of the then Bengal society where education of women was a vile crime and even it was considered against their society's norm. People always stigmatised to the women who did not obey their males and they had to face humiliation and torture. However, from the birth Rassundari had an everlasting desire of learning. She did not express it as she knew no body will permit her to do so. She kept on suppressing her desire in secret. When the opportunity came she started grasping it. This was clearly visible when she described that during the days of her in her parent's house there came a missionary woman to teach the boys in her colony. She was a little girl and due to this she was not allowed to be the part of that teaching. The missionary woman taught the boys and Rassundari curiously hid himself from the distance and tried to overhear the boys repeating alphabets on the blackboard. This was her first encounter with education. From there, she learnt Persian. But unfortunately it also ended due to the unfortunate burning down of the missionary schools.

The lives of women are not a very straight one; it was clearly experienced by her when she was married at the age of twelve. She had to leave all her ties from her parents and lived far away from her mother. Earlier everything was alright but when her mother-in-law fell ill, all duty came upon her shoulder. Her condition became even worse when she died. She felt the painful detachment from her beloved mother but she had to accept her fate resting faith upon God. Rassundari Devi wrote that at that time women were not allowed to get education. They did not even have that much time to spend their leisure time after their domestic work. After work they had to stand up meekly in front of their husband. People believed that women had no duty except looking after their family. Rassundari Devi's deep hearted pain was also the pain of plenty of women all over the world at that time. In one of her finest texts, *A Room of One's Own*, Virginia Woolf illustrates how women were subjugated within a family giving reference through the fictional character of Judith as Shakespeare's sister. She was not allowed to assert her creative potential. Women were bound to work inside the house having a large veil covering her face and they will remain silent all the time. If they were able to follow the decorum, they were applauded by a good wife.

Though there were the pains and sufferings in the life of the women, they adjusted themselves with the situation. They worked like beasts all day and at night they had to please their husbands. They unquestioningly did all their work hiding their battered self. A great regret was always in the heart of Rassundari Devi that women had no right to enter into the school life at her time. They were not able to cry out vindicating their urge to learn, to educate themselves. Like the helpless animals they are the prey of this male dominated society whose burden they were being carried down throughout the ages. She discussed how the grey hairs showed their abhorrence seeing the women holding papers in their hands.

The burden of family increased consequently from household affairs, attending of guests, and most importantly bearing her twelve children. She did not protest against these rather did them wholeheartedly with a smile. Only dissatisfaction inflected her severely and was not given allowance to do something of her desire to literate. Being a devotee of God, her profound wish was to read *Chaitanya Bhagavata* and shape herself according to the divinity. Her devotion led her to enter the spiritual world of *Chaitanya Bhagavata*. She found the book when her husband one day left it in the kitchen. Her passion became so irresistible that she detached a sheet from the book and then used palm leaves on which her son practiced handwriting. She compared both the writing and then thought deeply assimilating them with her previous learning which she stored within her mind from childhood. That's how she developed the skill of reading at the age of twenty six. Her interest in religious books let her reading all the religious texts like *Chaitanya Charitamrita*, *Jaimini Bharaata*, *Gobinda Lilamrita*, *Bidagdha Madhaba*, *Prema Bhakti Candrika*, *Balmiki Purana* which were already in her house. She had read the first parts of *Balmiki Purana*, she tried to find out the seventh part of it. Her fifth son, Darakanath brought this to her. Though the font was very small, her irresistible desire made her possible to complete. After that, she started reading the letters sent by her sons recognising the letters of the alphabet but her animosity was why not the society giving a free space for them. Why did they have to struggle a lot? Why are people idle about women's education? Her only aim was to have a society where would sustain no restriction of women education. They can pursue education not as their strife or struggle rather as happiness.

Though the society considered educating women was a violation of their society, she never lost her hope. Rather, she had the curiosity that motivates all the time to investigate and quest for identity. She understood really well the society in which she belonged would never be supportive of women education. To create women identity in such society, they need to literate themselves. So, she started her fight within the family by going against her husband's will not by radically but following the path of secrecy. She started denying the social taboos and stepped forward from her ignorance to knowledge. She always thanked God for providing her courage to pursue her passion. It was clearly visible how her desire of reading *Chaitanya Bhagavata* led her to the ability of reading. She also told how she started writing as well. It was when her son expressed his anguish for not replying to his letters. Her seventh son Kisharilal before returning back to the town requested her mother that she must send him a reply. It was painful for him when he found no reply from her mother after writing so many letters. So, before his return, he bought paper, pen, and ink pot for her mother. This led her desire to write and she became successful in writing too.

Rassundari Devi talked very little about her relationship with her husband. She expressed how her husband played a vital role in her life when he died. She told he was a kind of golden crown in her life with his death he lost that dazzling crown. This suggests that though there was no such exchange of time and views between them, she was not tortured by her husband. She had a very peaceful relationship with him. We have noticed how deeply the wives showed their respect to their husbands. Though it will seem very ridiculous but a great devotion was shown by the wives has been witnessed with the incident of her not coming in front of Joyhari, a horse owned by her husband. She believed to come in front of the horse was to stand in front of her husband.

Rassundari had great resilience and perseverance and it has been found throughout her marriage life undertaking plenty of family duties, caring everybody and sacrificing all her desires and freedom. She accepted the difference between the phases of life of a lady before and after marriage. She considered her life after marriage as a prisoner imprisoned in the prison matrimony. Her condition was like a handmaid in the hands of her husband. It was when her mother was seriously ill and she wished to take care of her, her husband did not allow her to return because he believed her returning may hamper their domestic works. She was not even allowed to see her mother for the last time. But Rassundari never convicted her husband for this. She rather criticised herself being born as a woman in this society. Through her writing, Rassundari questions that the necessity of women education was not only perceived by males but also the females of her time did not even realise that they have a self of their own. Although Rassundari understood this still she did not even think deeply about that. It was only after her husband's death, she started assimilating her own pains, sufferings, feelings with the all other women who had been the subject of subjugation like her. She realised apart from familial bond and responsibilities, there exist a greater world which was waiting for the women to enter.

Being women in a patriarchal society, women should shed out their self-caused immaturity to face the world outside the four walls.

To sum up, Rassundari Devi, being the first full-fledged autobiography writer in Bengali language, stands first among the writers in Bengal to talk about the plight of women in such a heart rendering way. Her *Amar Jibon* is a testimonial of the biased 19th Century Bengal society. A society completely controlled and ruled by the males who considered them to be the superior one upon whom all the responsibilities of the outer world rest upon. A society which never showed respect to the women, their wishes, pains, freedom, decisions. They are the worst sufferer in the ladder; they are treated as the machines in the hands of their males doing all the activities unquestioningly. But Rassundari Devi realised really well that their empowerment will not be possible without education. She understood that the pains and sufferings of women are the plights of every woman who like her lived an ignoble life. She unlike the most of feminist thinkers believed in the liberal empowerment of women. She established a glaring example to all the women that if one has the passion for anything, she or he should pursue it till its fulfillment. The journey may not be in favour of us and even the whole society may stand against us. But if our journey is a true one and we are striving for it from the core of our heart, the impossible will not remain any more impossible. In her autobiography, *Amar Jibon*, Rassundari Devi proved exactly what she believed.

Works Cited

Arnold, David. *The New Cambridge History of India: Science, Technology and Medicine in Colonial India*, Cambridge University Press, 2004.

Chakrabarti, Sumit. *Feminisms* (Ed), Hyderabad: Orient Blackswan Private Limited, 2019.

Chatterjee, Enakshi. *My life*, Calcutta: Writers Workshop, 1999.

Rassundari Devi. https://en.m.wikipidea.org/wiki/Rassundari_Devi. Accessed on 2nd March, 2021.

Salim, Saquib. *The Story of A Woman who stood Up Against Patriarchy in 19th Century Bengal*, Youthkiawaaz. https://www.youthkiawaaz.com/2016/11/rassundari-devi-autobiography/Accessed on 3rd March, 2021

Sarkar, Tanika. *Words to win: The making of Amar Jibon, A Modern Autobiography* (ed), New Delhi; Kali for Women, 1999.

Swarup, Ram. "Education System in Ancient India Before the British Raj-Sanskriti-Hinduism and Indian Culture," *Sanskritimagazine.* https://www.sanskritimagazine.com /india/ education-system-in-ancient-india-before-the-british-raj/ Accessed on 5th March, 2021

Vallath, Kalyani. *What About Theory?* A Useful Book for the Perplexed Student (Ed.), Kerela: Bodhi Tree Books & Publications, 2019.

Waugh, Patricia. *Literary Theory and Criticism*, New Delhi: Oxford University Press. 2006.

10

The Need for Decolonising Trauma: A Reflection on the Dominant Eurocentric Concepts of Trauma

Abhilasha Phukan

The term trauma was first defined by Cathy Caruth in her text Unclaimed Experience: Trauma, Narrative and History where she mentions a psychoanalytic approach of memory and trauma, 'traumatic memory' and 'traumatic repetition'. Caruth claims:

> What returns to haunt the victims, these stories tell us, is not the reality of violent event but also the reality of the way that its violence has not yet been fully known (Caruth 6).

The concept of trauma comprises of wounds inflicted on human's psyche that changes an individual's course of life or its perception. Traumatic events impact the human psyche in such a manner that the past continues to resurface itself time and again. Traumatic events may comprise of historical traumas, socio-political traumas, personal traumas, economic and displacement traumas, etc. Traumas of partition, colonialism, racism, discrimination, slavery have impacted the minds of the non-westerners in such a way that they are yet to be free from the shackles of the past. Many writers have found Cathy Caruth's theory of trauma to be very narrow and unidimensional as it doesn't pay its emphasis on the colonial trauma. Eli Park Sorenson, in his text *Postcolonial Studies and the Literary* finds her theory to be inadequate "due to its emphasis on melancholia, which results in a crippling self-reflexivity" (Sorenson 14).

Colonialism which started primarily as a means of gaining political and economic control became an ideology for oppression. Because of the trauma and oppression associated with the process, the term 'colonialism' began to be viewed synonymous with oppression and exclusion. Even after years of gaining independence from the British, the minds of the colonised people are still haunted by it. Colonialism is a part of that trauma process. Achille Mbembe remarks, "In African self-writing the colony is depicted as an original scene which does not merely occupy a space of remembrance, as if reflected in a mirror" but also "one of the significant matrices of language, operating on the past and the present, identity and death" (Mbembe 11). While postcolonialism deconstructs and refocuses on the colonial ideologies, their hidden objectives and tries to understand the methods used by the westerners of establishing control. It focuses on the fact how the British internalised the Indian people on their favour and forced them to accept their exploited state. This theory of internalisation focuses how the colonised accepted their powerless and subjugated state of life. This process was carried out through several methods such as slavery, discrimination, imposition of language and making them feel unworthy and how they suffered lack.

In the Western texts it is rarely found that colonialism is depicted in a negative manner. Many writers even justified colonialism as something which was necessary for the uplifted of the barbaric tribes. They famously called the process of colonialism as 'the White Man's Burden'.

> What saves us (the British) is efficiency – the devotion to efficiency. But these chaps (the Romans) we not much account really. They were no colonists; their administration was merely a squeeze, and nothing more, I suspect. They were conquerors and for that you want only brute force – nothing to boast of, when you have it; since your strength is just an accident arising from the weakness of others. Their grabbed what they could get for the sake of what was to be got.... The conquest of the earth, which mostly means the taking it away from those who have a different complexion or slightly flatter noses than ourseleves, is not a pretty thing when you look into it too much. What redeems it is the idea only. An idea at the back of it; not a sentimental pretence but an idea; and an unselfish belief in the idea – something you can set up, and bow down before and offer a sacrifice to.... (Conrad 6)

Here Conrad attempts to justify colonialism on the grounds of being methodical and effective. In the *Heart of Darkness* Conrad selected two explicit criteria – efficiency and the "idea" – to judge imperialism. He himself did not espouse these values but he chose them because they were widely held in England (Hawkins 287). As far as the European texts are concerned, they portray the colonised as 'savages'. Although a brief portion talks about their trauma, they tend to justify imperialism which is the root cause of trauma for the colonised nations.

In order to acknowledge colonial trauma, it is imperative to decolonise the whole model of 'trauma' which is dominantly Eurocentric. Michael Rothberg, states that "trauma theory is tied to a narrow Eurocentric framework, it distorts the histories it addresses such as the Holocaust and threatens to reproduce the very Eurocentrism that lies behind those histories" (Rothberg 227). The process of decolonisation started as a political liberation from British colonialism which later became a culmination of several other psycho-social processes. The psychological stressors of colonialism included many unspoken exploitations, occidental dominance, fragmentation/partition, slavery, racism, etc. These events were a part of systematic dismantling of the Orient's 'psyche' which forced to perceive themselves as 'the other' and inferior in front of the colonisers. The totalising and hierarchical worldview about colonialism being only a political invasion while ignoring the psychological dimensions; make it vague and partial. While writing history, the Western writers have a very selective and partial representation of trauma. It is seemed as if the whole model of trauma is significantly Eurocentric. The significant historical events of slavery, colonialism, racism and discrimination are ignored in their narratives of trauma or simply represented in half-baked truths.

In order to explore the psychological dimensions of colonialism in an impartial manner, it is important to decolonise the trauma theory. Decolonising would redress the marginalisation of the non-Western and minority trauma. Decolonising the Eurocentric model of trauma, it would pave new dimensions and help reflect in the historical traumas from a new perspective without adhering to any Eurocentric ideology. Many such Eurocentric ideas are countered by writers such as Aruna Roy, Sarojini Naidu, R.J. Mitra, R.L. Bhandarkar in their texts. Frantz Fanon is another example who decolonises trauma his works. "For Fanon, the end of colonialism meant not just the political and economic change, but psychological change too. Colonialism is destroyed only once this way of thinking about identity is successfully challenged" (Mcleod 11). His texts like Peau Noire, L'an Cinq, de la Revolution Algerienne and Les Damnes de la Terre explores such psychological traumas of colonialism and asserts on the fact that decolonisation of trauma can only occur when the colonised refuses to accept their position as a passive victim and establish his subjecthood. Therefore, decolonisation of trauma leads to a stronger sense of identity and renewed social cohesion among victims. It provides us an unbiased and untampered perspective of histotical voices by brings out those marginal voices which were silenced, ignored and s for a long time.

Works Cited

Caruth, Cathy. *Unclaimed Experience: Trauma, Narrative and History.* Baltimore: John Hopkins University Press, 1996.

Conrad, Joseph. *Heart of Darkness.* New York: Norton, 1971.

Mbembe, Achille. "The Colony: Its Guilty Secret and its accursed Share." *Terror and the Postcolonial.* Malden : Wiley-Blackwell, 2010.

Mcleod, John. *Beginning Postcolonialism.*

Rothberg, Michael. "Decolonising Trauma Studies: A Response". *Studies in the Novel.* 2008.

Sorenson, Eli Park. *Postcolonial Studies and the Literary: Theory, Interpretation and the Novel.* Basingstoke: Palgrave Macmillan, 2010.

11

Modern Need for Reinforcing Identities in the Select Novels of Chitra Banerjee's *Sister of My Heart* and Anita Rau Badami's *Tamarind Mem*

P.K. Smitha

The study focuses in the select fiction of Chitra Banerjee and Anita Rau Badami who are acclaimed as the foremost among the contemporary modern Indian Women Writers. It traces how the concept of marriage is apt to study the conflict between tradition and modernity and how it serves as a tool to reposition the states of women in a patriarchal framework. The study attempts to show the feminist trend in the writers whose central characters carve out the identity of the new women within the ambit of tradition. The struggle of the writers is to synthesise tradition with modern value and the focus is on the psychological aspect of the inner conflict – experienced by women. The writer Chitra Banerjee Divakaruni in her novel *Sister of my Heart* explore the dynamics of the joint family the bonds of friendship love and realities of arranged marriage. In the *Tamarind Mem* Anita Rau Badami novels how culture restricts and shapes one's personal life and aspiration, desire of the character. There is a never ending conflict between daughter and mother.

The paper also deals with the east-west encounter against the backdrop of the realities of arranged marriages and the adjustment needed did for modern life in the west.

Introduction

Indian English writing is a vast arena today with new trends emerging, new novelists with great talent making a mark in their creative writing and various critical branches sprouting in with thematic varieties technical experiment and new linguistic innovations. The old writers indeed proved to the world that their creative writings were not only intact but were living constantly being polished. The last two decades have witnessed in the emergence of diasporic women writing, which has created a large number of women writers who contributed in making their history in Indian diasporic literature. There is a long list of writers who emerged in the scene during this period for e.g., Salman Rushdie, Amitav Ghosh, Upamanya Chatterjee, Vikram Seth, Shashi Deshpande, Bharathi Mukerjee, Sobha De, Arundathi Roy, etc. The Indian writing novelists have created a new world wide trial of winning critical appreciation and international recognition. These writers have succeeded in retaining their position and identity. The primary work of these writers has been to reconstruct the traditional existing forces (demands) the Indian patriarchal family system and the new approaching demands of modernity.

Marriage locates itself in romance, sexuality and social environment. The ambivalence that is built into family relationships works at several levels and pulls the individual in different directions. On one hand the need for independence and on the other the need to belong. The individual responds to their needs differently by at different stages of life. Social roles and social constrains influence family relationships in multiple ways. Paradoxically just as the women in at the centre of the quality of family life, she is enclosed within it. The movement from and towards her is both centripetal and centrifugal. Familial roles denote enclose or confine the man in any comparable manner.

Man-Women relationship in modern times has undergone a sea change. However with the advancement of education, women started taking up job's is addition to their household duties. However this upshot has changed the conditions of women. Formerly the Indian Women was atypical product of tradition. She was destined to become a shadow of her husband. Indian women started realising their individuality and learnt to establish their separate entities. Not only socially but also in domestic circles. This socio-economic uplift in their status resulted in a change in their behavior pattern. Their attitude towards sex and sexuality also underwent a notable change.

Modern English novels like Arundathi Roy, Manju Kapoor, Chitra Banarjee Divakaruni, Anita Rau, Badami, Shauna Singh Baldwin etc., have tried to underline their significant changes by creating illustrative situation and characters in different contexts. So, these writers tried to chart out the advancement of women from tradition to modernity. The modern Indian man and modern women have now become acquisitive the age of "Go-Getters" has now set in. The novels of these modern writers focus on issues like marriage. Commercialisation, destitution, communalism, crisis of the individual alienation and general dilution of values once held dear.

Women were destined to follow certain behavior patterns that conformed to the norms laid down by society. It is also observed that a women status in Indian society is determined by her faithful adherence to the prescribed code of behavior.

During the ages, it has been ingrained in the mind of the Indian women that marriage is the ultimate goal of her life her husband's home is her only abode. Indian society is still conventional in its approach to marriage and despite numerous contradictions; husband and wife strive to maintain an outward show of balance and harmony.

Feminism

Feminism is the belief in full social, economic, political equality for women. Feminism largely arose in response to western traditions that restricted the rights of women, but feminist thought has global manifestations and variations. (So what does feminism mean to us?)

It is quite simple feminism is about all gender having equal rights and opportunities. It is about respecting diverse women experience, identities knowledge and strengths and striving to empower all women to realise their full rights. True equality leaves no one behind

About the Authors

Chitra Banarjee, Divkaruni a poet, Novelist and short story writer was born in India, migrated to United States in 1976. She re-evaluated the role of Indian women. She draws from her own experience and those immigrant Indian women to write novels and verse, including the award winning Leaving Yuba City: New and selected poems arranged marriage a collection of short stories and the Mistress of spices a novel Divakaruni also published two works *Neela, Victory Song* and *The Conch Bearer*. Divakarunie's second novel, *Sister of My Heart* is a realistic – treatment of the relationship of two cousins. *The Vine of Desire* is sequel to *Sister of My Heart*.

Anita Rau Badami was born in Sep 24, 1961 at Rourkela, Orissa. She was educated at University of Madras and then at Mumbai. In her childhood, she stayed at various places of India as her father's job was shifted to different places. She migrated to Canada and got her degree from Calgary University Badami has written four novels viz *Tamarind Mem*, *The Hero's Walk, Can You*, *Hear the Night Bird Call* and *Tell it to the Trees*.

Analysis: Chitra Banarjee Divakaruni made her to speak about Indian men in various ways because of their exploitative native in the household; Women have always been portrayed in certain roles as daughter, wife, mother and daughter in law.

The Sister of My Heart begins with the emotional story of two protagonists. Anju is daughter of a family of distinction. Sudha belonged to an impoverished family. Sudha is stunningly beautiful and Anju is not beautiful. The two girls are born in the same day but half an hour apart.

Anju and Sudha are raised in the same family with a household of three women. Sudha is stunningly beautiful whereas Anju has a fierce spirit and enjoy reading and challenges tradition. One day the girls are caught skipping school when they go to a cinema. This event along with a health scare in the family, unfortunately changes their plans. The mothers plan for their marriage. They are compelled into arranged marriages. Sudha marries her mother's choice Ramesh. But misfortune courts them during their marriage ceremony; Sunil reveals his infatuation with Sudha. Sudha will move in with her husband and in laws who live another part of India. Neither marriage results in happiness. Sudha had learnt a dark secret about the family. Their friendship and love is shattered...Instead distrust and suspicion set in.

Anju tries to fit into the new life. Later the two friends learn they are pregnant at the same time. Sudha's mother-in-law insists to have an abortion and husband will not oppose his mother. Sudha takes refuge with her family and is divorced for "desertion" Sudha, who was patiently bearing everything, stands boldly and defend her child inside her. She is forced to run away but she knows nobody would entertain her. Her mother will not understand her predicament. Her mother more traditional can never come out of the belief that a married women should live under the shelter of her husband.

Nalini, Sudha's Mother does not hesitate to sacrifice her own daughter's happiness. Pishi-the great upholder of family tradition, comes to the rescue of Sudha. She renders Sudha support. The three traditional women in the family do not allow Sudha to abort the girl baby to save the families face in the society. They bless her like the Rani of Jhansi, The Queen of Swords. Pishi mourns for the tyrannical rules of the society. When a girl is divorced/or becomes a widow.

When tragedy strikes them again, they realise that in spite of distance of marriage they feel comfortable when each turn to the other. All though Sudha's girl could love proposes to her. He does not want her child. She refuses him and comes to Anju in America. Anju caught up with also marital difficulties. When Anju becomes pregnant, Sunil discovers she has been secretly working at the campus. They fight, this leads to miscarriage. Sunil blames Anju. These marital difficulties are complicated due to Sunil's infatuation with Sudha. Sudha's arrival in America is the end of the novel.

Chitra Banerjee's novels are confined to the study of women of all races who share a common female experience he female characters struggle, in their balance between female responsibilities and individual happiness. Anju and Sudha suffer and where America gives a promising possibilility for Anju, who can work dress in the western style. Whereas Sudha would live a long with her child and face discrimination in India. Sudha honors and admires all that is Indian. She feels sad and subordinated in order to lead a comfortable life. This means that something that can enable to create a new atmosphere and to face challenges as a women.

Anita Rau Badami's novel *Tamarind Mem* is a family saga. Anita Rau Badami's novel *Tamarind Mem* is divided into two parts, first part is about Kamini, the daughter of Saroja, the second part is about the mother Saroja. There is an endless conflict between the mother and the daughter. The novel is set both in India and in Canada. The mother is nicknamed "Sour tongued", and is in India and her daughter in Canada. Saroja is a very ambitious women wanted to become a doctor. On compulsion from her parents, she got married. Saroja begged her parents to permit her to pursue her studies. Sarojas's mother replied, "A women without a husband is like sand without the river, No man to protect you and every evil wind will blow over your body" (TMA 158). Marriage does not bring happiness for her. Her husband is always busy with his work as an engineer. There is no sharing of her feelings and communication with his wife. She could not escape from the bondage of culture. She was her Sour tongue to scold others. She protects her daughter from the traditional rules. She was imprisoned with the traditional rules and cultural heritage. Saroja wanted her daughter to be a free bird. Saroja, as a protagonist does not accept Paul's offer. She just maintains her daughters sake and for their future. Saroja has all the necessary characters of an Indian women and she lead her life in as a candle in order to give light to their next generation. She grants her daughter whatever she missed in her life Saroja nick named Sour tongue. She was this tongue to protect her daughter's from the scorn of relatives in her family. Saroja after her husband's death takes up a journey she travels throughout India visiting places like a Sanyasi. Now this journey fulfilled her life. Saroja never allowed anyone to live under her shelter. Anita Rau Badami portrays Saroja as a frustrated women trapped in cultural expectations. Anita Rau Badami presents Saroja as a women escaping from the traditional prison to the modern independent world. She gets out of her traditional values taught by her orthodox parents and from her disappointed married life. She very slowly and gradually escapes from her motherly duties. She becomes an independent woman.

Empowerment points out to women the need to fight for their privileges. Sudha has to confront and tackle the problem of pregnancy and abortion. Sudha emerged as independent women. She is able to confess, convince every one of her actions. She does not regret or sentimentalise as an ordinary woman. She has the determination, courage learnt to outlive the situation in which she is placed. She neither acts as a daughter of the Chaterjee family nor as a daughter-in-law of the Sanyals. She discovers that she cannot allow being dependent on man and so she searches out for an independent life. Anju also mustered the courage that is essential for her to survive in the world. The characters of Chita Bannerji make and the interaction they maintain with the immigrant community force them to question their existence and morality. Chitra Banerjee has created a new empowering image for women. The hall mark of this transition was the emergence of the new women which would change the dynamics of the Indian society forever and for the better.

Works Cited

Divakaruni, Chitra, *Sister of My Heart*. Great Britain: Doubleday, 1999.

Parameswaran, Uma. *A Study of representative Indo-English Novelists*. Delhi: Vikas Publishing House, 1976.

Chetty, Rajendra and Pier Paolo Piciucco. *Indias Abroad The Diaspora Writes Back South Africa*, 2004.

International Multidisciplinary Research Journal.

An International Refereed e-Journal of Literary Exploration.

12

Depiction of Wounded Women in Partition Stories of Sadat Hasan Manto

Shivani Sharma

The date of India's partition and the birth of Pakistan, August 15, 1947, marked the culmination of a mass exodus of Hindus to India and Muslims to the newly established Pakistan. This time was also remembered as the period of India's worst communal unrest. During the partition, the fulminations on family, faith, national position, and defence exaggerated the conflicts over ownership and dignity of female sexuality, contributing to horrible brutality against women in both cultures. The sexual violence that occurred during the partition of India and Pakistan represented an intense manifestation of society's attitude toward women's sexuality, especially the desire to control and own her. The violence also depicted how women's sexuality symbolically represented power in gender relations in India's Hindu and Islamic communities. This chapter would look at these ideas about sexuality by looking at the division of India and Pakistan as a point, where, due to the heightened emotion of the circumstance, sexuality and power were particularly entwined. Partition, one the saddest moments of India in twentieth century, is a dominant sad theme in Indian literature, either English or in Vernaculars. The sadness can be imagined by the fact that around 10 to 12 million Indians displaced during the event that is followed by butchering, killing, prostitution and even in rapes of women of opposite religion.

It was the selection of shocking and real life stories which makes Manto one of the most controversial short-story writers of the time. In his small career of some 20 years, Manto never afraid to expose the madness, nakedness and hollowness of the society around him. His theme somewhere surpasses the Progressive Writers' Association and other place over take the social-realism. In short, he was more progressive and more realist than any other author of the time. Manto, the more real than realists or to say socio-realists, tragically showcased the real life stories of the victims exposed to the partition, both from India and Pakistan. Manto's short story "Toba Tek Singh," written shortly before his death, is a live example of it that has its setting in the environment surrounded by the Partition of India. Manto had been implacably opposed to partition and had refused to go to the newly formed Pakistan. One evening he was sitting drinking with his Hindu colleagues at the offices of the newspaper where he worked when one of them remarked that, were it not for the fact they were friends, he would have killed Manto. The next day Manto packed his bags and took his family to Lahore, and it was here that he wrote the stories that revisited the brutality and absurdities of partition. In "Toba Tek Singh", one of his most famous stories, Hindu and Sikh patients in a Pakistani asylum are moved to India. One of them, a Sikh, is so enraged that he stands on the border between Pakistan and India. Manto said Partition was madness he adds "Don't say that 100,000 Hindus and 100,000 Muslims have been massacred," and he wrote "say that 200,000 human beings have been slaughtered. And it is not such a great tragedy that 200,000 human beings have been butchered but the real tragedy is that the dead have been killed for nothing." The legacies of partition are still with us – in both the subcontinent and in Britain – and the need to understand it has not diminished with time. "How does this happen? How is it that people who have lived on the same street for centuries turn on each other?" asks Hanif. "How do you kill your best friend? He is one of the few writers who picked on these themes and he wrote ferociously, and he wrote fearlessly."

Women were considered to be the most dangerous casualties of partition. All types of degradation, brutality, torture, and barbarism were accepted. Women's mutilated breasts landed in cars, where they were captured, molested, abused, and murdered. People were ultimately duped that the best way to inflict vengeance on the opposing group was to dishonour their women. When they squandered their blamelessness, they may adversely harmonise to their primary residences. When Sundari, a newly married bride, was heading to Gujranwala with her benedict on the fourth anniversary of her engagement, Khushwant Singh explains the hollowness of societal expectations and pointless procedures. Their bus was overrun by Muslims on the road to Pakistan. Her husband was stripped nude, and she was physically molested by the ferocious crowd.' The literature of the partition is fraught with themes and stories about tyranny, violence, and insanity for no particular cause. The plot takes one back to some 2-3 years after the partition, and the story can be seen as a slap on the face of governments of Pakistan and Hindustan. Both, during this critical time, decided to exchange the lunatics across the border. This remains the theme of Manto's story.

Saadat Hasan Manto, unquestionably one of modern India's most questionable Urdu authors, has a special place in the hearts of literature lovers. 'His compositions are well-known for depicting human nature in a savage and blunt but cohesive way. His tales are characterised by gloom, evil, and social taboos. However, he stands out because of his precision and strong degree of character insight and detail.

During the partition period, Saadat Hasan Manto was published regarding women being abused. In order to escape rape, several people attempted suicide or were killed by their husbands. Other scholars, such as Urvashi Butalia of Zubaan Books, have written about the violence against women during Partition, but far later. Manto, on the other hand, was well ahead of his period in terms of questioning culture and writing against its hypocrisy.

In "Thanda Gosht" (Cold Meat), one of his fiction short stories set during the continuing war between Muslims, Hindus, and Sikhs, a man rapes a woman out of contempt towards the other religion. He eventually discovers that he raped a dead body. When his wife attempts to seduce him after he comes home, he is not physically aroused by her. He can't get his mind off the lady he assaulted. Enraged, the wife murders her husband.

Kalwant, Eeshwar's wife, is depicted in "Thanda Gosht" as a woman who seeks revenge through her organisation. She isn't described as vulnerable or afraid. Kalwant's anger reflects her willingness to confront her husband. She uses her influence to blame him for his infidelity, rather than becoming submissive and subservient. The narrative often illustrates how women were treated as artifacts, and how their dignity was viewed as an extension of men's honour. As a result, rape was seen as a weapon to undermine the opposing community's honor.

In another short tale, "Khol Do" (Open It), a girl kidnapped in East Punjab (now Pakistan) is eventually found in a hospital by her father. She's been raped by her kidnappers as well as rescuers, and she's been wronged by men from all walks of life. As rapes were conducted in secret, hushed up from public culture, his portrayal of abuse against women was an apt reflection of society. At the moment, women claimed that stopping suicide was better than preventing abuse. In this narrative, the definition of honor, which can be interpreted as a reflection of culture, is prominent.

Since his stories dealt with subjects that were mostly deemed taboo, Manto was branded as crude and vulgar. He freely addressed women's sexuality and did not hesitate to use words such as breasts, which was deemed very brazen at the time, particularly by a male. Rather than treating women as sexless objects or having repressed their sexualities, Manto is known to have portrayed women as he saw men without creating distinctions in their morality or making judgments about them despite their roles. As sexuality is combined with incorrect conceptions of dignity, women's position in India becomes especially complicated. Women have a special role in all religions and it is this virtue that contributes to redemption, whether in the form of a better heaven or regeneration, and this honor is reflected in women. Honor is correlated with personal modesty, chastity, and loyalty, and the individual is required to maintain her honor and the honor of her male relatives by these ways. Controlling female sexuality, whether by her parent, spouse, brother, or son, determines the social and moral order of all cultures, and the regulation of sexuality is justified by describing chastity as pure and holy and sex as impure. As a consequence, maintaining male honor becomes inextricably connected to preserving female honor. Controlling sexuality and preserving honor contributes to the development of conventional paradigms of the perfect woman, and any woman who deviates from this construct, whether through coercion or choice, is stigmatised as immoral." Controlling her sexuality and her body becomes the most powerful way to preserve or kill dignity. "This element of female identity was skewed during the division, which further magnified pre-existing perceptions of women as property that had already pervaded the communities.

Right at the start of the field, work by Das (1995), Butalia (1998), and Menon and Bhasin (1998) showed that the brutality of partition for women ranged from gender relationships within the family to those with the nation/state. During division, women were exposed to inhuman acts of sexual abuse, demonstrating the insecure role of women in society's patriarchal arrangement.

Furthermore, victimisation of people from the other culture was not the only kind of abuse women were exposed to. No one hesitates to denounce women's kidnapping and torture, genital mutilation, and tattooing of their reproductive organs with images of the other faith' (Butalia 1998: 204). Communities, on the other hand, are much less likely to debate how many women were murdered by their own kin to 'save their dignity,' how many committed suicide for the same cause, and how many women and infants, along with often elderly men, were 'martyred' to 'secure' them from forced conversion. They were far less likely to address any individual who had fled martyrdom and 'honourable death' in order to endure abuse and kidnapping. As a result, Bhasin and Menon write of 'permissible' abuse against women by their own families and kin in order to preserve their dignity. Although 'the lines between option and coercion' are complicated to draw in this sense, Butalia questions that 'such events [of noble death and martyrdom] qualify as violent incidents nowhere in the discourses on partition' (1998: 212-214). 'As a consequence, we are guided to explore the past, contours, and function of the idea of honor, which is related to oppressive notions of female sexual modesty and chastity.

The regime, too, duplicates the brutality of setting a woman's worth in terms of her sexuality and using her solely as money in an honor economy, as the past of partition reveals. Das, Butalia, Menon, and Bhasin draw our attention to the Government of India's Recovery Activity, especially The Abducted Persons Act, which was passed in the Indian Parliament in December 1949. They find out that the concept of an abducted individual in the Act was originally a male child of sixteen years or a girl of any age (Menon and Bhasin 1998: 71, emphasis added). While the Act provided police wide powers to arrest anybody they accused of being kidnapped after March 31, 1947, it refused to accept women as legitimate subjects with their own views. Regardless of the reality that the circumstances of their 'abduction' differed greatly, some were left behind as captives for the safe passage of their families and others. These images of women made violence toward women perfectly appropriate, and they expressed the universal visceral emotions that men in all cultures have and have against women. Fifty-seven years later, not much has improved, both in terms of the general view of women as intrusive sexual creatures that must be regulated and in terms of abuse aimed at them during periods of communal tension. For example, after Islamic extremists set fire to trains carrying Hindus in Gujurat only two years ago, Hindu men committed virtually equivalent forms of violence against Muslim women. According to the Human Rights Study on Sexual Abuse against Women. A Global Viewpoint, conflict and sexual violence are not special to India. 'Women have traditionally been abused for sexual harassment during periods of civil and foreign war. As a means of fighting, troops raped and otherwise physically assaulted people on the opposite side; rape helped to demoralise and execute the opponent. Another aspect leading to women's sexual abuse during periods of combat was men's socialised views about women and women (like other objects) became spoils of battle and therefore sexually accessible to them during times of conflict." Furthermore, soldiers were not afraid of being disciplined if they perpetrated sexual abuse against a section of the civilian community that, particularly in periods of stability, had an unfair or reduced position in contrast to men.

Thus, Saadat Hassan Manto, Manto's characters come from a fallen class, the class of people who have been rejected by society under the assumption that they are somehow morally degraded. Through this story of Manto implicitly criticise collective madness of the then leaders whose misdeed invites apocalypse future.

Works Cited

Bodh, Prakash. "*Nation and Identity in the Narratives of Partition*". Postcolonial India: History, Politics and Culture. Eds. Vinita Damodaran and Maya Unnithan Kumar. Delhi: *Manohar,* 2000. *1220. PDF*

Issar, Devendra. "Manto: *The Image of the Soul in the Mirror of Eros." Tr. M. Asaduddin and Alok Bhalla Conference; Life and works of Saadat Hasan Manto. Ed. Alok Bhalla*. Simla: Indian Institute of Advanced study, 1996. 184-190. PDF

Panthi, Dadhi Ram. "Moral Condemnation of Partition Violence in Manto's Toba Tek Singh." *International Journal of Humanities and Cultural Studies* ISSN 2356-5926 2.3 (2015): 700-09. PDF

Selden, Raman. "Art and Objective Truth." *The Theory of Criticism*. 1990 ed. Vol. 1. New York: Longman Group, n.d. 40-78.

13

Re-reading J. K. Rowling's *Harry Potter*: Postcolonialism and the British Empire

Giangthuiliu Gonmei

The Harry Potter series has been receiving praises and admiration to a great extends from children and adults alike since its first publication in 1997. It is easy to see at first sight that they are for children where good triumphs over evil. If we step past the pleasurable reading of children's literature, in their courses in the book, we see social themes and issues play out. In children's literature, colonial and postcolonial observations are prevalent. This paper will explore the subject of magical creatures in the wizarding world, the subject of humans other than English wizards, and Harry's characterisation in the Harry Potter novels from a postcolonial perspective with particular reference to Othering, hybridity, and ethnicity. This will provide us to find proof of imperialism and postcolonialism inside the narratives of J. K. Rowling. By investigating instances of identity, hybridity, and Othering, one can relate without difficulty the impacts of imperialism to the storyline and characters in the books.

The Harry Potter series by J. K. Rowling consists of seven novels with witches and wizards and animals that are not regular animals. The events in the books of Harry Potter take place during the 1990s in Great Britain in both a wizarding and a non-wizarding society (Fransson). Harry Potter, a famous teenage wizard, is the protagonist of the story. In the first book, Harry was not aware that he possesses magical abilities and that he is the son of a witch and wizard and lives with his non-magical aunt and uncle in a suburb of London. We can look at this kind of novel for children just as they are without extensive observation.

On multiple previous occasions, the Harry Potter novels have been studied using various hypotheses and objectives. As in previous studies, the Harry Potter novels have been used to analyse the topic of gender, patriarchy, feminism, etc., in conventional literature reviews and classrooms. In this paper too, we will take a look at the famous *Harry Potter* novels by J. K. Rowling and analyse them to obtain a more profound message. This paper would do so by taking two novels from the Harry Potter novel series – *Harry Potter and the Philosopher's Stone* and *Harry Potter and the*

Goblet of Fire and examining them to find proof that supports the hypothesis through the lens of postcolonial theory.

While the Harry Potter novels have been studied from several viewpoints before, they are so nuanced that it is still possible to discover various subject matters. Together with reference to Postcolonial theories, this paper will demonstrate how certain events in the two novels of the Harry Potter series mentioned above can be used to investigate unjust problems that can arise in society. Through the term Othering, few themes of discrimination are also examined in this paper. The argument in this paper will be divided into three parts: the subject of magical creatures in the wizarding world, the subject of humans other than English wizards, and the characterisation of Harry Potter in the novel(s).

Postcolonial Criticism was originally established to analyse how colonisers affected postcolonial countries. Some of the ideas used in postcolonial critique can be used to describe how prejudice is depicted in novels. In the Harry Potter books, there is a clear hierarchy between non-magic and magical beings, and it may be claimed that magical humans and animals are the dominant race or groups who oppress and discriminate against non-magic humans and animals. Through children's literature, many European nations of the eighteenth, nineteenth, and twentieth centuries have instilled the colonial and colonising ideals of the adult population (Anatol 165). Through her novels, Rowling has built a world parallel to contemporary Britain in which she can explore colonialism and class problems. Under this context, it incorporates characters, artifacts, and events reflecting colonial dominance and the post-colonial powers that resist it (Sorensen 104).

In their essay, "Images of the Privileged Insider and Outcast Outsider," Elizabeth E. Heilman and Anne E. Gregory examine the power dynamics portrayed at the metaphorical level of Harry Potter's books. They state, "the Harry Potter books legitimise numerous forms of social inequality and their related cultural norms, rituals, and traditions" (Heilman). The authors address power dynamics by social status, peer groups and community, heredity, and nationality. The writers also note that the "non-dominant cultures" portrayed in the books play a parenthetical role in the plot, suggesting a strong imbalance of power. Heilman and Gregory briefly mention educational opportunities focused on these power structures (Heilman). Pseudoscientific theories like phrenology and race classification theory also greatly influenced racial thinking in the British empire.

Barbara J. Fields, a history professor and general scholar writes in *Ideology and Race in American History* that "classes may have struggled over power and privilege, over oppression and exploitation, over competing senses of justice and right; but in the United States, these were secondary to the great, overarching theme of race" (Fields 143). This, too, can be seen to be true in Rowling's wizard world, where the issue of racial inequality becomes all-encompassing and essentially contributes to (and in some cases creates) class struggles as well as other social problems.

In the magical world of Harry Potter, there are witches and wizards as well as animals and other beings that are not normal and do not associate or get together with the prevalent human races. There are the house-elves who serve the witches and wizards household, the goblins who serve as bankers, the centaurs who are held in the forests, and the merfolk in the lake. The dwarves were recruited by Lockhart as Hogwarts entertainers, and there are the veelas who work during the quidditch world cup as exotic dancers (Goblet of Fire). The centaurs and the giants lost their native lands to the humans of Hogwarts and were forced to live in reservations reminiscent of the Native Americans (Green). The giants and the centaurs were not portrayed in a particularly sympathetic light in the book. The centaurs were portrayed as being violent and even uncooperative towards any humans who attempt to have contact with them. The giants, as well, were described as being unreasonable and ignorant that they are bringing themselves to death by killing each other.

On the other hand, the other groups of creatures or species that do remain on good terms with the witches and wizards each have much to give to them for having accepted them into their magical community. Goblins are valuable to have around in view of their hold over the financial business, and the house-elves are valuable as domestic servants. Then Veelas are exoticized as the other again, and they have only appeared in two roles in the books: as entertainers and as married to wizards (Goblet 253). There is also the merfolk whom Dumbledore advocates for their entitlement to exist in their own isolated areas of land, and consequently, they will support Dumbledore. Merfolk will permit themselves and their home to be utilised as deterrents in the tri-wizarding competition, and the centaurs will let wizards trail through their forest.

What about the humans in the magical world? All of them are not created equal either. The other magical world of wizards and witches and its conditions outside of Britain are not shown in great lights in the books. The global wizards we do see are additionally nearly as much stereotyped and generalised as the creatures. We can see that the French witches and wizards from Beauxbatons are presented as conceited and showy, whereas the ones from Durmstrang are depicted as being rough and brutish.

There is additionally an unmistakable divide between the muggles and wizards. The wizards indeed are compelled by a solemn obligation from their superior position to secure the muggles. The novels shed a light that there was a division between the magical world and the non-magical world, not for the protection of the people of the magical world, but for the muggles who, in their obliviousness, kept burning other muggles during the period of witch-hunting. The probability that muggles were to win the war if they were confronted with an existential danger like the death-eaters and their genocidal instincts is not even passed on as a concept. There is no discussion of the moral ramifications of keeping the muggle community unaware of a section of the UK population that wants to destroy them and has participated in many terrorist attacks against the general population.

In order to keep the magical community hidden from the non-magical folks, witches and wizards clearly have the authority and power to endanger the muggles' existence. Those from the magical community who display some fascination in muggles do so in the most patronising manner possible. Arthur Weasley, who was Head of the Misuse of Muggle Artefacts Office for years, was unable to say the word electricity correctly and has no idea of what is a rubber duck. How is it possible for one to work for affairs concerning muggles while being fully unaware and unfamiliar about it? How is it that all muggle-born people clearly prefer to follow the ideology of wizarding without any underground muggle-born culture running against the state of pure blood? Hermione Granger wishes herself to be seen not as someone with a cultural awareness of muggles which may be a power in itself, but as one of the witches, and this reminded us of Fanon's *Black Skin, White Mask*. Rowling really needs readers to believe that it is naturally so ideal for the British wizarding world that no counter-cultures have been born inside it or that there might ever be some other problem than that muggle-born cultures are prohibited from accumulating in it.

At first glance, Harry Potter seems to be the underdog battling against the wizarding world's unfair establishment. But when we take a careful observation at how the story goes, Harry is not an underdog, as he was able to inherit a great amount of wealth from his deceased parents during the first part of the novels (Philosopher's Stone p.85). Extreme wealth tends to be a derogatory trait in any other character, but Harry's status as an heir to inheritance is not at all adequately addressed in relation to his moral nature.

Harry is also the son of two respected and powerful parents; both of them are well-known in the wizarding community. Harry can recollect his relationship to an old pureblood ancestry on his father's side, rendering him a member of the foundation of pureblood wizarding. The wealth and bloodline that the Potter family has inherited ensure a place for young Harry in the upper class of magical society. Even the highly racist Draco Malfoy seems willing to make friends with Harry in the first novel (Philosopher's Stone p.120). It was only Voldemort who took his natural heritage and rights from him and pushed him into hiding with his cruel and brutish (muggle) relatives (Mendlesohn 369).

In the wizarding world, there are structures and establishments that are similar to those found in the British empire but not those issues of such systems. At last, they were able to go back to their normal life where 'everything is well.' The house-elves now have regulations and laws which protect them from being mistreated by their master as it regulates the master to be punishable if found mistreating them. In their segregation, the goblins proceed, and a pledge of no genocide is made to the Centaurs and Merfolk. The British muggle-born are promised a spot in the dominant wizarding community, considering they follow the pureblood noble and do not display muggle culture. The dominance of the British wizard form has been proven, and they live benevolently over their less developed subjects, ensuring that in peace, they are able to serve their positions in society, as they naturally wish. There are no rebellious creature-rights activists wreaking disorder out in the public space. There is no muggle-born who wants to side with the wizards against the muggles. No dictatorship exists; only the natural order of things exists.

Works Cited

Anatol, Giselle Liza. "The Fallen Empire: Exploring Ethnic Otherness in the World of Harry Potter." *Reading Harry Potter: Critical Essays*. 2003. pp. 163-178.

Fields, Barbara J. "Ideology and Race in American History." *Region, Race, and Reconstruction. Eds. Kousser and McPherson*. New York: Oxford UP, 1982.

Fransson, Sophia. "Using Selected Novels of Harry Potter as a Tool for Discussion in the English as a Foreign Language Classroom with Postcolonial and Marxist Perspectives." *The Institution for Culture & Learning, Södertörns University*. 2015.

Green, Amy M. "Revealing Discrimination: Social Hierarchy and the Exclusion/Enslavement of the Other in the Harry Potter Novels." *The Looking Glass : New Perspectives on Children's Literature*. 2009.

Heilman, Elizabeth E. and Gregory, Anne E.. "Images of the Privileged Insider and Outcast Outsider" New York, *Harry Potter's World: Multidisciplinary Critical Perspectives* (2003)

Mendlesohn, Farah. "Crowning the King: Harry Potter and the Construction of Authority." *The Ivory Tower and Harry Potter. Columbia: University of Missouri Press*. 2002. pp. 366-384.

Rowling, J. K. *Harry Potter and the Goblet of Fire*. Bloomsbury, 2010.

.... *Harry Potter & the Philosopher's Stone*. Bloomsbury, 2018.

Sorensen, Christian. "Education at Hogwarts: Colonising the Muggle." *Inscape*: Vol. 21: No. 2, Article 5, 2001. pp. 103-115.

14

Postcolonial Caribbean Rootlessness and Identity Quandary: Mapping Walcottian Cultural Resistance in *Omeros*[2]

Bame Jude Thaddeus Tomnyuy

Introduction

This chapter investigates and discusses how Derek Walcott in the poem *Omeros*, exposes and resists the quandaries suffered by Saint Lucian identity contrived by their cultural rootlessness engineered through imperialist epistemology as well as practices like slavery and colonialism. In effect, the chapter seeks to map out the various ways in which the poet's cultural resistance enables him to (re)construct a newfangled identity for his compatriots. Premised on the mutuality between cultural roots and identity as well as understandings of resistance, the chapter will argue that, the various afflictions suffered by Saint Lucians as a result of rootlessness, warrants Walcott's cultural resistance aimed at (re)constructing a distinctive identity for them.

The institutions and practices of slavery and colonialism established an observable power dynamic whose objective was domination and exploitation implemented through physical violence. Nonetheless, Western epistemology by emphasising the uncivilised state of indigenous peoples, justified the effacement of their cultural roots and of course, their identity. In fact, "colonialist literature was informed by theories concerning the superiority of European culture and the rightness of empire" (Boehmer 3). This is because such literature, perceived of the native as "a quintessence of evil" and a "negation of values" (Fanon 41).

A true sense of self and identity within the inhabitants of the Caribbean islands was scraped as a result of "the experience of enslavement, transportation, or 'voluntary' removal for indenture labour. Or...destroyed by *cultural denigration*, the conscious and unconscious oppression of the indigenous personality and culture by a supposedly superior racial or cultural model [original emphasis]" (Ashcroft *et al.* 9).

2 Alternative Title: Mapping Walcottian Cultural Resistance in Omeros

Sadly, the abolition of slavery and the feat of independence did not resolve the effects of rootlessness. The variegated ethnic and cultural morphology of the West Indies generated socio-cultural and political tensions. The lack of a unique Caribbean identity resulted to a lack of social cohesion among the racially and culturally diverse peoples of the islands.

This lack of commonality and the resultant identity crisis is attributable to the pluralistic racial backgrounds of the region's peoples as well as a general sense of rootlessness. In fact, the West Indies was misshapen because of these racial divisions that scored no sense of unity to transcend the people's differences (Marshall 287). To solve such problems, there must be a merging of all Caribbean experiences in order to overcome 'historylessness' in the process of fashioning national identities that take into account, the racial and cultural heterogeneity of the islanders (Glissant 153-4). The various cultural quandaries occasioned by slavery and colonialism especially related to roots and identity, still saturate postcolonial scholarship today because many a nation still suffers from them. The continued affliction of a people's identity licences a renewed sense of and a desire for cultural resistance in a poet like Walcott since his country and region still bear the negative impact of such problems that sustain the painfulness of the postcolonial condition.

But what is identity? It is "a cultural attribute enabling people to find meaning…through a process of individuation" (Castells 94). There are three main categories of identity *viz.*, "legitimising identity", "project identity" and of course, "identity of resistance" which is my focus in this chapter. Identity of resistance involves reactions by a "human collective" that feel culturally, economically or socio-politically marginalised. This kind of identity is created through materials of history and self-identification that empower this collective "to…[resist] what would be its…assimilation into a system in which its situation would be structurally subordinated" (Castells 95) or completely annihilated.

Since the processes of slavery, indenture and colonialism eroded the ancestral and cultural roots of Caribbean islanders, the process of identity (re)construction for them, becomes a serious quandary. To overcome such rootlessness within the brackets of postcolonialism and defeat 'historylessness' as Glissant captions it, there is need for a scrutiny of the process of erasure that should climax in the restitution of lost roots, culture and identity. The desire for reclamation must be typified by a "renewed quest for native roots and [a] distinct self-identity" that can be viewed "as a move from 'imposed innocence' to 'awakened conscience'" (Digole 129) through a process of cultural resistance.

Another important concept that this chapter explores is resistance/cultural resistance. Resistance is a "rejection of [the] power of the political over-structure and a sense of…solidarity against that structure" (Davis 12). The base for cultural resistance lies in counter-cultural discursivity within the process of contesting institutions and practices of denigration and exploitation. As a result, resistance cannot occur without the readiness of the afflicted to project ideas of liberation (Said 200). In this light, Derek Walcott through his poetry demonstrates his unwavering readiness to resist the cultural pains of his people in an effort to construct for them, a true Saint Lucian and Caribbean identity. Unequivocally, Walcott articulates through his poems especially *Omeros*, his rejection of, and his solidarity against the structures, discourses and practices that continually foment the affliction of Saint Lucian and Caribbean culture and identity.

From Caribbean Rootlessness to Identity Crisis

One of the major setbacks faced by Caribbean writers with the question of identity is that of their lost cultural roots. The dislodgment of native Africans through slavery and Asians through indenture to the Caribbean islands marked the beginning of the abrasion and denigration of their roots, identities and cultures. Walcott captures this loss of roots in *Omeros* through the poem's characters by stressing the role of dislocation in its obliteration when the speaker in the poem allegorically intimates that:

> Men take their colours as the trees do from the native soil of their birth,
> And once they are moved elsewhere, entire cultures
> lose the art of mimicry, and then, where the trees were,
> /...a desert place / widens in the heart. (207-8)

Through metaphor, Walcott emphasises that, men inherit their racial identity from their place of birth as depicted by the word "colours" and "native soil" in order to make clear that, once Caribbean islanders were removed from their native land, they lost their ethno-cultural roots.

The abrasion of identity and culture occasioned by the loss of roots infuriates Philoctete who, in the poem, is mad at the bad yam yields that he associates to their lack of roots. The yams' lack of roots figuratively becomes his personal lack of ethno-cultural roots and consequently, a loss of his identity. As the speaker reports, Philoctete "cursed the yams: / "Salope! / You all see what it's like without roots in the world?" (21). Poor Philoctete unleashes his exasperation on his yams, and to buttress his cultural frustrations, he "hacked" the yams and abusively refers to them as "salope" meaning 'slut'. The pathos evoked by the line; he "sobbed, his face down the slaughtered leaves...[and] A sap / trickled from their gaping stems like his own sorrow", conveys Philoctete's afflictions occasioned by the loss of his ancestral roots and consequently, his cultural identity.

Like Philoctete, Achille has lost touch with his African ancestry and is constantly afflicted by his inability to reconcile his African-Caribbean culture and his new identity. Achille's sense of loss is echoed through dialogue when he has an epiphanic encounter with his dead father who asks him the meaning of his name – "Achille". His failure to say what it means or the meaning of Afolabe – the name he was given at birth (136-7), demonstrates the amnesia all islanders suffer and which accentuates the consequential abrasion of their personal as well as national identity. Achille is aggrieved by the loss of his identity for, after his failure to respond appropriately to his father's questions, the speaker says "Achille nodded / the tears glazing his eyes, where the past was reflected / as well as the future" (139).

Manifestly, it is only through his epiphany – his encounter with his father during which he experiences fragments of the Trans-Atlantic Slave Trade (134-5), that he seems to recover from his amnesiac state. Philoctete like Achille, is afflicted by slavery and consequent loss of his ancestral roots as well as cultural identity as captured through the incurable wound on his leg–a lesion that is interpreted here to symbolise the horrors of the Middle Passage because "He [Philoctete] believed that the swelling came from the chained ankles / of his grandfathers. Or else why was there no cure?" (19). Philoctete's apparently incurable wound can be read as a metaphor that captures the afflictions caused by slavery and colonialism on him and other characters in the poem and by extension, the people of the Caribbean islands in general. The wound can also be read as both physical and psychic to stress the multidimensional afflictions of slavery and colonialism whose effects can also be perceived on Achille and Ma Kilman.

Walcottian Cultural Resistance: (Re) Constructing Caribbean Roots and Identity

From the previous section, the correlation between dislocation, roots, loss, culture and identity has been established. Nevertheless, there still remains an unanswered question: how does Walcott go about his cultural resistance against the afflictions identified and discussed in an attempt to (re)construct the identities of his characters in *Omeros*? David William Lucas' submission that Walcott "takes up the task of liberating his islands, his language, and himself from that history of colonisation and enslavement", is of significance because the identity he seeks to forge is symbiotically linked to his characters' roots (214-5). Thus, the catharsis of his task lies in his construction of his compatriots' Caribbeanness through cultural resistance.

It is to be noted that, epistemological representations of slavery and imperialism that orchestrate cultural denigration and annihilation, can only begin "to loose their justification and legitimacy", when "the rebellious "natives" impress upon the metropolitan culture the independence and integrity of their own culture" (Said 200). It is during this counter-cultural discursive phase of resistance that efforts are made to reconstitute a shattered community against all the pressures of oppressive systems (Said 209). Of course, this is what Walcott enables his characters in *Omeros* to do. In the poem, such characters like Achille, Philoctete and Ma Kilman, make efforts to resist their different states of cultural rootlessness.

The Walcottian cultural resistance technique in *Omeros* is buttressed in what can be termed, the psychic journey motif. Through it, Walcott is able to contest and subvert the cultural afflictions suffered by West Indians. He does this by presenting his principal characters as subjects with agency rather than the erstwhile faux depictions of the enslaved, indentured and colonised as primitive object or "other" within some Western mega-narratives. Walcott is thus, through this psychic motif, able to free his characters of African descent, from the fetters of rootlessness and consequently, the identity quandaries they suffer.

Achille in *Omeros* for instance, is capable of overcoming his amnesia and ruin of his racial and cultural identity through an epiphanic reconnection with his ancestral roots. It is through this transcendental journey that his father appears to him and from the discussions that ensue, he comes to understand that his real name is not Achille but Afolabe; brought from Africa to the islands through slavery. Through this voyage into his genealogy or ancestral roots, Achille becomes an acting subject who resists the prior devastation of his selfhood by pursuing the information necessary for ascertaining his identity. His coming to terms with who he really is despite the obliviousness imposed by the processes of slavery and colonialism, crystallises with his father's wise counsel when he explains and warns that:

> No man loses his shadow except it is in the night,
> and even then his shadow is hidden, not lost. At the glow
> of sunrise, he stands on his own name in that light.
> … / but you, / if you're content with not knowing what our names mean,
> then I'm not Afolabe, your father, and…/…you,
> nameless son, are only the ghost / of a name. (138-9)

From the intimation of Achille's father, a man only loses understanding of who he is, during nightmarish moments like slavery, the Middle Passage and colonisation as suggested by the phrase, "in the night". Despite this, a man's shadow, interpreted here to mean identity, is merely "hidden, not lost" during such moments. Thus, any man who experiences setbacks in understanding who he is during moments of affliction like those suffered by Caribbean Islanders, has the ability to reassert himself. As the old man explains further, such a man must stand "on his own name" at "the glow / of sunrise" that is, when he comes to self-realisation of the pains he has endured as can be linked to his ancestral roots, culture and identity.

Of course, Achille/Afolabe overcomes his amnesia through this epiphanic journey that permits him to interact with his father. From this instant on, he becomes Afolabe for he now understands his pains, where he comes from, and who he really is. Moreover, it is this coming to terms with his selfhood through his ancestral and cultural roots that cause him to become emotional for the speaker reports that, as he nodded to the wise words of his father, the tears glased his eyes "where his [afflictive] past was reflected as well as the future" (139). Apparently, "the future" here, connotes his return from the journey as a new Caribbean man – one who understands who he is despite the afflictions that may continue to arise.

Now on to Ma Kilman the obeah, who, like Achille, undertakes a journey in order to find a cure for Philoctete's sore. Unlike Achille's however, Ma Kilman's journey is corporeal. Nonetheless, it has a tinge of the psychic, the spiritual or supernatural too. She is guided into the woods by ancestral ants to uncover the curative herbs whose seed had been carried from the Bight of Benin over the ocean to the Caribbean shores by a sea-swift hundreds of years ago (237-9). The subversive apotheosis of the priestess' journey comes when, in order to spiritually reconnect with her ancestors and visibly nature in a way that preserves the potency of the curative herbs, she has to strip for the speaker reports:

> Ma Kilman unpinned the black, red-berried
> straw-hat with its false beads, lifted the press
> of the henna wig, made of horsehair, from the mark
> on her forehead. Carefully, she set both aside
> on the green follicles of moss in the dark. (243)

Symbolically, this stripping signals Ma Kilman's defiance because her shading of alien ornaments, invigorates her cultural resistance that occasions her distantiation from the false identity created for her by Western cultural prescriptions. In this instance, Kilman can be said to have taken a voyage into the culture and tradition of her native Africa, and by stripping, she is resisting out of her sullied selfhood into her African culture as well as tradition. By so doing, she is able to assert her true Africano-Caribbean identity.

Kilman's journey and reconnection with nature as well as her ancestors carry both individual and collective implications for it signals hers, and all West Indians' rejection of the foreign cultural ways that have alienated them from their ancestral and cultural roots. Also, her stripping can be read as her acknowledgement of the fact that, through her unquestionable acceptance of alien cultural values, she has lost her rights and ability to commune with her African ancestors and deities who cannot recognise her, and she herself cannot understand their language through the spiritual ants. Kilman's alienation from the ways of her ancestors, justifies why she must cleanse herself by stripping and rubbing her forehead on the ground as a means of resisting the negative impact of alien cultural practices on her African culture before she can religiously connect with her ancestors and get hold of the curative herbs.

The Walcottian psychic journey motif as discussed here, presents his readers with an opportunity to perceive how through a reconnection with roots, tradition and environment, they can overcome the quandaries suffered by their own identities, cultures and traditions. The poet's engagement with the afflictions of lost roots, offer subversive perspectives of resistance against the denigrating (mis)conceptions of non-Western culture and identity especially within orientalist epistemology such as that projected about negroes and Africa claiming that, "there is nothing harmonious with humanity to be found in... [the negro's] character" or anything that brings him "within the range of culture" (Hegel 111).

By giving agency to his characters in *Omeros*, Walcott sets the base for his cultural resistance in the process of recuperating the lost African roots of the Caribbean and the revitalisation of the region's culture and identity. Finally, the reciprocity between cultural roots, identity and understandings of resistance, justifies the argument that, the various afflictions suffered by the identity of Caribbean islanders as a result of rootlessness, warrants Walcott's cultural resistance whose aim is the building of a true Caribbeanness, that is, a distinctive identity for Saint Lucia and the West Indies as a whole.

Works Cited

Ashcroft, Bill, et al. *The Empire Writes Back.* Routledge, 2002.

Boehmer, Elleke. *Colonial and Postcolonial Literature: Migrant Metaphors.* OUP, 2005.

Castells, Manuel. "Globalisation and Identity." *Quaderns de la Mediterrània* vol. 14, 2010, pp. 89-98.

Davis, Lennard. *Resisting Novels: Ideology and Fiction.* Methuen, 1987.

Digole, D.P. "Postcolonialism: An Aesthetic of Subversion and Reclamation" *Proceedings of National Seminar on Postmodern Literary Theory and Literature.* 2012, pp. 128-134.

Fanon, Frantz. *The Wretched of the Earth.* Grove Press, 1961.

Glissant, Édouard.. *Caribbean Discourse.* Trans. Michael Dash. Virginia UP, 1989.

Hegel, G.W.F. *Introduction to the Philosophy of History.* Trans. J. Sibree. Batoche Books, 2001.

Lucas, David W. "The Self in the Song: Identity and Authority in Contemporary American Poetry." University of Michigan, 2014.

Marshall, Peter J. Ed. *The Cambridge Illustrated History of the British Empire.* Cambridge UP, 1996.

Said, Edward. *Culture and Imperialism.* Knopf, 1993.

Walcott, Derek. *Omeros.* Farrar, Straus and Giroux, 1990.

15

Representing the Oppression of Indigenous Women through Storytelling: A Study of Bessie Head's "The Collector of Treasures", "Heaven is Not Closed", "Looking for a Rain God"

Mohonlal Patra

African literature is constituted with three sections – East Africa, South Africa, and West Africa. Disintegration of South African indigenous cultures affected the literature of the country due to racialism and the dominance of the white settlements there. The renowned South African writer Bessie Amelia Emery Head is commonly known as Bessie Head. Bessie Head in her writings projects the humdrum life, folktales, rituals and socio-economic condition of Botswana. In her fictions as well as in short stories one can find the saga of weal and woe of Botswana. Head upholds several themes in her writings like identity, exilic consciousness, oppression, relationships between men and women. She depicts in her short stories the live experience of the oppression of the native women of Botswana. I have taken three stories of Bessie Head to explore the oppression faced by women of Botswana and how their conscripted roles shape their identities. The stories of Bessie Head taken for discussion are "The Collector of Treasures", "Looking for a Rain God" and "Heaven Is Not Closed". All the three stories have been published by Heinemann Educational Books in 1977 in an anthology of 13 magnificent short stories named *The Collector of Treasures and Other Botswana Village Tales.* The stories I have taken for my study are generally depicted through oral storytelling. Every indigenous culture has various literary products in oral tradition. The aim of this paper is to show the plight, suffering, and the grim condition of indigenous women of Botswana under shade of marriage, family system and dominance. To make the paper relevant I have analysed the stories under important theoretical views like Feminism and Spivak's Subaltern Studies. The objective of my research is to explore how the women of the indigenous society are oppressed in the name of social system. The three stories have different dimensions of oppression against women. Bessie portrayed the African male and female through the mode of fictional narration i.e. through story telling.

These stories lead us to make out what kind of oppression the indigenous women have faced and endured. "The Collector of Treasures" begins with Dikeledi's imprisonment. Dikeledi's tragedy is based on an actual story told to Bessie Head by the family of the emasculated husband. At the very outset of the story, Head makes one thing clear that Dikeledi is one of many African women convicted of murdering their profligate husbands. Garesego, husband of Dikeledi is a sex-maniac who deserved to die; is not a single and isolated individual but a type whose numbers are multitude in independent Africa. In this aspect one can take Kebonye's husband for another example of this type. Kebonye's husband, a school administrator chastises the male teachers for making sexual advances toward their female students, but he himself is impregnating school girls. Moreover, he is guilty of spousal abuse. "The Collector of Treasures" is a very gender oriented stories. In this story, Bessie projects two types of man. The first one regards sex as a means of exerting power over his wife. He is not faithful and he has sex with his women like dogs, out of pure carnal lust. Garesego is an example of this type. The second one makes care of everything so that his wife never has a day of worry. He makes sexual life enjoyable for his wife. Paul is an example of this second type. "The Collector of Treasures" upholds the oppression against African women and their struggle against ghost-ridden pasts. Dikeledi's decision of killing her husband, Garesego is one type of reaction against this life-long extreme oppression. Dikeledi cannot tolerate her husband's sexual abuse and torment no longer. Therefore, she has taken such bold step to come out from the clutch of chronic domination and oppression and she has no prick of conscience after committing this crime. She strongly retorts about the crime,

> "I cut off his special parts with a knife." ("The Collector of Treasures")

Dikeledi's going to the prison is not a mode of confinement for her but a taste of liberation or an experiment of freedom for the first time.

The story "Looking for a Rain God" is also an oral account told by a member of the village about history and people of Serowe, a large village in South Africa. In the story "Looking for a Rain God" Mokgobja and his son, Ramadi kills the family's two young daughters, Neo and Boseyong to bring rain in their village. Actually, Mokgobja sacrifices her daughters just for the ritual belief or practices. Question may arise in the reader's mind why the girls should be victimised for this kind of ritual practices? Why doesn't Mokgobja take his son, Ramadi for this ritual practice? Bessie Head tries to solve this type of evergreen critical question. Head suggests that at the time the story was written society as well as the villages were steered by the male members. The ideas or desires of women also controlled by the male members in the villages and the male members take decisions as per their own interests and actions. Two young girls, Neo and Boseyong have been killed just based on Mokgobja's traditional beliefs. The most important thing is that Mokgobja has no sense of repentance for this crime. But to him, this is one kind of sacrifice for the greater good of the family, because of that his family may survive the drought and his crops might grow. Mokgobja also stated a lie that Neo and Boseyong died of natural causes. In this story the general tendency of the society of victimising the women is depicted through story telling.

In the story "Heaven Is Not Closed" we have seen the pathetic situation of a devout Christian woman of Botswana. The protagonist of the story, Galenthebege becomes a victim of society's insensible rules and spiritual hypocrisy. Galenthebege wants to marry Ralokae who is not Christian by religion. Therefore, Galenthebege asks for advice from the church missionaries. The missionaries vehemently discard the proposal of marriage to Ralokae. Not only that, the Church also proves its inhuman stature by kicking her out from the Church. During the passage of time, Galenthebege succumbs to death and cannot fulfill her dream of marrying Ralokae. Several changes had taken place in the Botswana society because of colonial domination. Bessie surveyed the impact of generations of colonial domination on African men and the opportunism licensed by the postcolonial atmosphere in Botswana in the years following its independence.

Women in the postcolonial society is dominated and oppressed by several means. Generally, they are oppressed in the name of domestic violence, in the means of sexual abuse, through the mode of patriarchy or social system. Subaltern women, means tribal, lower-caste, dalit, indigenous women are oppressed by the power politics and masculine superiority. We can view a glimpse of grim reality of masculine superiority in the short stories of Bessie Head. To comprehend the situation of indigenous women in the postcolonial society one can remember the words of Kebonye. Kebonye said,

> "Our men don't think that we need tenderness and care. You know my husband used to kick me between the legs whenever he wanted that. Because of this I once lost a child. He wanted to sleep with me even when I was sick. And he would not take no for an answer. I once said to him he could even take another woman to sleep with when I was sick." ("The Collector of Treasures")

P.K.Nayar in his *Postcolonial Literature – An Introduction* very aptly theorised the condition of Subaltern women.

> The woman in postcolonial society is doubly colonised, as noted before. However, in the hierarchy of structural oppression, there are women who are placed further down the scale. Tribal, 'lower caste', differently abled, lesbian, lower class women all come in at the lower end of the hierarchy of women (Nayar:p.150).

Gayatri Chakravorty Spivak in her highly celebrated essay, "Can the Subaltern Speak?" argues that the Subalterns cannot raise their voice for their selves because of the impact of colonialism and clutch of patriarchy. Therefore, they need another intellectual voice to project their position and to bring them centre from margin. Bessie Head projects the voice of the African indigenous women through her short stories.

Bessie Head is very unwilling to categorise her writing as African or feminist, because she wants to make her writings global or universal. But we can analyse her writings under feminist theoretical view point. The selected stories of Bessie Head can be analysed through gynocriticism. If gynocriticism means the literary criticism concerned with women authors and the representation of women's experience with the aim of transforming the canon by privileging women writers, Bessie Head provides an excellent opportunity to develop its methods. The motto of gynocriticism is to unravel the tenets of women's writings by ascribing the woman's experience as being at the centre of both writing and criticism. In Head's writings the experiences of oppression of indigenous women of Botswana have been presented meticulously. Bessie's women characters also come under the shades of radical feminism. In radical feminism a common link works over the whole class of women and that is patriarchal oppression.

> Radical feminism treats women as a class, or a collective subject. They see all women as linked by a common structure: patriarchal oppression (Nayar.p.101).

This kind of patriarchal oppression also one can find in Alice Walker's *The Colour Purple,* where Celie is the victim of that oppression because of her stepfather and her insensible husband. In Chinua Achebe's *Things Fall Apart* Okonkwo's wives also face the same kind of oppression belonging to the indigenous society.

In "The Collector of Treasures" Bessie Head projects more dilemmas about the human condition. "The Collector of Treasures" is a complex story that does not condone Dikeledi's own 'crime of passion' but tries to understand why someone who is so good is denied to use the treasures she has collected on her journey. "Heaven Is Not Closed" is a story where people are placed in the colonial era where Christianity is slowly rendering the indigenous religion. If we visit the story from feminine perspective we can know that in society women have been said not 'to know their own minds, Galenthebege in this story is finest example of one woman who does not know her own mind. Bessie Head like a feminist theorist includes in her writings the identity of women, demanding rights for women and representing the experience of women. If women are considered as a radical force that subverts the construction of patriarchal phallocentric discourse, Bessie is famous for creating such characters, Dikeledi as for example. If anyone examines Bessie's writings from gynocritical perspectives he or she must find in her writings direct feminine experiences and longings, women's point of view and radical women-oriented transformation of society. Through these stories Bessie Head displays that the colonial oppression and postcolonial torment had equal devasting effects on indigenous women of Botswana. Karen Bernardo has justified this by commenting this following statement.

> It makes a fascinating link between African postcolonial independence and political freedom as well as feminism and the liberation of African women. It is a unique opportunity not to be missed. It has been said that for better or worse, her female

characters are willing to leave the oppressions of the past behind, all of them, and go forward into the future without looking back (Bernardo 2004).

On the basis of feminine approaches and women's rights the oppression against women should be eradicated from indigenous society, not only from indigenous but also from every society. If character like Paul emerges then the oppression, torment, violence against women cannot get a place to occur. It is the responsibility of every intellectual both male and female to raise voice against the oppression of women takes place in every society especially in indigenous society. Bessie Head was not like other feminists who believe that women will never achieve total liberation until they separate themselves from their oppressors.

Works Cited

Achebe, Chinua. 1958. *Things Fall Apart.* New York: Anchor Books, 1994.

Bernardo, Karen. (On-line). *Bessie Head (1937-86). South African writer.* Consulted at: http://www.sotrybites.com/head1.htm. [26/07/2004a].

.... (On-line). *Bessie Head's "The Collector of Treasures."* Consulted at: http:www.storybites.com/headtreasures.htm. [26/07/2004b].

Guha, Ranajit. 1997. *A Subaltern Studies Reader* 1986-1995.

Head, Bessie. *The Collector of Treasures and other Botswana Village Tales.* London: Heinemann, 1986.

Nayar, Pramod K. 2008. *Postcolonial Literature An Introduction: Pearson India Education Services.*

Nayar, Pramod K. 2010. *Contemporary Literary and Cultural Theory From Structuralism to Ecocriticism: Pearson India Education Services.*

Showalter, Elaine.2003. 'Feminist Criticism in the Wilderness'. In *Lodge and Wood* 2003.

Spivak, Gayatri Chakravorty, 1988. 'Can the Subaltern Speak?' in *Cary Nelson and Lawrence Grossberg*(ed.)

Walker, Alice, 1983. *The Color Purple: Orison Books* Ltd. ed. Weidenfeld & Nicolson, 2014.

16

Arundhati Roy's *God of Small Things*: A Postcolonial Feminist Critique

Rafraf Shakil and Mehak Fayaz

The determining nature of postcolonial projects cannot be attributed to single splinter group of writers; it was assessed by men and women invaders as well as men and women among the invaded. The elements produced by these sections were gauged by the positions they confronted. All these groups produced antithetical writings. The literature of invaders proclaimed invaded nations to be their own; their writings could not justly portray the complete real phenomenon. They said their procedure of ruling was free of any illicit system. But in real it was not even handed. This is understood by the following words, "Such texts can never form the basis for an indigenous culture nor can they be integrated in any way with the culture which already exists in the countries invaded. Despite their detailed reportage of landscape, custom, and language, they inevitably privilege the center, emphasising the 'home' over the 'native', the 'metropolitan' over the 'provincial' or 'colonial', and so forth" (Bill et al. 5).

On the other hand the invaded population traced everything critically: the custom, the language and the property. Hence they created Postcolonial literature with evocative descriptions and facts. Diverse groups of the academia and reformers took a chance of rephrasing their positions, one such group was that of women writers. They at sub level even started indicating the faults of the fellow men who proved to be unreasonable as they still inscribed fellow women as inferior and even neglected their roles. As in the words of Carole Boyce Davies, "where are the women in the theorising of post coloniality?" (Davies 80).

This chapter in particular observes the incompetence of Indian men of the postcolonial time who disregarded women and followed no promise. As KetuKatrak states "Gandhi's specific representations of women and female sexuality, and his symbolising from Hindu mythology of selected female figures who embodied a nationalist spirit promoted [...] a 'traditional' ideology wherein female sexuality was legitimately embodied only in marriage, wifehood, domesticity – all forms of controlling women's bodies" (Katrak117).

Recuperation from this state was advanced by various female postcolonial writers who felt that only a certain group of women enjoyed privileges and benefit while others are left unseen which gave rise to movements like women's liberation and feminism, conferring into better evaluation and exchange of ideas. As mentioned; "Postcolonial feminist historians' interest in colonialism is reflected in research that involves the recovery and examination of the role of women in freedom struggles and, further, in understanding the ways women's social roles, the symbolic meanings of femininity and female sexuality (such as "mother-hood"), and the relations among women of different castes, classes, and religious communities, were "recast" under colonial modernity, chiefly by way of the colonial state's reformist legislations. The first enterprise led to the realisation that the expansion of the sphere of activity and the increase of political influence that participation in anticolonial nationalist struggles had made possible for women, were invariably not sustained into decolonisation, except for a small class of elite women who had benefited from access to education and the professions under these conditions. How the demands of nationalism and feminism were reconciled or set at odds with one other, is an important and continuing site of inquiry for postcolonial feminism"(Schwarz and Ray 61).

Gradually the development in colonial and post-colonial writing was seen in the 1980s as at this time various reformists, liberation movements had emerged. Some receded while as few of them achieved desired results. Moderately there was a rise in awareness among women who reexamined the social structures formed after the conquerors rule. They observed various dissentious changes. The developments understood were; "Just as the advent of British rule prompted the reconstitution of Indian patriarchy, so too did its withdrawal from the subcontinent. Governing relationships and resources within the family, personal law formed an important lynchpin for many Indian social structures on which colonial power had depended. Changes in family law were therefore tied to and reflected shifts in the operation of colonial authority. Though the policies and networks of alliance pursued by the early colonial state varied between localities, regional studies of gender relations in this period have shown that the expansion of colonial rule was accompanied by a reconsolidation and heightening of existing social hierarchies and relationships of dominance throughout India" (Newbigin127).

Among this conscious category were the female fiction writers and essayists of India who presented the situation before followers in various forms. One among them is Arundhati Roy who wrote essays as well as novels with persuasive technique, the one which is to be discussed in this chapter is "The God of Small things" a novel consisting of "the layerings and interconnections of contrasting experience, of national turmoil and personal suffering, of physical wounding and linguistic artistry, of pain accented by play, and play hollowing out pain, were considered as being further elaborated in the cultural and political layerings of the narrative: the minglings of Hindu ritual, especially Kathikali dance, Marxist activism and Christian proselytising that characterised social life in Kerala in and around 1969" (Boehmer 64).

The main focus through this chapter will be on some hardships and harassments faced by the female residers of the Indian state, Kerala. "When interviewed about her novel, *The God of Small Things* shortly after winning the Booker Prize in 1997, Arundhati Roy made the point that her work had been conceived as a single defining image, and subsequently written out of sequence; "I didn't start with the first chapter or end with the last I started writing with a single image in my head: the sky blue Plymouth [car] with two twins inside it, a Marxist procession surrounding it [The story] just developed from there''. And, true to Roy's non-linear method, this ''single image'' is divided across the second chapter of the novel, forming the centre-piece of a larger episode which recounts a family outing to Cochin in the southern Indian state of Kerala, during which Roy's protagonists, middle-class Syrian Christians who run a failing pickle-factory, find their car surrounded by a trade-union demonstration at a rural level-crossing" (Tickell 73).

This single image which is fixed on her mind helped her to write this piece. She tries to come out of the early adapted form of assimilated English to an Indian form which indicates her coming out of the dominion system and hence returning to it through her mother tongue. The actions and etiquettes of female characters in the novel seem to be intimidated and restrained. The main female characters who are going to build up this analysis are Mammachi, baby kochamma, Ammu and Rahel who are dictated by men like Pappachi, Chacko and Baba. These are their tag names which the novelist has used. It is in itself an indication of the precocial state in which she wants to write and reframe her ideas. The male character Pappachi develops as a harsh husband and one sided father, he has been an imperial entomologist at the Pusa Institute, an unsympathetic husband and father, who dresses in a methodology habituated to him by several English men he worked for, even in the bad hot days of Ayemenem he continues wearing the English styled woolen wear. He is valiant and confident while beating his wife Mammachi. Pappachi is seventeen years older than Mammachi, a character who never avoided quarrels and confrontations in his house. "Pappachi worked hard on his public profile as a sophisticated, generous, moral man. But alone with his wife and children, he turned into a monstrous, suspicious bully, with a streak of vicious cunning. They were beaten, humiliated and then made to write the envy of relatives as well as friends for having such a nice partner and father.'' (Roy 180)

Mammachi has Conical corneas yet Pappachi is resentful towards her achievements be it her success as a pickle maker or her love towards playing the violin. Mammachi gets nothing in return, be it as a mother of Chacko or as a wife of Pappachi. This whole idea of improbability towards women arose from the traditional ideas they were still caught up in. Ammu who is Pappachi's daughter describes him as, "Pappachi was an incurable British CCP, which was short for chhi-

chhi poach and in Hindi meant Shit-wiper, Chacko said that the correct word for people like Pappachi was Anglophile" – The God of Small Things." (Roy 51-52) The Indian men lagged adequately in raising their homes. Ammu noticed his father who used to be "Urbane with visitors but gruesome with his family" which also suggests that being the defeators, the men had adapted seclusion and were captured in dreams. Loomba expresses," Colonialism intensified patriarchal oppression, often because native men, increasingly disenfranchised and excluded from the public sphere, became more tyrannical at home. They seized upon the home and the woman as emblems of their culture and nationality. The outside world could be Westernised but all was not lost if the domestic space retained its cultural purity" (Loomba 167).

Mammachi is dictated by a man of political considerations which shows how English Men had produced several clones who propagated the same agenda as they did. As earlier in the chapter women are mentioned as intimidated because she always receives beatings with different frequencies and yet quiet and cried profusely at his funeral. Roy's narrative that "at the funeral of Pappachi she mourns because she was used to him than because she loved him." (Roy 50) Mammachi as a mother of Chacko and Ammu is also very proclive, Chacko is a person who is not able to run his mother's small pickle factory profitably, yet his mother thinks that he is one the cleverest men in India. As he was told by someone in Oxford that "he was made of prime ministerial material", Ammu always felt impartial about that. As mentioned in the novel; "All Indian mothers are obsessed with their sons and are therefore poor judges of their abilities" (Roy 56).

Ammu is a beautiful, young, cheeky woman of stillness and severity who is considered to be left unlearned by Pappachi. Her husband turns out to be "Not just a heavy drinker but a full blown alcoholic with all of an alcholics deviousness and tragic charm." (Roy 40) She initially develops as a single parent of Rahel and Estha in the novel, who stoically desires every good thing for both Rahel and Estha, "A woman that they had already damned, now had little to lose, and could therefore be dangerous." (Roy 44) Her life revolves around motherhood and divorce-hood. Her children are considered as waifs in the novel who cannot fit in the Syrian Christian society of Kerala. As defined by French naturalist Buffon; "Mixed objects which it is impossible to categorise and which necessarily upset the project of a general system" (Tickell 78).

The novel has socio political desires which the male members want to fulfill by keeping women stagnant. The actions of men like Pappachi and Chacko represent male domination. Chacko is mentioned in the novel as "Self Proclaimed Marxist". By calling women Comrade he would call them to the factory, forced them to sit with him. Roy narrates the personality of Chacko as, "Self-proclaimed Marxist who would call women who worked in the factory to his room, and on the pretext of lecturing them on labor rights and trade union law, flirt with them outrageously. He would call them Comrade, and insist that they call him Comrade back (which made them giggle). Much to their embarrassment and Mammachi's dismay, he forced them to sit at the table with him and drink tea" (Roy 65).

The novel would be incomplete if we do not touch the up-burst produced by Ammu when she falls in love with a Velutha, a paravan, a toddy tapper who was never allowed by Pappachi into the house. Paravan's were expected to crawl backwards with a broom so that they could sweep away their own foot prints. This love for Velutha changes her love towards her children. This whole incident shows the caste system even prevailed in postcolonial India which never wanted to get deducted and this is how Kerala was made. "It is Ammu's braided 'unmixable mix[ed]' subaltern consciousness of 'tenderness' and 'rage' that drives her feelings toward her children, toward the Untouchable Velutha, and her disapproving mewling family and local culture and society" (Saldívar 360).

The novel's actions are set around 1969 and 1993, this a time when India had newly acquired freedom, here the motivation of changing the unfair things should have been more but the internal colonialism was still very abounding. "The terms external and internal colonialism suggest viewpoints of colonised people. External colonialism includes the domination and exploitation of indigenous people by foreign invaders, and indigenous responses (Spencer-Wood 2013a, p. 399). Internal colonialism colonises minorities within a polity. When colonies rebelled or used political mechanisms to become (semi-)independent polities, such as the United States, Australia, New Zealand, and African countries, external colonialism of indigenous groups often transformed into internal colonialism" (Spencer 479).

Rahel is the abandoned daughter of Ammu, who is also divorced, she comes back to see her brother Estha. She holds curious questions, which aren't suitable. She is even black listed in Nazareth convent at the age of eleven. She and her brother are treated as illegitimate. She always prevents herself from morality. She grows up "Without anybody to arrange a marriage for her. Without anybody who could pay her a dowry and therefore without an obligatory husband looming on her horizon." (p. 17) She feels a certain danger of dignity, She is often seen giggling and yearning for fresh air. "Rahel wasn't sure what she suffered from, but occasionally she practiced sad faces, and sighing in the mirror." (p 61) Rahel is subverted, as a kid she is under strong supervision of Baby kochamma, she was in charge of their education, had read them a version of "The Tempest" abridged by Charles and Mary Lamb. "Where the bee sucks, there suck I," Estha and Rahel would go about saying. "In a cowslips bell I lie" (Roy 59).

Baby kochamma wants them to understand and comprehend the highest level of English; it was a sub conscious act of herself being a high brow person. Baby kochamma, a character who destroys the lives of many people in the novel. She creates all the bitterness around. She is a destroyer and a controller. She likes English language, English television operas and everything related to them. She also joins

English institutions against her fathers will. She even falls in love with a man named Father Mulligan, tries to seduce him and would call him with a different smile but remains unmarried throughout her life, which gives her a chance of commenting on love, marriages and divorce. Her experiences and views are very different from other women in the novel. Her views on marriage and divorce are like this "She subscribed wholeheartedly to the commonly held view that a married daughter had no position in her parents' home. As for a divorced daughter according to Baby Kochamma, she had no position anywhere at all. And as for a divorced daughter from a love marriage, well, words could not describe Baby Kochamma's outrage. As for a divorced daughter from an intercommunity love marriage. Baby Kochamma chose to remain quiveringly silent on the subject" (Roy 45-46).

Baby kochamma's role as a daughter, Sister in law or as an aunt is very unsympathetic. She cares about nothing, neither the house nor the residents. This novel has individual aspects of everything; characters face different situations and have different methods of resolving emotions. Colonists after ruling the Eastern mainland taught people to arbitrate at sublevels. As a postcolonial feminist critique this novel shows how men sabotaged women of their indigenous groups. This chapter has sliced the inhumane behavior of men in the Indian households where inter caste marriages were still treated as dishonorable and if women would stream higher than men they were censored even if they brought surplus advantage to the homes. The novel is bestowed with so many threats, the outside as well as the inside atmosphere is that of command. All the characters have a past but all are not treated equally. Chacko and Ammu both are divorced but receive varied attention, the internal colonialism prevailing in the novel helped develop the insight for this piece. There are colonial traumas and behaviors adopted differently by people in the novel. Silence is traced among females like Mammachi, Ammu, Rahel and even Kochamma which shapes their conduct, making it a novel of postcolonial milieu both semantically as well as historically.

Works Cited

Bill, Ashcroft., et al. *The Empire Writes Back: Theory and practice in post-colonial literatures*. 2002

Boehmer, Elleke. "East is East and South is South: The Cases of Sarojini Naidu and Arundhati Roy." *Women: A Cultural Review*, vol.11,no.1/2, 2014,doi.org/10.1080/09574040050051424.

Davies, Carole Boyce. *Black Women Writing and Identity: Migrations of the Subject*, 1994.

Katrak, Ketu H. *Politics of the female body*. Rutgers university press, 2006.

Loomba, Annie. *Colonialism/Post Colonialism*. Routledge, 2015.

Newbigin, Eleanor. "A post-colonial patriarchy? Representing family in the Indian nation-state." *ModernAsian Studies*, vol 44, no.1,2010 http://www.jstor.org/stable/27764649?seq=1&cid=pdf-reference#references_tab_content.

Roy, Arundhati. *The God of small Things*. Ink India, 1997.

Schwarz Henry, and Sangeeta Ray. *A Companion to Postcolonial Studies*. Blackwell, 2005.

Saldivar, José David. "Unsettling race, coloniality, and Caste." *Cultural Studies*, doi.org/10.1080/09502380601162563. 2007.

Spencer wood, Suzzane M. "Feminist Theorizing of Patriarchal Colonialism, Power Dynamics, and Social Agency Materialized in Colonial Institutions." *International journal of Historical Archeology*, DOI 10.1007/s10761- 016-0356-3. 2016.

Tickel, Alex. "The God of Small Things: Arundhati Roy's Postcolonial Cosmopolitanism" *The Journal of Commonwealth Literature*, DOI: 10.1177/002198940438100. 2003.

17

Quest for Identity Assurance in Mulk Raj Anand's *Untouchable* and Need for Identity Saving in Abhijit Sen's *Rohu Chandaler Har* in a Caste and Race Burdened Society

Amitava Das

Casteism and Racism in India in both Colonial and Post-colonial period has remained a favourite theme among Indian storytellers to expose reality of the hypocrisy of the society that boasts for the necessity of casteism and racism to hold the balance and identity of Indian society. From Mulk Raj Anand and Rohinton Mistry in English to Bama and Perumal Murugan in Tamil, Urmila Pawar in Marathi, Manoranjan Byapari in Bengali have all tried in their own way to bring out the pain, suffering and questions of the so called "lower class" people being awed at the hypocritical and double-standardised social customs and behaviours.

In fact Racism based on casteism and religion has been remained the most favourite weapon of the prejudiced society to manipulate the so called lower castes and marginalised people in the name of tradition and customs. At the same time racial discrimination and related behaviour also has generated in the victim/s a crisis of identity being not able to be the part of the mainstream of the society. The crisis is sometimes felt in personal level and sometimes in social level. This crisis of identity generates questions that are sometimes part of existentialist views.

According to Peter Weinreich, "A person's identity is defined as the totality of one's self-construal, in which how one construes oneself in the present expresses the continuity between how one construes oneself as one was in the past and how one construes oneself as one aspires to be in the future"; this allows for definitions of aspects of identity, such as: "One's ethnic identity is defined as that part of the totality of one's self-construal made up of those dimensions that express the continuity between one's construal of past ancestry and one's future aspirations in relation to ethnicity" (The operationalisation of identity theory in racial and ethnic relations: Peter Weinreich)

The crisis of identity and quest to find identity both in personal level and in social level against the background of caste and race defined society can be traced in two novels discussed hereafter. The first one, "Untouchable" written in English by Mulk Raj Anand, tells the story in colonial time and the another "Rohu Chandaler Har" (The Magic Bone of Rohu), written in Bengali by Abhijit Sen tells the story that starts in Colonial; and ends in postcolonial period, around 1970s. In both of these novels, we experience the eternal human striving to announce the purity of the human soul and its struggle to exist against all odds.

Mulk Raj Anand's celebrated novel *Untouchable* was published in the year 1935.It depicts the happening of a single day in the life of an outcaste, the latrine cleaner, 18 year old Bakha and his world from dawn to dusk on a very significant day, the day he sees and listens to Mahatma Gandhi. Bakha lives in the outcastes' colony where live "the scavengers, the leather workers, the washermen, the barbers, the water carriers, the grass cutters and other outcastes from Hindu society" (Text) which is no better than a hell. The continuous neglect and hatred of the upper caste has sprouted in him 'an overwhelming desire to live' the life of the rulers, the "Tommies". He tries to copy them in almost everything. He secretly tells himself: "I will look like a sahib" and "I shall walk like them". He "could sacrifice a good many comforts for the sake of what he called 'fashun'. He dresses, sleeps and smokes like the white rulers. Because of this, his father abuses him and his best friends Chota and Ram Charan mockingly calls him "Pilpali Sahib" (Imitation Sahib), but it adds to his pride more. Though he knows "that except for his English clothes there was nothing English in his life. But he kept up his new form, rigidly adhering to his clothes day and night guarding them from all base taint of Indianness, not even risking the formlessness of an Indian quilt, though he shivered at night". (Text)

Bakha's identifying himself with British way of life and trying to grow comfortable with it is the direct result of his contempt and disapproval of the Indian way of life, specially the Hindu ways. It may remind us that. It was the Hindus, that had created the four varnas – Brahman, Kshatriya, Vaishya: all of whom had` the right of the Vedas but not, the fourth Varna, Shudra, which is regarded as the lowest of all. They are the Sevakas (servers of all the three). But the most interesting thing is that a person like Bakha doesn't fall even into the category of these four but of the outcastes and even more, he falls into the lowest of the Untouchable hierarchy: The sweeper. In the preface of Untouchable E.M. Forster writes "The sweeper is worse than a slave, for the slave may change his master and his duties and may even become free, but the sweeper is bound forever, born into a state from which he cannot escape and where he is excluded from social intercourse and the consolations of his religion".

For generations people like Bakha had silently put up with the atrocities of the higher caste taking it as the ordeal of fate. But Bakha was the child of modern India and his choice to be "pilpili Sahib" has come out of the counter-contempt against the higher social classes in India. Bakha knows though, it is nothing but a false consolation. His inability to find his true identity torments him bitterly. Even the words of Mahatma Gandhi at first could not reassure him. Had he not overheard the conversation between the poet Iqbal Nath Sarshar and the barrister Mr. R.N.Bashir; Perhaps Bakha could not learn about the flush system in toilet soon to be introduced in India. Unlike Gandhi, the poet thinks that, it is the machine that could save the future of India, both from it's state of British dependence and the present state of poverty. The poet also said "We must recognise an equality of rights, priviledges and opportunities for everyone. The Mahatma didn't say so, but the legal and sociological basis of caste having been broken down by the British-Indian penal code". (Text) He hopes that when the sweepers can change their profession, they will no longer remain untouchables or will be regarded so. With the introduction of machines like the flush system" the sweepers can be free from the stigma of Untouchability and assume the dignity of status that is their right as useful members of a casteless and classless society."(Text)

On one side Bakha hears Mahatma's speech about human equality and that scavenging is actually a noble task, while on the other the words of the poet generates hope in him about the future when machines would clear the human excreta. Now Bakha is assured of his identity "Yes, said Bakha, 'I shall go on doing what Gandhi says." He starts to think himself not an outcaste but an essential part of the society. The prospect of the flush system also made him hopeful about his freedom to choose any trade he wanted in future. Now Bakha doesn't need to wear the dresses of the rulers assuming a false identity. It doesn't matter to him that he doesn't look like a sahib. Bakha is now calm and reassured as he now walks homeward. He has been successfully able to shed off his false assumed identity of being a "pippali sahib" in search of a truer identity, a more meaningful one.

Abhijit Sen's Bengali novel *Rohu Chandaler Haarh* was published in the year 1985 and claimed "Bankim Puraskar" for the year 1992 (the Annual Bankim memorial award for novels written in Bengali). It is the story of a nomad group popularly called 'Bajikar'; by others and even by themselves. This is due to the fact that they earn their bread primarily by showing magic tricks, juggling, acrobats and stunts. They called their work as "vikh mangar kaam" (the work of begging) The story of their repeated quest to settle in a place permanently, to become householders and the failed attempt time and again is described by the grandmother Lubini to her twelve years old grandson Shariba; is the main essence of the story. The 'Bajikars' are also outcastes here. They have no specific religious and racial identity, as defined by tradition and society which can be clearly discerned in their names. They have Hindu names like Pitem and Pratap and Muslim names like Jamir and Yasin but all of them bear the same surname 'Bajikor'. Even in terms of appetite they can't be grouped into any religious identity as they are equally attracted to cow and pig for meat. It seems as they don't have any sureity of settlement, they have no choice upon their appetites. They are just like the primitive humans for whom food was simply consumed to live and not to support religious vanity.

The exact origin of the Bajikars is not known to even them. Lubini tells Shariba the story of an unknown land. The language of that land has been forgotten long ago by the Bajikars. The holy river Gharghara flows there. On a black Saturday a great earthquake made the land upside down. The land of the Bajikars of Gorakhpur went into the river. The headman Pitem tried to settle in the north with the clan members but were driven away by the local milkmen. At night Pitem was directed by his dead father Danu to move towards the land of the east. Thus from Gorakhpur to Dehrighat, then Siwan, and a few years later Danapur, Patna, Munger and numerous other places, the Bajikars tried to settle but failed and finally they came to East. From here the story starts weaving. First Rajmahal, from there Malda, then Namankurri, Rajshahi, Amunara and finally in Panchbibi. The story flows from Lubini to Sariba as if Lubini is in trance and is compelled to pass on the quest..... ......" You know Shariba, Your grandfather (Jamir) yearned to settle, to be a farmer in his farmhouse. He would have cows and buffalows; a plough of his own, a piece of own land. He despised begging" (Translated from Bengali text)

But what lacked in this quest is their having no religious and ethnic identity. As Lubini discloses "Bajikars learn language through travelling. Wherever they go, make the language their own, their religion and rituals their own. Bajikars don't have any own religion". In this context Bajikars have their own myth that thousands of years ago when the forefathers of the Bajikars lived beside a great river; one of their male named Pura was attracted to one dancer named Pali and married her who was supposed to be his sister. At this the curse of the gods fell upon them that they could never settle anywhere on the land, could never eat fruits from the same tree and drink the water of the same pond twice. Even they couldn't visit the same land once visited. From then on Bajikars are homeless and away from the gods and religion. They are unwelcomed to the people having home and religion.

This absence of religious identity tolls heavy on the Bajikars again and again. Sojan Bajikar loved and secretly weds Pakhi Halder, a lower caste Hindu girl of "Jhalo" caste. He brings Pakhi, his wife, into the clan and is welcomed by all. Jamir is happy at the prospect of the expansion of his clan into other root, which in the future might find a stable identity. But the Halders take Pakhi back without accepting the marriage as valid. Jamir's dream to increase and to find identity remains a dream. The clan decreases in number as members are dying untimely. In a battle to claim their rights on the crops, Rupa kills and flew for years. His wife and Shariba's mother Shajadi changes her house and becomes his cousin Yeasin's wife. Jamir has to decree people like Matin. "No Matin, Pasra is the daughter of your sister; You can't marry her." Matin queried, then who he would marry? How he would marry? Jamir advised Matin to bring another girl from any other clan. For the last six generations the Bajikar blood is being mixed with itself and being polluted. Jamir told others that they must try to give their daughters marriage into other social groups and encourage their sons to bring bride from other places because mixing up of same blood brings destruction and death. He thought that this might bring settlement. Or settlement might bring solution to the problems of marriage. But Jamir's dream was yet to be fulfilled in his lifetime. Shariba thinks that Jamir had destroyed all the Past of the Bajikars and left them only the Present and the Future for his descendants.

On the other hand, Hanif, the road roller driver befriends Shariba and according to him. "You people are having a good life. You don't have religion. You don't have problems. I am Muslim. I despise Hindus. Hindus despise us. We kill each other. My mother and brother die in riot, my sister goes missing. And I build this road on which all the religion walk away." He marries Palbi Bajikar even after knowing her dark past. (Translated from Bengali text)

Omar Bajikar and Malati Namashudra of Mohar village elopes. The Namashudras are unable to find them and arrest the Bajikar headman Yeasin. Their leader Vairo questions Yeasin about their religion. Yeasin feebly requests, "Master, take us into your caste. You are respected by people here. They obey you". But Vairo laughs and says he doesn't have the right to include them in Hindu religion. He also passes the judgement that Malati should be brought by the Bajikars and the cost of her remarriage must be borne by Omar. Both Omar and Malati do not agree and remain hidden in a broken boat and then in a desolated temple afterwards. But their days of love are temporary. On one moonlit night when Omar and Malati are sitting by the riveside, they suddenly find armed people silently encircling them. Soon Omar's head is separated from his body. Someone throws away the head into the river. One of them carries senseless Malati upon his shoulder and all start returning. Shariba remains the silent spectator of all these hidden behind a bush.

But finally the Bajikars are separated into two parts. At the suggestion of the Haji and with the assured help of Sonamian of Mohar village to get them shared land for agriculture and stable identity, most of the Bajikars agree to embrace Islam. Yeasin is happy with this prospect. He meets Rupa and they discuss about all their pasts learnt from the forefathers. Even before Gorakhpur, they were regarded as the Untouchables. They had to beat drums while walking on the roads to warn others of their coming. Their works were limited in graveyards and crematoriums or to look after the cows and buffalows or to scavenging. During wars they served the kings and died in thousands. They were taken as slaves in other countries. They are bereft of any home, any respect, any land. Rupa remembered that his father Jamir wanted them to be stable, to have a home and a piece of land. He had observed that their accent matches with the Gujrati shopkeepers in Malda. But Rupa had married Sharmi who worships "Maa Manasa" (the Hindu deity of snake). He asks pardon from Yeasin to let her family including Shariba to be spared from this conversion.

In the year 1966, on the day of Muharram, Of the Bajikars of Bada-Kismat, around 200 people, from children to youth and elders are converted into Islam at the mosque yard. A feast is arranged. They took new names or surnames and only six families that remained the same Bajikars also enjoyed the feast with others. Before the day at evening; Shajadi, Rupa's ex wife and wife of Yeasin visits Rupa. Rupa laments" our forefathers want us to settle. But now we are unsettled even more. From one land to another land, from one caste to another caste, I think me as Hindu, You think Yourself as Mussulman. In reality We remain that same Bajikars. It is all due to our sins" (Translated from Bengali text). They touch each others' hand in dark. A deep darkness remains constant.

The quest of identity and the search to claim one's assured place in society thus finds individualistic story in Mulk Raj Anand's "Untouchable" where Bakha becomes the representative of all the Untouchable Youths like him, who moves homeward at the end not with identity assurance but with the hope of finding his claimed position in future when machine will replace human predicament. And in Avijit Sen's "Rohu Chandaler Harrh", the Protagonist Shariba observes that even after the conversion, Old Yeasin complains of the same problems of marriage and work still hovering in their society. Shariba proposes and marries Omar's widow Malati and takes her son as his own with his inner assurance that rare people like Hanif are still there, for whom human beings are more important than their religion.

Works Cited

Weinreich, Peter (1986). "14: The operationalisation of identity theory in racial and ethnic relations". In Rex, John; Mason, David (eds.). *Theories of Race and Ethnic Relations. Comparative Ethnic and Race Relations.* Cambridge: Cambridge University Press (published 1988). pp. 299ff. ISBN 9780521369398. (Wikipedia: Identity (Social Science)

Anand, Mulk Raj: *Untouchable.* Penguin Random House India (published 2001) ISBN 9780143027805 (Text excerpts).

Sen, Abhijit: *Rohu Chandaler Har.* J.N. Chakraborty and Company (4th ed: December 2016) ISBN 9789380411125.

English translations from the original Bengali text excerpts of Rohu *Chandaler Har* is done by Amitava Das.

18

Intersection between National and Individual Identity English Language Reshaping the Dalit Identity: Reading *Untouchable* – An English Bahujan Colonial Narrative in a Postcolonial India

Manashi Singh

Introduction

To see a nation that was born after hundreds of years of rebellion finally being established as a sovereign union that resulted in thousands of deaths, in a context that is not only undermined in the mainstream social debate but viciously considered unfit to discuss, is an in-depth unlearning process. For many, the notion of identity is a subject that doesn't require too much consideration and can be explained in a few short sentences, as and when needed. But for an entire section of Indian society, such is not the case. It sure has some traits that could've been altered to exert more inclusivity and justice for a country that has existed since time immemorial. One of the many elements that define the modern-day Indian Hindu society is said to be descended from the ancient Sanatana Dharma. For all we know, it may or may not have clearly stated how Hindus must be divided to continue on a path of Karma, which will result in their ultimate salvation. Nevertheless, our society is divided into five sections that become the five castes (four main castes and Dalits at the bottom-most fifth one), and caste appropriate jobs are allotted to each. Such a division becomes the prototype of how an Indian society functions, and to this date, not even a single national or regional party of India has objected to it. Consequently, one of the five sections, Dalits, became the caste responsible for every task the top four castes refused, and soon came to be identified as Untouchables.

Even Gandhi, who detested everything western and insisted on Home Rule, when asked about his perspective of civilisation by a news editor, admitted in his *Hind Swaraj* that Indian evils like child marriage, widow shaming, systemic prostitution, untouchability, and so on, are not a part of the Indian civilisation. The civilisation he exerted too much pride for was full of the above mistakes that needed to be rectified. Then again, when one reads *Anandmath* after reading *Hind Swaraj*, maybe one realises that this might be the reason why Bankim Chandra Chatterjee wanted the British to stay a little longer. A question might arise that these two texts were written several decades apart, but Gandhi's *Hind Swaraj* offers ample evidence that nothing much changed in the Indian social scenario, which was published more than two decades after *Anandmath*.

Postcolonial India, as we see it, is the linear historiography studied by many theorists and critics. On the other hand, from a literary point of view, postcolonial literature, fiction or otherwise, is marked by the writers like Manto, Chutgai, and many other post-partition writers, reflecting on India premising the Partition of 1947 as an experience of mixed feelings, but some emotions related to the partition nevertheless. Dalit Literature around the same timeline was founded on narratology, not in sync with the modern European historiography Indian writers grew so keen on. Dalit literature hung on to the oppressed community members' lived experiences who resided and timelessly faced oppression in India. This type of literature did not only defied western conceptualising norms but made many Indian writers uncomfortable with the choice of narratives that didn't sync with the classic sentimental tone of the 1947 partition. However, it invoked a kind of contextual reading that still doesn't make it to the mainstream Indian literature dominated by socio-economy-political dynamics. As understood by Anand and many rising Dalit writers, English has provided them with the sense of much-needed memory loss, a tool of expression that intervenes right through the dominant hegemonic communities, and situates the Dalits at par with other peoples of India, offering them the equity of language they're denied in their mother tongue.

This research attempts to have two focus points: one, rooted in the doctoral research of Gajarawala, is reading Hazari's *Untouchable* like a privileged *savarna* in a westernised critical format of contextualising, and then shredding off all the prejudices to read the text as and how the author directs and wants the readers to read it. The research aims at working more on the foundational work by Gajarawala and explores the lack of temporal and spatial rigidity around nationalism and national identity in Dalit writings. Two and not the least concern of this literature is that it attempts to find leverage in Anand and Kothari's arguments, who make exceptional points in favor of a tool chosen by the Dalit community to answer oppression in the language that it understands the best – English.

As most western writers emphasise on three timelines while analysing a text, it is imperative to highlight that *Untouchable: the Autobiography of an Indian Outcaste* is based on the early 20 Century, a period that encapsulates Hazari's journey from childhood until he becomes a young adult; the book is written in the second half of 20 Century most probably after Hazari attained a formal education and assumed employment opportunities denied to his caste; last and foremost, the text is read in the early 21 Century, a century after the time these incidents occurred in. Besides, Hazari, well versed in more than one Indian language, opts for English to write his biography must be understood as a statement in itself considering the socio-economic position he dwelled in, in the initial years of his life. Hazari learns many languages and experiences all three major religions of India in the 1900s in his teen and adult ages, only to feel more alienated from his identity in this world and less interested in any religion whatsoever. The highlight of his autobiography, however, is when he receives financial assistance from a British professor and an offer to pursue higher studies in Paris.

As part one of this research, originated from Gajarawala's doctoral work, it is essential to read this text as a typical *savarna* (dominant caste Hindu) would in order to grasp a perspective, which needs to be contested later in this paper. As Dasgupta makes some of the most sensitive remarks on Anand's defense for English as an adoptive language of Dalits, the *savarna* reading of this text will entail his arguments converged in Hazari's book. Dasgupta questions the context in which Indian readers read English and their own mother tongue or how differently communication happens in both these languages. One of Dasgupta's many remarks is that the everyday discourse, the primary education, the only requirement to exist in every region of India, can be achieved only in the mother tongue, that is, the hundreds of Indian languages that people use in day to day life. This is also the case in the early years of Hazari's life when he couldn't comprehend English. His mother tongue helped him get by to the effect that it could also have become his language for the autobiography, had he stayed in India for formal education in his dialect of an Indian language.

Then, Dasgupta goes on to accuse English of stripping off the users of their native background baggage, should they choose English as their mode of making sense of the world and communicating. One might find merit in this argument invoking a period in Hazari's biography when he was restless even after he was living a life of a middle-class student in Lucknow. Verbatim, he could not feel included in the city where he could not reveal his real identity of an untouchable to anyone for two reasons – one, they'd need a lot of context and information to understand his position, and two, his newly found brothers, Muslims, and Christians might not care enough to know about his background in the first place. To a *savarna*, the latter might sound like a perfect solution to an Untouchable's problems. Still, to a person who comes from a community where everyone has lived like an inferior to the same species of animals all their lives assuming it as their karma, it felt like a severe blow to the young Hazari when he realised it doesn't even matter in the real world.

To summarise Hazari's book as a *savarna*, he was unfaithful to a language and a religion that gave him and his community a path to righteousness. Even after becoming a Muslim, Hazari couldn't find the peace he was looking for. Ultimately, he ended up leaving the country for good exactly when individuals like him were needed to fight for India's independence. Lastly, he became friends with the very people who came to India to oppress and rule over him and contributed toward propagating western education and culture on Indian land.

Moving towards the second and the foremost part of this paper, to explore the role of English as a language that addresses the Dalit community in a different light, a language that, by not acknowledging the persistent caste discrimination, enables the community to have a fresh perspective of their existence in a society that unanimously oppresses them. Hazari, who hails from the colonial United Province, describes his village as a cluster of muddy houses that have the stench of all kinds of refuse coming from all direction, surrounded by almost barren land where there is nothing to appreciate apart from the love and care he received in his community in many years of his life. Noting the book was published in 1969 and written around that time, the intention of the book was not just to recount events of the past but to invoke an authority over the identity of a community that was once again attempting to drift away from the religious and social identity imposed on them. Here community means many writers and thinkers like Hazari who voiced a similar opinion, and by once again, I mean to bring your attention to the time when these events actually occurred – the 1920s. This paper's most aspirational argument is that even if the book is read in 2020, the only change in the Untouchables' identities is made in a book, which is read only by a meager fraction of people of our Indian society – The Constitution.

Dasgupta, in all his arguments, conveniently ignores the importance of a neutral language for a group of people who are forced into becoming a domestic subaltern and suppress their thoughts. His statements are full of practical applications of language but miss the social implications an Untouchable meets with once s/he adheres to the regional language and thereby, surname. Hazari, through his autobiography, questions those very social implications he grows up in and meets with confusion and frustration when he learns that the members of his community have wholeheartedly accepted their fate as the inferior, less fortunate, least deserving, third-class citizens.

In the 1920 context, the mother tongue Hindustani didn't do much to improve Hazari's life as against Urdu and English, which played an important role in shaping his thoughts during his youth. Not only him, but most people from his community, at that time, were seeking servant jobs for Europeans and Englishmen who readily took them in without giving a second thought about their caste. The Untouchable community was able and needed to learn broken English, and at the same time, experience a space where they were at par with any other caste of Indian society as they're judged on the basis of their skills and references, and nothing else. In 1969 and in 2020 too, English as one of the many official languages of India could be favored more than regional languages in any circumstance as the English speakers make to the most educated circles and provide a direct pass to be in a social standing with any other people, at least officially. Why, then, Dasgupta would undermine a series of Dalit writers themselves who will readily shred their mother tongues off and adopt English as their foster language (Kothari, 65)?

The problem with regional language as a language of expression for the Dalit community is that the language has already taken away too much from the community as the language functioned as a mode of discrimination, a weapon for suppression, and a tool of oppression. Why then wouldn't an Untouchable want to leave his/her mother tongue way behind and accommodate a language understood by the oppressors and the oppressed alike? Why then would the Dalit community want to be attached with a background that has exercised not only verbal but physical abuse on its members? The way native Indian Languages have barred equitable participation of all communities alike by fostering social and cultural apartheid, it contributed to infusing differing national identities among the most suppressed lots. A close reading of Hazari's autobiography offers the readers an insight into his idea of national identity, which in his case has only earned him a title of an untouchable, who can best his life by fulfilling his duties of putrid manual labor as his *Karma.* In a *savarna* reading of this book, it is easy to point out Hazari's hypocrisy around nationalism and his lack of interest in the freedom struggle by invoking his disloyalty towards a nation that provided him food, clothing, and shelter. However, the minute this patronising thought crosses our minds, Hazari's contradictions start making more and more sense. The oppressors never understand the extent of their oppression until an autobiography like this one makes it to mainstream communication. Consequently, a Dalit writer like Hazari and many others running the same race, sometimes against and sometimes for each other, had no other option but to realise their individual consciousness only by shredding every bit of their national identity.

As a textual analysis of Hazari's biography, it can be inferred that the author wasn't disturbed due to the alienation he felt even after converting into Islam and living everyday life. The reason for his unsettled thoughts was the question that he repeatedly asks throughout the book – why were his people treated as untouchables when it was so easy to fit into this society the moment that untouchable tag leaves the body? Even if Dalit writers use their mother tongue for literary work, what is the guarantee that the essence of their work won't be lost in translation (Kothari, 62)?

Conclusion

Reading Hazari's *Untouchable: the Autobiography of an Indian Outcaste* offered a subtly put prominent perspective of the Dalit community on the notions of identity as an individual and national citizen, the world they live in, and most importantly, how they experienced an event that holds the most important place in Indian history – the Partition. Skipping the traditional historiographical method of recounting a lifetime, Hazari's book enables its readers to experience the margins of an important political event that helps in realising the non-binary nature of human identity and existence. Reading a work written by an oppressed community member in a language that is not only foreign but is revered in the Indian circle helped in acknowledging the voice that would otherwise have been silenced by translation or due to some godforsaken religious tradition.

Works Cited

Anand, S, ed. *Touchable Tales: Publishing and Reading Dalit literature*, Chennai: Navayana Publishing, 2003.

Anderson, Benedict R. O'G. *Imagined Communities: Reflections On the Origin and Spread of Nationalism*. Rev. ed. London; New York: Verso, 2006.

Dasgupta, Probal. "Sanskrit, English and Dalit." *Economic and Political Weekly*, vol. 35, no. 16, 2000, pp. 1407-1412.

Gajarawala, Toral Jatin. "Sometime between Revisionist and Revolutionary: Unreading History in Dalit Literature." *PMLA,* vol. 126, no. 3, 2011, pp. 575-591. JSTOR, www.jstor.org/stable/41414131. Accessed 16 Nov. 2020.

Hobsbawm, E. J. and T. O Ranger. *The Invention of Tradition*. Cambridge, UK ; New York: Cambridge University Press, 2012.

Hazari, *Untouchable: the Autobiography of an Indian Outcaste*, London: Pall Mall P, 1969.

Kothari, Rita. "Caste in a Casteless Language?" *Economic and Political Weekly*, vol. XLVIII, 2013, pp. 60-68.

19

Amitav Ghosh: *Sea of Poppies*: Disseminating Diasporic Discourse

Kalyan Pattanayak

Etymologically the word 'diaspora' came from the Greek verb *diasperirein* signifies "to dissipate" or "to spread about", which is formed by the expression of *dia* intends to disperse or to isolate and the word *speirein* signifies 'somewhere else'. As per the antiquated Greek perspective the word as recommending augmentation through outward movement and settlement. 'Diaspora' rapidly procured a more heartless and sad significance. In the Greek interpretation of the Old Testament it had been utilised to portray the persuasive scattering of the Jews.

The demolition of the Temple in Jerusalem in 586 BC prompted the subjugation and relocation of the key military, common, and religious leaders of Judah and their outcasts in Babylon. Priests held that this destiny was anticipated in Deuteronomy where God had cautioned that anyone who resisted his law would be dissipated to all or any finishes of the planet. There they might 'discover no harmony'.

The historical backdrop of the term 'diaspora' compares to this organic interaction of transplantation and migration. It was initially utilised in the *Septuagint*, the Greek interpretation of the Torah, and was applied to the Jewish experience of the outcast which was taken in before examines 'as the paradigm for both exile and diaspora' (Baumann 19). Quickly the term conveyed the negative meanings of dispersal and disintegration. "The Alexandrian Jewish-Greek translators of the Hebrew Scriptures adopted precisely the disastrous connotations of current philosophical discourse" (Baumann 21). It was a reviled word and show expulsion by God.

Providing the mainstream critical views just as the critical impression of diaspora in contemporary basic examinations, William Safran contends in his article *Diasporas in Modern Societies: Myths of Homeland and Return* that Diaspora Studies need to change its basic substitute courtesy of a more unique discernment. He broadens Walker Connor's wide working meaning of 'diaspora' as "that segment of a people living outside the homeland" (Safran 83) by offering six essential trademarks generally shared by the diasporic groups.

'Diaspora' alludes to the dislocation of individuals from a particular unique 'center' (Safran 83) to at least two or more 'peripheral' (Safran 83) or regions. The dislodged individuals 'retain a collective memory, vision, or myth about their original homeland – its physical location, history and achievements' (Safran 83). They capture that they are not maybe welcome in the host country and subsequently, feel estranged from it. They appreciate the longing to get back to their hereditary country, 'their true, ideal home' one day at a suitable time. They have a firm conviction that they ought to be focused on the "maintenance or restoration of their original homeland and to its safety and prosperity" (Safran 84). They keep on relating, actually or vicariously, to that country somehow or the other, and 'their ethno communal consciousness and solidarity are importantly defined by the existence of such a relationship' (Safran 84). Regarding the above highlights, Safran refers to the Armenian, Maghrebi, Turkish, Palestinian, Cuban, Greek, and maybe Chinese diasporas as of now and of the Polish diaspora of the past, although none of them completely adjusts to the "ideal kind" of Jewish Diaspora (Safran 84). This is certainly not a comprehensive rundown however considering when Safran published the article (1991), it ought to be viewed as the start of the way toward recognising the diasporic gatherings.

Robin Cohen properly recognises the significance of William Safran's definition and develops his hypothetical situation on it. He offers changes of two of the previously mentioned highlights set by Safran and adds four more, "mainly concerning the evolution and character of the diasporic groups in their countries of exile" (Cohen 6). The two alterations are concerned with the diasporic gathering's relationship with the native land. He expresses that the journey from the centre to the periphery is "often accompanied by the memory of a single traumatic event that provides the folk memory of the great historic injustice that binds the group together" (Cohen 6). He changes the fifth component by moving the concentration from the support or reclamation of the country to its 'very creation' which 'covers the cases of an "imagined homeland" that only resembles the original history and geography of the diaspora's natality in the remotest way' (Cohen 6). Other than the adjustments of these two trademark highlights, Cohen likewise gives some extra highlights. According to him, the diasporic mass may 'disperse for colonial or voluntarist reasons' (Cohen 6). This is a most controversial take-off from the 'prototypical Jewish diasporic tradition' (Cohen 6) and, widens the extent of the term by including the individuals who moved deliberately since the beginning to look for work abroad and can be applied to 'imperial and colonial settlers' (Cohen 7).

Cohen causes us to notice the positive parts of diaspora. This adds up to a paradigmatic shift in Diaspora Studies. He declares that 'tension between an ethnic, a national and a transnational identity is often creative, enriching one' (Cohen 7) and offers the case of the diasporic Jews who added to the fields 'medicine, theology, art, music, philosophy, literature, science, industry and commerce' (Cohen 7). This they did regardless of the way that they endured a level of 'subterranean anxiety in the diaspora' all through the ages and in numerous spaces.

Cohen discusses the dislocation of an aggregate mass with regards to "solidarity with co-ethnic members in other countries" (Cohen 7). Cohen's observation of the lateral dimension of the ethnic relationship motions towards a transnational turn in Diaspora Studies to be examined instantly. Roger Rouse, in his article *Mexican Migration and the Social Space of Postmodernism,* offers a fascinating contextual investigation of the improvement of a parallel relationship of a Mexican ethnic local area from the rustic *municipio* of Aguililla since the mid-1940s. This *municipio* turned out to be important for an energetic organisation of monetary and sociocultural exercises because of the transcultural development of its occupants, the majority of whom got comfortable in the metropolitan neighbourhood of Redwood City on the edge of the Silicon Valley of California. Rouse's investigation shows that they stayed in contact with their local space through familial, sociocultural, and monetary organisations. Subsequently, they keep up "these spatially extended relationships as actively and effectively as the ties that link them of their neighbours" (Rouse 29). They add to the dynamic cycles in the family and the local area back home. Rouse comments, indeed, through the persistent dissemination of individuals, cash, merchandise, and data, the different repayments have gotten so firmly woven together that, from a significant perspective, they have come to comprise a solitary local area spread across an assortment of destinations, something may be alluded to as a "transnational migrant circuit" (Rouse 30). Now and again, in this way, diasporic dislocation of a specific ethnic local area to an alternate, especially an adjoining, nation may bring about the improvement of an enthusiastic organisation of monetary, social, and social exercises. Such exercises thrive without severe administrative advances taken by state specialists. Commencement of observation by the state normally controls such ethnic developments and systems administration.

The extra highlights referenced by Cohen vouch for the lateral dimension discussed by Rouse and accordingly update the idea of diaspora. These attributes explicitly destabilise what Clifford calls "localising strategies" by which he signifies limited local area, natural culture, and periphery. Clifford, indeed, accepts that 'it is not possible to define "diaspora" sharply, either by recourse to essential features or to private oppositions' (Clifford 254). Rather he proposes his concept of "a loosely coherent, adaptive constellation of responses to dwelling-in-displacement" (Clifford 254).

Amitav Ghosh's outstanding novel *Sea of Poppies* (2008), shortlisted for the Man Booker Prize and which is the first of an extended set of three books known as *Ibis Trilogy*, manages a disorganised journey across the Indian Ocean to Mauritus Island getting back to a self-reflexive inquiry regarding the country. Its story unfurls in north India and the Bay of Bengal in 1838 just before the British assault on the Chinese port, generally known as the first opium war. Set in 1838, not long before the opium war (1839-1842), this novel typifies the colonial history of the East. In the novel, Ghosh amasses the mariners, voyagers, and sailors from various corners of the world aboard the ship *Ibis*. This, a slaving yacht currently changed over to the vehicle of coolies and opium to China. In carrying his group of characters to Calcutta out of the dark water, Ghosh furnishes the readers with all way of stories, and outfits himself with the workforce to man.

In the backdrop of the opium trade, which is an energising story all by itself, laden with insatiable covetousness, power-mongering, and racism, *Sea of Poppies* expands the meaning of diaspora as a third space, neither home nor metropolis, yet where a background marked by its own is unfurling. In the novel, Amitav Ghosh addresses multilingual groups of India on *Ibis*, with the vivid characters, the novel is the conflict and blending of dialects: Bhojpuri, Bengali, Lascari, Hindustani, Anglo-Indian and so on. The blending of these dialects makes a distinctive feeling of living voice just as the phonetic cleverness of individuals in diaspora. Ghosh has confidence in Eastern Humanism and shared points that pervade irrespective of race, class, and culture. Political commitments decide a significant number of relationships in the novel, however generally neglect to extinguish the substance of individual human feelings, recollections, dissatisfaction, and yearnings.

The novel is a critic of the socio-cultural advancement of Indian diaspora, of battle by the downtrodden and outcasts of colonial India, and the impartial record of the Indian peasantry constrained into opium development. It is a novel of disporic sensibility and recreation of identity. The possibility of diaspora as migration and colonisation implies an aggregate injury, a banishment where one longs for home yet lives in exile. Diaspora is a transnational organisation of scattered political subjects. The *Ibis*, which was a transport for slaves, is being refitted to take an enormous mass of indentured migrants called '*girmitiyas*' to Mauritius. On one hand, it is a vessel to ship the '*girmitiyas*' from India to the plantation estate settlement of Mauritius, however on the other, it is a microcosm of the ranch province itself. Paul Gilroy, in *The Black Atlantic: Modernity and Double Consciousness* (1993), has called the ship which transports labourers while in transit to plantation colonies "a living, micro-cultural, micro-political system in motion" (Gilroy 4). Deeti portrays this "as a vessel that was the Mother-Father of her new family, a great wooden mai-baap an adoptive ancestor and parent of dynasties to come" (Ghosh 356-57) is reminiscent of their new assenting country, the manor province of Mauritius.

Ibis dwells of individuals of various identities, castes, customs, doctrines, and practices, some escaping from the troubles at home, some being moved as convicts. It is loaded with a large number of characters both high and low, including a blended race fledgling mariner from Baltimore, a Rajah in debt to a British, a Chinese crook, a French stowaway, a Malay crew member, ranchers, troopers, and a horde of contracted Indian labourers. As the travellers of the Ibis sail down the waterway Hooghly into the Indian Ocean, their old family ties are washed away and they start their lives once more. The ocean turns into their new country as the shipmates form new obligations of sympathy and comprehension. They abandon the constructions of social caste, geographical location, and religion; rename themselves as 'jahaj bhais' and 'jahajbahans' (Ghosh 356). Wretched from their habituated life and finally uprooted from their homeland, the travellers forced to resettle, went through a horrible transformation that changed their feeling of subjectivity and influenced their point of view toward their general surroundings.

The excursion of the voyagers on the ship *Ibis* appears as a model of the local community involved trading off with social and social conduct in another life changing the circumstances to new facilities of having a place. In the novel, practically all the characters feel the feeling of longing and belonging. Indeed, they long for the region where they had come from. The boat turns into a substitute space for individuals to shape their new identities, personalities, and new networks too. Travel uncovered new places and causes the travellers to account new narratives. Regarding this, Robert Dixon properly says of Ghosh that the reality Amitav Ghosh has had the option to move uninhibitedly in his composition "between anthropology, history, and fiction is symptomatic of the extent to which traditional boundaries between those disciplines have themselves broken down." (Dixion 13) The characters on the boat experience new places and occasions, contrasting them and the previous occasions, and live the past in the present in an alternate area.

In his novels, Ghosh has depicted his diasporic emotions, loss of identity and rootlessness. While experiencing *Sea of Poppies* we can analyse the vexed diasporic encounters of colonial India with that of a similarly bothered history of Africa. A predicament was experienced by 'jahajbhais' of the Ibis while they were crossing the abyss of darkness where the Ganges vanished into 'kalapani'. Inside the novel the power of Käla-pani taboo to deconstruct territorialised types of personality is reached out past the South Asian characters of the novel as both the horrible "third" space of diaspora and a phase by which novelty enters the world through worldwide maritime ecologies. The boat turns into a vehicle for the enunciation of polyphonic diasporic relationships across a culture that survives yet doesn't completely remove territorialised types of Identity. On the Ibis, people of different groups or sorts start to form among the travellers. Relationships are manufactured or separate, clashes explode and singular predeterminations experience alter of course. Cut off from their foundations on the way and searching ahead for a new beginning, the migrants are inclined to design new names and identities.

The diasporic cognisance is firmly connected with the issue of identity and feel longing. The characters in Ghosh's novel have decided to traverse the Indian Ocean to a weird island where they should rebuild new identities. Being from various layers of Indian culture, these characters oppose the hard colonial setup and outline their game-plan to cut a special identity out of the traumatic conditions. In any case, it is a character in motion since every one of them is over in a hurry toward self-arrangement and recreation. In *Sea of Poppies*, there is another discovery that individuals relocated themselves in constrained but chosen condition since they were not owing a decent status in their country and therefore they acquired by and the large new characters of 'jahaj-bhai' and 'jahaj-behan' to characterise their existentialism. In the novel, every one of the characters attempts to interface his/her past with the present, memory with want, old binds with new affiliations, and moves to arrive at their objective with a solid level of vacillation.

Victims of diaspora are not at the edge constantly. They do not bring out self-centeredness for being alienated from home but instead attempt to be accustomed to new circumstances. The issue of identity has in reality been a significant distraction with Ghosh in the current novel. It seems, by all accounts, to be affected by the ethno-political dimension that continually changes characters' directions to recreate new personalities in the new milieu. In his books, individual identity is demonstrated to conflict with aggregate or collective identity. To recover the subaltern voices, Ghosh approaches a transcendental humanism by building up certain postmodern qualities like fictionality and ease of every desultory arrangement.

In the novel, individuals who are strongly rooted in the beginning, follow a slow interaction of separation and dislocation. Maybe obliging the inquiries of personal identity and recognisable proof, we come across a genuinely exceptional assortment of characters. Inside the layers of strangeness, we face different questions of dedication and identity, questions which are, partially, imperative to the development of the obscure future that this novel leaves us with. Ghosh maintains a strategic distance from familiar figures from history and takes the marginalised class of society that can give him a superior purpose of fictionalising and to his end.

Ghosh enriches the character of Deeti with the conventional qualities of upper-class Hindu while Kalua, the untouchable Dalit, carries on like one from the lower strata of society. Even though Deeti accepts another name and caste and hence removes her caste identity, she is unmistakably conspicuous for her hereditary caste consciousness. It was her conventional elite class that empowered her to accept the leadership of *girmitiyas* on the *Ibis* and, by suggestion, on the plantation settlement of Mauritius. She acquaints herself and Kalua with other *girmitiyas* as "Chamars" (234), of the leather labourer caste. All in all, Deeti's high caste Hindu identity is coded regarding her leadership. In the hierarchical caste system and privileged caste and traits of authority and order being equivalent to one another, Deeti's higher rank proceeds to exist and is regarded in any event, even when she assumes a lower caste. Ghosh must cause Deeti to lose her upper-class identity as opposed to elevating Kalua to a higher rank. Ghosh, a social anthropologist, recommends that having endured disgrace, affront, and maltreatment for millennia, untouchables could not carry on like upper caste individuals, for in India the caste that decided then how a specific individual would act towards different castes in the public eye. Kalua's submissive conduct with Deeti's husband Hukam Singh, daffadar Ramsharanji,

Gomusta, subedar Bhyron Singh and others plentifully demonstrates this view. His imaginary rise to higher standing would unquestionably have made him helpless, and drove both Kalua and Deeti to death, for the novel shows that "family's honour won't be restored till they're dead" (Ghosh 224).

Through Deeti's narrative of endurance and survival as an indentured worker, Ghosh endeavours to reproduce through the historical fiction the lost individual records of the main flood of South Asian coolie after the end of British bondage. In doing so, he also endeavours to make up for an obvious shortcoming in the advanced history of work dislocation and relocation. Ghosh proposes that for the abroad Indian migrants in the quest for their lost roots, revelation of some disgusting story at the root of their precursors' movement from India as contracted workers. Lately, as the Indian demeanour to abroad diaspora has gone through significant changes, and as an ever-increasing number of Indians came into contact with them, the abroad diasporaics have energetically responded to the Indian motion. Obviously, the memory of lost roots forces the Indian diaspora to think back with nostalgia to their motherland.

Works Cited

Baumann, Martin. "Exile." *Diasporas: Concepts, Intersections, Identities* Ed. Kim Knott and Seán McLoughlin. Rawat, 2010.

Clifford, James. "Diasporas." *Routes: Travel and Translation in the Lay Twentieth Century*. Harvard UP, 1997.

Cohen, Robin. *Global Diasporas: An Introduction*. Routledge, 2010.

Rouse, Roger. "Mexican Migration and the Social Space of Postmodernism." *Transnational Spaces*. Ed. Peter Jackson, Philip Crang and Clair Dwyer. Routledge, 2004.

Safran, William. "Diasporas in Modern Societies: Myths of Homeland and Return." *Diaspora: A Journal of Transnational Studies* 1.1,1991.

Dixon, Robert. "Travelling in the West: The Writing of Amitav Ghosh." *Amitav Ghosh: A Critical Companion*. Permanent Black, 2003.

Ghosh, Amitav. *Sea of Poppies*. Penguin Books. 2008.

Gilroy, Paul. *The Black Atlantic*. Harvard UP. 1993.

20

The Predicament of the 'White Cockroach': The Paradoxes of Belonging in *Wide Sargasso Sea*

Animesh Biswas

Introduction

Neo-Victorian studies are not identified clearly as academic studies. Neo-Victorianism reflects our on-going attitude towards Victorian literature and culture. It reveals the past in which women were presented as peripheral. Neo-Victorian literature criticises Victorian culture through postmodern angle. The emergence of Neo-Victorian literature as an academic discipline can be seen as a reaction to a historical age or position that is no longer with us. With the publication of Jean Rhys' *Wide Sargasso Sea* (1966) and John Fowles' *The French Lieutenant's Woman* (1969), Neo-Victorianism gained traction in the 1960s.

Wide Sargasso Sea by Rhys is the popular adaptation of Victorian literature. Adaptation is a polyphonic practise involving "both memory and change, persistence and variation" (Hutcheon). Neo-Victorian adaptation challenges Victorian construction of empire, gender and sexuality. Through *Wide Sargasso Sea*, Rhys adapts Charlotte Bronte's *Jane Eyre* criticising the ideas and ideologies of the past represented in the text. Sandra Gilbert and Susan Gubar consider Bertha Rochester as the 'veiled' sexual self of Jane. Rhys brings out the problem of sexual repression into the open. Antoinette's madness is the result of her sexual castration and lack of adequate human interaction. Rhys takes her heroine Antoinette from the marginalised position and makes her appear most prominent. While doing so, Rhys remodels Bertha and offers Antoinette a centralised role rather marginalised.

Jean Rhys' articulation of race in *Wide Sargasso Sea* is a very complicated one as the problem is inherently tangled with gender, class and national identities. The novel which portrays Creole Jamaican society at a moment of crisis presents a unique network of colour, culture and hierarchical power relations. Colour that is consciousness of skin viewed as a metaphor for social creation of race. It is woven with the issues of gender and national identity. Whites born in England differ from white Creoles, who are descendants of Europeans who have lived in the West Indies for a century or more. Since white slave owners in the Caribbean and Americans were notorious for raping and impregnating female slaves, there is a large mixed-race population. However, the central character Antoinette, who is based on the madwoman Bertha from Charlotte Bronte's *Jane Eyre*, is caught in a larger paradox. Though one step removed from racial injustice this white Creole woman is bestowed with fractured identities and an implicit fear of belonging. Antoinette is an exile within her own family, a disdainful servant's "white cockroach," and an oddity in her own husband's eyes. She never finds a place that belongs to her and to which she belongs. The historical situation that dominates the novel is the Emancipation Act of 1833 that liberated all slaves in the British colonies and the ethnic conflicts, social upheaval and economic instability that accompany it. This paper is going to look into the plight of the white Creole woman, who is an outcast and is shunned by both Europe and England, with whom she shares blood, and the Black West Indian people, whose culture and home she has known for two generations or more.

Ambivalence of the Creole Identity

Through a reading of some old colonial photographs, Derek Walcott's poem "Jean Rhys" paints a vivid and imagistic picture of the decaying grandeur of early nineteenth-century white Creole society, in which the people have "drifted to the edge," as if marginalised in both time and space. It locates the unbelongingness of the white Creole space trapped between the two racially divergent cultures. In Rhys' novel *Wide Sargasso Sea* "this position becomes a position of anxiety which makes manifest not a direct confrontation, but the ephemeral qualities of a melancholic sigh that strives to make relation through the rhetorical hush that divides the two sentences or two rapidly dividing cultures" (Burrows 26). This was the culture to which belonged Jean Rhys herself and her upsetting unforgettable character – Antoinette. The question of race and identity was definitely the most critical fact of the society. Consequently, *Wide Sargasso Sea*, a neo-Victorian adaptation of Bronte's *Jane Eyre* that questions the Victorian construction of empire, gender and sexuality, uses race as a ground on which meanings and significance can act upon one another. Bronte had a sensitive understanding of the plight of disenfranchised women, but she had been unable to see her own Creole heroine, the first Mrs. Rochester, as completely human as a Victorian English resident. Rhys in contrast has created interconnected but increasingly complicated perspectives on the story of Bertha Mason. The reason might be that Rhys, "opened up space for exploring the over determining strands of her protagonist's subjectivity" (Simpson p. 111). Part one of *Wide Sargasso Sea* takes place within the Creole's head, and it explores the factors that contribute to her apparent insanity. Rhys' text also thwarts literary critics' attempts to depict Antoinette as an outsider whose native resistance stands alone in the face of English hegemony. Actually, the whole issue of race and identity in *Wide Sargasso Sea* is much too complex to be reduced to a simple response to Charlotte Bronte's letter.

According to Savory, Rhys' most provocative theme in *Wide Sargasso Sea* is "race: this, too, is a kind of positioning, a political and economic identity that, motivated by the past of white racism, may be the most challenging field for a white writer to try to unravel" (Savory 134). Some critics, such as Spivak, Hite, and Gregg, find Rhys' depictions of the West Indies and race to be offensive. Every non-white character in *Wide Sargasso Sea*, according to Veronica Gregg, is based on historical white stereotypes of black people: Tia as a stealing, hostile nigger; Amelie as a lusty wench; Daniel as a hateful mulatto; Christophine as a black mammy. White commentators may also blatantly promote racial stereotypes. Tia and Daniel, according to Carole Angier, reflect "the power and gaiety (and also treachery) of the primitive" and "the half breed, neither black nor white but yellow," "the wolf-like other," respectively. (Angier 566). On the other hand, Jeremy Hawthorn claims that the plot summaries of Wide Sargasso Sea and Faulkner's Absalom, Absalom are strikingly similar, and that they both "give fascinating accounts of the ways in which vast conflict between society and race create internal contradictions in their members" (Hawthorn 92). The irony of Antoinette's dual role as oppressed and oppressor is lost on Hawthorn. Joline Blais' assertion that Tia "stands for all the ambivalence of Antoinette's identity across the race line" is more useful (Blais 105). Rhys represents the biases of her day, both in terms of race and class, but she also paves the way for white authors. Rhys was ahead of her time in terms of her ability to deal with race in several respects. Her job, however, is not especially admirable since race was inextricably linked to issues of gender, ethnicity, language, and class. A proper examination of Rhys' portrayal of the protagonist of *Wide Sargasso Sea*, Antoinette Cosway Mason Rochester, as ambivalently caught between the ideologies of coloniser and colonised, oppressor and oppressed, and the menacing anxiety of being neither white nor black, requires a thorough understanding of Jamaican society at the time of crisis.

Rhys' *Wide Sargasso Sea* is set in Jamaica and takes place between 1834 and 1845. This was a period of great political and social instability and at a time in which the local meaning of white was in great flux as power relations shifted in England's colonial domains as a result of the passing of the British Emancipation Act of 1834. The abolition of slavery caused a temporary state of ruin on West Indian plantations. It was a period of colonial history, and there were various levels of whiteness within the power system. Their status in this structure was largely determined by their position in the imperialist enterprise. At the end of the novel Antoinette suddenly realises that for imperialist such as her husband, "Gold is the idol they worship", without it, as she has now learnt to her cost the credibility of White Creole position is lost. The racial tension of bitterness was especially pervasive in the four years (1834-38) of the so called apprenticeship system established as a transitory measure between the abolition of slavery and the implantation of waged-labour structure. Disowned by England the white Creoles are now openly hated by newly freed slaves. For the white Creole slave-owner, slaves were property that with the passing of the act became worthless. The suicide of Antoinette's only friend and white neighbour in *Wide Sargasso Sea* is symbolic of the result of white Creole post-Emancipation desertion by the English. Those powerful and rich plantation owners such as the widowed Annette Cosway and her children around whom the narrative revolves are overcome by poverty, and now black hatred mingles with utter contempt: "old time white people nothing but white nigger now, nigger better than white nigger" (WSS 14). The whites are derided, openly jeered at and despised. However, it is the act of abandonment by their own race that adds the extra edge of bitterness and despair. Rhys herself visited Dominica with her second husband in 1936. Her account of the visit in "the imperial road" shows she found hostility to herself as a local white Creole and reminded strongly of the way race and racism informed her childhood. The doubt and dilemma that marks the existence and authenticity of British culture in the novel can be traced back to Jean Rhys herself. Rhys shares with other twentieth-century authors of postcolonial literature a deep distrust of authenticity and the cultural identities. If Antoinette and Christophine are unsure whether England exists, Rhys is unsure if Englishness exists in the first place. "Place, displacement, and a prevalent concern with myths of identity and authenticity are a characteristic common to all postcolonial literature in English," according to Bill Ashcroft (Ashcroft, p, 24). Rhys writes in her journal about some of her experiences as a teen. Rhys documents some of her childhood memories in her journal:

> My romantic relationship Working with 'real' little English boys and girls was strange (the real ones).
>
> They were almost always something I despised. I immediately noticed their peculiarly arrogant demeanour, as if they were convinced that I was inferior in some way. That's how I come across! Is it true that I spent every morning and evening in the tub? It is crucial. I'm proud of the fact that I once slapped a young English girl across the chest. I soon found out about something else as well. If I said I was English, they automatically contradicted me or implied a contradiction – no, a colonial – you are not English – inferior being. Colonials, in my mother's opinion, are not ladies and gentlemen.
>
> On the other hand, if I said exasperated, I'd be lying. "All right then I am not English as a matter of fact I am not a bit. I'd rather be French or Spanish than American. They'd be even more shocked at that. I was a scumbag. They'd say you're British because you're not one thing nor the other. I never liked their voices any more than they liked mine" (quoted in O'Connor, p. 19).

In this passage, Rhys' emphasis on "the real" succeeds in undermining both the English identity she is compelled to reject and the alternate national identities to which she is exposed. She is ultimately denied claim as a "British" subject.

One of Rhys' novel titles experiments, "Sargasso Sea (The Wide) Crossing Across" (Letters, p.204), aptly illustrates the novel's frequent movements, as seen in contrasting and shifting points of view, authorial voices, and narrative frames. Inside the fictions of colonial identity and English imperialism, there are struggles for meaning and supremacy recalled in such movements. In Wide Sargasso Sea, Antoinette's challenge is to strike a balance between British colonialism's conflicting logics while navigating Creole culture and post-emancipation English society, both of which she continues to elude. Antoinette explains:

> The narrator describes a white cockroach. That's me up there. Some of us are referred to as "slaves" because we came before our own people in Africa sold us to slave traders. I've heard the word "white niggers" used by English people, but between the two of you, I'm never sure who I am, where I belong, or why I was born at all" (61).

It's not quite English, and it's definitely not "native." The Creole woman in Rhys' film blurs the boundaries between human and savage, core and periphery, self and other.

Other factors to consider include the importance of the plantation economy and England's growing contempt for slavery and colonial slaveholders, making it more difficult to become a British subject in the West Indies Antoinette Cosway, who is played by Rhys, must traverse the perilous worlds of Creole, Caribbean, and English identity. In other words, long before Rochester appears on the scene, the violent conflict between Rochester's narrative and hers, his vision and hers, his historical memory of pre-emancipation vices and her cultivated forgetting and fears about herself and her place in the world has already begun. Rochester's response:

> "[Antoinette] was unsure, oblivious to the reality. "Not those," she said when I asked if the snakes we used to see were poisonous. 'Of course, the fer de lance,' he said, 'but how can they be sure?' 'Do you think they're aware of what's going on?' "Of course, our snakes aren't poisonous," he adds (52).

By being forced to move between the different knowledge circulated in the text, Antoinette dramatises the ontological contradictions that are constantly playing out on both the visual landscapes and psychic space of the *Wide Sargasso Sea*. Rochester is worried about the ambiguous Creole language that appears so often in Rochester's narration here and elsewhere. He is adamant about resolving Antoinette's ambivalence into the singular tones of English womanhood, then into the similarly singular tone of a barbaric otherness, until his failure to cast Antoinette as the chaste mother of English sons is fully apparent.

On the other hand, Antoinette's response to Rochester's attempt adds to the equation's complexity and perplexity. Rhys' Edward Rochester illustrates the mechanism by which English men and women are rendered by trying to incorporate Antoinette into nothing less than an English civilising narrative whose racial logics are so elegantly mystified by Charlotte Bronte in *Jane Eyre*. The variations between English and Creole, White and Black, man and woman are addressed in *Wide Sargasso Sea*. It also looks at how such a politics of consciousness is entangled in social logics that transcend national, racial, and historical boundaries. Rochester's reimagining of Antoinette as "the redheaded, wild haired stranger who was my wife" is connected to the domestic economy of England (89). Unlike the Creole crazy girl, who has a "lust for someone-not for me," she can loosen her black hair, chuckle, coax, and flatter (a mad girl). She is unconcerned with who she is in love with (99).

However, the traumatic relation between Antoinette and Rochester lacks sincerity on the part of both. While Rochester remains thoroughly doubtful about the plausibility of the whole effort, Antoinette herself masques her own closer bond to the blacks and the oppressed quite unsuccessfully in a tangible form of ambivalence. According to Sandra Drake, "the satisfactory resolution of Antoinette Cosway's crisis of identity can come only with a satisfactory resolution of her relationship to the part of Caribbean that is not derived from Europe-in this novel, particularly the black Caribbean" (Drake 194). It is not only just her connection with the black Caribbean characters but also her leaning towards Afro-Caribbean belief system as well as the culture and background which rarely provides a willing shelter to her troubled soul. It could account for the ambivalence in Antoinette's plight as "white cockroach".

The immense complexity involving dependency and alienation, desire and disgust that marks Antoinette's connection with black Caribbean is best illustrated by her relationship with characters: Christophine, Tia and Sandy Cosway. Antoinette who is a Caribbean, colonial and female is portrayed in the novel economically and psychologically powerless by European colonialism and patriarchy. Support comes from Christophine, former slave, model of female freedom. In part two of the novel Antoinette seeks support from Christophine:

> "But I cannot go. After all, he is my husband."
>
> She (Christophine) spits over her shoulder. "All women, all colours, nothing but fool...(I have) no husband, I thank my God. I keep my God. My money is safe with me. I don't give it to no useless man."
>
> "When must I go, where I must go?"
>
> "But look me trouble, a rich white girl like you and more foolish than the rest. If a guy treats you poorly, pick up your skirt and leave..." (66).

For Antoinette, this declaration defines Christophine as a paradigm of female freedom and dependency, as she reacts to her situation in patriarchal terms: "He is my husband after all" (66). "The benefit of not being a rich white girl but a former slave woman for knowing the undesirability of dependency and obedience, and links together the equation in the novel between the colonial state and the state of the slave in either sex in a discussion that often highlights the disparity in two women's situation," this extraordinary passage implies (197). Antoinette, on the other hand, couldn't agree with Christophine's astute psychological evaluation of Rochester or follow her advice on how to get out of it.

Christophine and Sandy fight the battle for Antoinette's survival against European patriarchy and empire, which they seem to have lost to Rochester. The resultant loss and defeat is strongly captured by Rhys with metaphorical cadence of a series of religio-cultural signifiers of Afro-Caribbean origin. The definition of zombie and its close connection with the practise of obeah is arguably the most important of them. A Eurocentric understanding restricts and regulates Rhys' use of the metaphor of marooning and references to zombification in *Wide Sargasso Sea*. The figure of the zombie reflects the African perception of death in its own cultural context. "The zombie, or living dead, dies only in appearance and is revived by those who have created the illusion of his death," wrote Maximilien Laroche (Laroche 49). However, when the zombie symbol was applied to the enslaved situation of Africans in the Caribbean, it became a symbol for slaves who were forced to work for a master (Laroche 55). According to Laroche, zombies can be identified by their "vague appearance, dull almost glazed eyes, and above all, the nasality of their voice" (Laroche 51). The zombified Antoinette in *Wide Sargasso Sea* embodies all of these traits. Rochester's 'possession' of her turns her into a puppet incapable of autonomous action, a doll with a nailed-on smile. Zombies are utterly unaware of their condition as slaves to their master because they have no memory of their former life. Rhys has invented a formula involving ghosts and zombies that suggests Antoinette for the part. "Does there seem to be a ghost or a zombie here?" Baptiste was questioned by Rochester. (63). Finally, the Thornfield Hall is plagued by a rumour about the imprisoned Antoinette. As a result, Rochester is to blame for Antoinette's descent into a zombie state, followed by an apparent death (insanity) and then a real self-inflicted death. "Antoinette's 'real death' is not a deranged suicide in the flames of Thornfield Hall...her 'real' death is Rochester's subjugation-the long slow process of her reduction to the zombie state chronicled in the novel" (200). The immensity of colonisation, a process that pervades with all authority, appears to have defeated her bond with Christophine and Sandy.

Conclusion

The novel comes to a close with a sense of ambivalence, which Walcott captures so well in his poem. The hush in Walcott's poem begins with a sense of movement suggesting that the child's sigh can carry across the sea between England and Dominica, but by the end of the verse the 'the white hush is caught between two sentences'. It is this final ambivalence which if not negates but at least partially subverts the totality of the triumph aimed by the white colonisation. The resistance itself is located in the form of dreamscape that gains its final shape in the vision of a deranged Antoinette. Antoinette's third and final dream proves to be her awakening and her relation with Tia seems to provide a clue into the final direction to which this White Creole woman turns her face. The scene that hints at resolution in part three is a significant reversal of sharp division and alienation by race, class and wealth so brutally yet beautifully captured in the scene of burning of Coulibri. When Tia threw a stone, it was a symbol of the Blacks' rejection of the White Creole. But, the girls equally hurt, one bleeding and the other crying made way for the last gestures towards a resolution at the end. Antoinette stands on the battlefield of Thornfield Hall in her third dream:

> "Tia was there," says the narrator. I hesitated when she beckoned to me, and she chuckled. I overheard her say, "Are you scared?" Bertha, I heard the man's voice! Bertha, Bertha! In a fraction of a second, I saw and heard everything. And the sky was a bright colour. Someone screamed, and I wondered why they screamed. I shouted 'Tia,' stood up, and awoke" (112).

The reader is given just the tiniest hint that could entice him to dig deeper into the plight of the "White Cockroach," but the rest is shrouded in a misty ambivalence that only adds to the perplexity of the White Creole woman's life. Between *Jane Eyre* and the *Wide Sargasso Sea*, between black and white, between coloniser and colonised, between Christian tenets and obeah magic's influence, between metaphors that appropriate and metaphors that proliferate, Antoinette Cosway Mason Rochester is trapped in an untenable situation. The white hush of Jean Rhys, resonant with a fleeting stillness, may be sandwiched between two sentences, but the hush implies that the sigh, like the paradox, will linger.

Notes

1. Derek Walcott. 'Jean Rhys' in his Collected Poems 1948-84. New York Farrar, Straux & Giroux.1986. 427-29.
2. Here, one must remember that Rochester is significantly left unnamed in Rhys' text. Gayatri Chakraborty Spivak observes "Rhys denies to Bronte's Rochester the one thing that is supposed to be secured in the Oedipal rely: the name of the father or the patronymic. In Wide Sargasso Sea the character corresponding to Rochester has no name".

Works Cited

Angier, Carole. *Jean Rhys: Life and Work*, Boston: Little Brown and Company, 1990.

Bronte, Charlotte. *Jane Eyre*. New York: Penguin, 1985.

Burrows, Victoria. *Whiteness and Trauma: The Mother-Daughter Knot in the Fiction of Jean Rhys, Jamaica Kincaid and Toni Morrison*. New York: Palgrave Macmillan. 2004.

Drake, Sandra. "Race and Caribbean Culture as Thematic of Liberation in Jean Rhys' *Wide Sargasso Sea*" in J. Raiskin ed. *Wide Sargasso Sea*: New York: W.W. Norton & Company, 1999.

Gregg, Veronica Marie. *Jean Rhys' Historical Imagination*. Chapel Hill: University of North Caroline Press, 1995.

Hawthorn, Jeremy. *Multiple Personality and the Disintegration of Literary Character*. London: Edward Arnold, 1983.

Rhys, Jean. *Wide Sargasso Sea*: New York: W.W. Norton & Company, 1999.

Rhys, Jean. *Jean Rhys Letters*, 1931-66. ed. Francis Wyndham and Diana Melly. London: Deutsch, 1984

Spivak, Gayatri Chakravorty. "Three women's Texts and a Critique of Imperialism Race, Writing and Difference". Ed. Henry Louis Gates, Jr. Chicago: University of Chicago Press, 1985.

Simpson, Anne B. *Territories of the Psyche: The Fiction of Jean Rhys*. New York: Palgrave Macmillan, 2005.

Vreeland, Elizabeth. "Jean Rhys: The Art of Fiction LXIV" *in Paris Review* 21:76. Fall Issue, 1979.

21

Krishna, the Shyamsundar: Semiotic Study of Krishna's Complexion in *Dhamashektra*

Priya Samni

In recreating a precolonial era mythical character; postcolonial Indian author is bound to go against the traditional representation of the character's complexion, resulting in the misconception of the legend. In ancient India, colour was not the root of killing and discrimination. The colour black was accepted as the skin colour of heroes and even gods. But with the invasion of Mughals and then the British, Indians developed 'snow-white syndrome', a craze for white skin which led to the prejudice that 'whites' were superior and powerful. The study aims to find out the significance which the relationship between Krishna and Draupadi lost because of the fair-skinned depiction of the dark puranic characters. The researcher will conduct a semiotic analysis of Krishna's complexion in the visual text, *Dharmashektra.* The studies done before on the colour symbolism of Krishna focused *Mahabharata's* 'dark one' as a justification for colour prejudice as a result of colonial influence whereas the postcolonial fair-skinned Krishna has not been analysed before. Hence, semiotic analysis of Krishna in *Dharmashektra* will give more in-depth knowledge of the postcolonial subconsciousness.

In constructing a Puranic character, the author is always conscious in assigning the kind of divinity, power, birth, colour, hierogamy and progeny. These features are significant as they influence the character's aura or mythical persona. Of the various features mentioned, colour symbolism is unique to each culture. Therefore, what a particular colour symbolises in one culture may not be true to the other. The specific culture or community which produces and consumes the text determines the colour complexion of the characters. In ancient India, colour was not the root of killing and discrimination. The colour black was accepted as the skin colour of heroes and even gods. But with the invasion of Mughals and then the British, Indians developed 'snow-white syndrome', a craze for white skin which led to the prejudice that 'whites' were superior and powerful. Thereby in recreating a precolonial era mythical character; postcolonial Indian author is bound to go against the traditional representation of the character's complexion, resulting in the misconception of the legend.

The study explores the semiotics of Krishna's complexion in the TV series, *Dharmashektra* against the precolonial description of Krishna as 'shyamsundar', meaning 'dark and handsome'. My analysis is attentive to understand why a postcolonial author is obsessed with 'white' as the colour of supreme power. *Dharmakshetra* is a mythological drama set in the court of Chitragupta after the battle of Mahabharata. Of all the other recreation or adaptations of *Mahabharata*, *Dharmakshetra* had an important reason to portray Krishna in black as the series focused each character of the epic closely to determine the true heroes and villains of the battle. But the colour symbolism, which is very important in understanding the true persona of the character, is ignored. By ignoring it, the series failed to understand Krishna and his action completely. The study aims to find out the significance of Krishna's complexion concerning the mysterious affiliation and co-association with Draupati which is lost in modern recreation.

In Hindu mythology, Krishna is always showered with praises of being "the dark one", he is called in various names like 'Shyama', meaning 'dark' or 'Shyamsundar', meaning, 'dark and handsome'. Devotional songs in all Indian languages praise Krishna as the dark god. Despite the dark complexion, Krishna is always adored for his beauty. "One of the most striking features of the cowherd Krishna is his fantastic beauty. Krishna is beauty itself-his appearance alone transcends the world of the ordinary. For of all the Hindu gods, Krishna expresses most completely all that is beautiful, graceful, and enticing in the other world of the divine" (Kinsley 172). There have been several works on Krishna in the precolonial India which includes Subramaniya Bharati's *Kannan Paattu,* medieval Bhakti movement work *Krishna Lila, Mira Bhajans,* Andal's poems and many more. These compositions hailed Krishna as the dark-hued charmer. Also, the portraits, paintings, and ancient literature depicted Krishna in blue, dark blue or black colour. "In Indian paintings, Krishna is normally blue or mauve in colour, though cases occur in which he is black, green or dark brown. Black would seem to follow from Krishna's name-the word Krishna meaning black" (Walter and W. G 269). It is evident from the above discussion that ancient Indians adored Krishna as the 'dark god', yet there is a discomfort in the postcolonial Indian minds to portray Him in dark skin.

Ancient Indians didn't discriminate based on colour. Ancient texts justified the tendency of Indians to accept the presence of power and beauty within all beings irrespective of skin tone. Some of the most beautiful princesses, heroes, powerful gods and goddesses of ancient literature were dark-skinned. During the precolonial era, dark colour did not carry any prejudice and was, in fact, used as a describing feature of beauty... Unfortunately, British colonialism in India created a race-based ideology in the minds of the nation's dark-skinned common man. Having been ruled by white-skinned masters for over three hundred and fifty years, who claimed themselves as "superior" and "intelligent" race, the common man started to associate white coloured skin with the ruling class, desirability, power and also with beauty. This craze for white has not ceased from the Indian postcolonial subconscious – even after so many years of Independence.

Fanon in *Black Skin, White Mask,* remarks that the black man desired to become white in order to prove the richness of his thought and the equal value of his intellect. "For the black man, there is only one destiny. And it is white" (Fanon). The craze for fair skin, 'snow-white syndrome' in Indian society can be traced back to the colonial period when the men and women tried to imitate their British rulers. Though Indians despised the British men in India, they looked up to the white rulers as the symbol of wealth, power and style. The Indian women of higher social hierarchy were in awe of the 'memsahibs' (white women of high social status living in India). However, the 'memsahibs' developed a prejudice towards dark-skinned Indians, primarily due to their interaction with the Indian domestic helpers employed in their households. "The servants' dark skin and their religious, social and linguistic differences contributed to the negative attitudes of the memsahibs towards them" (Chaudhuri 544). Chaudhuri in "Memsahibs and Their Servants in Nineteenth-Century India" details the Memsahib's prolonged rejection and prejudice over the Indians. Over the period, Indians were bound by a strong notion that 'white' was supreme. Chatterjee brought out the reason for the dark one's obsession over whiteness in his discourse, "Colonialism, Nationalism and Colonialised Women". "For a colonised people, the world was a distressing constraint, forced upon it by the fact of its material weakness. It was a place of oppression and daily humiliation, a place where the norms of the coloniser had perforce to be accepted" (Chatterjee 627). Shankar and Subish wrote in a similar line of thought that colonial legacy in India is one of the contributory factors in the belief that white is powerful and beautiful. Arnold elaborated on the factor as he explained East India Company's exclusion of Indians from authoritative positions in the administrative office and the army which were occupied by the 'whites'. "This legal and administrative revolution was, moreover, supported, among Europeans in India, by a discourse of racial discrimination and abuse that identified a non-white skin with every kind of unsavoury physical and moral attribute" (Arnold 264).

A vast body of literature strengthens the idea that colour prejudice is the result of the negative influence of colonialism. However, influenced by the postcolonial subconsciousness, heroes of the postcolonial era were portrayed as fair-skinned. While analysing why Indian consumers idealise fair skin, literature conveys that skin tone is a powerful tool in postcolonial India, where a lighter colour represents higher status and beauty. When most literature used the legend of Krishna as the 'dark one' to justify the absence of colour prejudice in precolonial India, the representation of Krishna as white-skinned in modern texts is hardly studied. But there must be such a study if we are to understand the significance of Krishna's dark complexion and its misconception in the postcolonial era. The researcher will conduct a semiotic analysis of Krishna's complexion in the visual text, *Dharmashektra.* The studies done before on the colour symbolism of Krishna focused on the 'dark one' of *Mahabharata* whereas the postcolonial fair-skinned Krishna has not been analysed before. Hence, semiotic analysis of Krishna in *Dharmashektra* will give more in-depth knowledge of the postcolonial subconsciousness.

Dharmashektra is a mythological drama series narrated from the perspective of various characters justifying their actions in the court of Chitragupta. The focus of this paper is episode 26 of *Dharmashektra,* where Lord Krishna testifies in the assembly the deeds he did on earth. Portrayed in fair complexion, Krishna explains the relationship he had with Pandavas and Draupadi. At this point, it is important to note that *Mahabharata* depicted Krishna and Draupadi as dark or black when all the other characters were something but black. Based on this shared complexion, the two characters develop a mysterious relationship. Constructed as fair-skinned in the drama *Dharmashektra,* this mysterious relationship lost its significance.

The major focus of episode 26 of *Dharmashektra* is to explain the relationship Krishna shared with the other characters of the epic, in particular Arjuna and Draupadi. Draupadi and Krishna are both dark-skinned and are known by the same name 'Krishna' meaning 'dark'. Besides sharing the same name, they develop a bonding which cannot be explained in definite terms and this bond is strengthened by their colour homogeneity. Draupadi states, "I was the only one, who never considered you as God. I always thought, I had a right to you. I've been stubborn with you. I used to debate with you" (*Dharmashektra* (26) 32:16-33:21). Though described in words, the magical attraction between Draupati and Krishna which can be termed as 'divine Maya' lost its significance in *Dharmashektra*. Krishna establishes that he is either a family member or a friend to the characters present in the court. He further adds that everyone needs kin whose words can be accepted wholeheartedly rather than a person who bosses around. When Arjuna lamented over his son Abhimanyu's death, Krishna consoled him as a friend and not as a God. And when Draupadi declared, "No matter what you are to anyone. But you will be my best friend" (*Dharmashektra (26)* 36:26-36:29), the bonding meant the same as that of Arjuna's friendship with Krishna.

Krishna, Draupadi and Arjuna of *Dharmashektra* were visualised as fair complexioned whereas the mythology presents Arjuna as fair as milk; Krishna and Draupadi dark coloured. Does this make any change? Krishna as a friend to Arjuna and as having a mythical attraction towards Draupadi was distinguished clearly in the epic with the use of colour. The epic identified Lord Krishna as Narayana and the chief hero Arjun as Nara, Hindu deity pair of back and white. Arjuna means white, like that of milk, silver, lightning and the dawn. To sustain this very same relationship in modern recreation it is necessary for Krishna to be dark-skinned. However, being portrayed in fair complexion this connotation becomes invalid in the drama. At the same time, Draupadi is said to have a divine bonding with Krishna which explains the miracle that happened when Druyodaran tried to disrobe her. What other justification can be given to the audience for this divine action than the shared colour complexion of Krishna and Draupadi. Unfortunately, the value of this special bonding between Krishna and Draupati last its significance, leaving the viewers in confusion.

Based on the shared colour, Krishna and Draupadi develop a series of mysterious affiliations and co-associations. The mysterious union, narrated in episode 26 of the TV drama when Draupadi saw Krishna in the eyes of her mind needs explanation. Hopelessly holding hands in prayer and crying bitterly while meditating Krishna's name, Draupadi saw Krishna by the blanks of a river telling her to "be furious". No other characters of the epic had this experience. This mysterious attraction can be termed as 'divine maya'. 'Maya' being the veil of reality, is "instrumental in disguising their divine self from all mortals, choosing to unravel their true identity only when they want" (Ramakrishnan). When the shared colour failed to explain the 'divine maya' as they were all fair and no uniqueness between Krishna and Draupadi, words came to explain. Pointing to the union, Krishna said, "But I wasn't with you, you were with me" (*Dharmashektra (26)* 34:04-34:09) and Krishna promised Draupadi that He would surrender Himself to the one who thought of him as a friend, a promise not made with any other character. He had suggested earlier that he is either a friend or a family to the characters. If all are the same, then what makes the words said to Draupadi mythical? The shared dark complexion that is absent in the drama is again the foundation of this mysterious relationship that Krishna shared with no other characters but Draupadi.

The series though tried to establish the unique relationship between Krishna and Draupati with words, the author didn't consider visualising them in the original dark complexion which would have given a better understanding of the bond. The postcolonial subconsciousness of the Indians was influenced by the colour prejudice that associates 'black' with slaves or domestic helpers and 'white' with supreme power. Krishna being the supreme power and hero of the epic is therefore constructed with a fair complexion. But with the negligence of Krishna's dark complexion, the relation between Krishna and Draupadi remains the same as Krishna's relation with other characters.

Works Cited

Arnold, David. "Race, Place and Bodily Difference in Early Nineteenth-Century India." *Historical Research*, vol. 17, no. 6, 2004, pp. 254-273.

Chatterjee, Partha. "Colonialism, Nationalism and Colonilised Women: The Contest in India." *American Ethnologist*, vol. 16, no. 4, 1989, pp. 622-633.

Chaudhuri, Nupur. "Memsahibs and Their Servants in Nineteenth-Century India." *Women's History Review*, vol. 3, no. 4, 1994, pp. 549-562.

Mehta, Dharmesh, director. *Dharmashektra*. EPIC (TV Channel), 2014.

Fanon, Frantz. *Black Skin, White Mask.* Grove Press, 2008.

Gurner, Walter. "The Loves of Krishna. In Indian Painting and Poetry." *Journal of the Royal Asiatic Society*, vol. 89, no. 3, 1957, pp. 268-269.

Kinsley, David. "Without Krsna There Is No Song." *History of Religion*, vol. 12, no. 2, 1972, pp. 149-180.

Mishra, Neha. "India and Colorism: The Finer Nuances." *Washington University Global Studies Law Review*, vol. 14, no. 4, 2015, pp. 725-749.

Shankar, Ravi, and Subish P. "Fair Skin in South Asia: an Obsession?" *Journal of Pakistan of Dermatologists*, vol. 17, 2007, pp. 100-104.

Venkataswamy, Sudha. "Transcending Gender: Advertising Fairness Cream for Indian Men." *Media Asia*, vol. 40, no. 2, 2013, pp. 128-138.

22

Presentation of Caste in Colonial Narratives: A Discourse on DK Chowta's Tulu Novel *Mittabail Yamunakka: The Tale of the Household of a Landlord*

Mridul C Mrinal

Caste is the predominant system of social stratification. This paper analyses the presence of caste and caste hegemony presented in DK Chowta's *Mittabail Yamunakka: The Tale of a household of a landlord* against the backdrop of the 1835 Canara revolt and Indian Independence struggle. It focuses on the regional system of social organising and the common communities. The connections and roles of these communities are discussed. It specially focuses on the emergence and establishment of Bunts as a hegemonial order over the regional social system and analyse the text correspondence with the hegemony. It analyses that cultural traits are the important element, which establishes the hegemony. Militancy is another element used in the developing a hegemonial order. The chapter also enquires the presence of different communities of the region corresponding to the novel and the social and cultural role undertaken in the light of the theme. It analyses the distinctive social subjugation of the untouchables and features social phenomenon such as temporary social upgradation. The paper also picks up some of the fanatic elements identified with in the novel. It also enquires how the social transformation is facilitated through the movement of Gandhian Principles.

Mittabail Yamunakka was published in 2005. It was later translated into Kannada by Muhammed Kulai in 2008. The novel has won the prestigious Paniyadi award for the best Tulu Novel in 2006. It was translated into English in 2017 under the title *Mittabail Yamunakka; The Tale of a household of a landlord* by Prof. B.Surendra Rao and Prof.K.Chinnappa Gowda. As the title proposes, the story revolves around a Bunt household near Manjeshwara in the ancient Kumble kingdom. It consists of several plots and sub plots. The main theme is the feud between two Bunt households of Bara bail and Mittabail. The novel consists of two narrations, an analepsis described as *Those Days* and *Now a Days*. *Those Days* are set in the 1830s, during the historical Canara insurgency whereas in *Now a Days* are set during the Indian Independence struggle. The time spans of both periods are about one and half century or four generations. Both the time periods are mainly consist of political turmoil. This include the historical invasion of Kalyanaswamy against the English East India company and the hostile climate it creates in the Mayippady Kingdom followed by the struggle for Indian Independence against the British which was gaining momentum under the leadership Mahatma Gandhi. The brothers Manjanaalva and Kinhanna establish the Mittabail Bail Guttu. They rebelled against their uncle and came out of Majalody Guttu. They found a piece of land and started cultivation. Eventually the land was prospered and transformed into an estate. Manjanaalva established wealthy the Mittabail Guttu estate. The king of Kumble, Ramanatharasu, invited Manjana into his army. The upcoming threat of Kalyanaswamy from Coorg held an uncertain fate over the kingdom of Kumble. Biranna Banta of Bara bail raises an insurgency and terrorise the Tulu villages by ransacking and looting them. Manjanaalva was promoted as the commander of king's army. They plan to face Kalyanaswamy, when his forces reached the neighboring Amara Sullia region. But Kalayanaswamy left out Kumble without attacking and in turn he appreciated the fight put up by Manjanaalva's forces. He neglected Biranna who created terror using his name. Biranna Banta was caught and killed. Kalyanaswamy moves north towards Mangalore and attacks the British garrisons. During the fight, he was caught and hanged. The British East India Company acquired the Tulu speaking lands and established the Company raj. Manjana was later anointed as the head of the new Mittabail Guttu. The enmity between Mittabail and Bara bail continued for generations. The present narration shows the continuing enmity even after generations. Yamunakka, the descendent of Manjanaalva was occupying the headship of Mittabail Guttu after the death of its head, Manku Rai. Yamunakka is defending Mittabail against the threats of Thyamapanna Shetty of Bara bail. Thyampanna Shetty was lobbying for Manku Rai's kin to be anointed as the head of the Guttu. Thyamapanna Shetty was the illegitimate son of Manku Rai and Achakka of Bara bail. He expects to control Mittabail once his bynames was anointed. Yamunakka keeps Thyamapanna Shetty away and waits for her younger brother, Subbayanna Alva to return. Subbayanna was the rightful heir, but he became a Gandhian and went to participate in the Indian freedom struggle. Bara bail was the tenants of Mittabail Guttu. Thyampanna tried to acquire the legal claim over the land but Yamunakka prevents it. She put blocks to every attempt by Thyampanna for gaining an upper hand over Mittabail. Yamunakka exterminates the entire Bara bail and kills Thyampanna Shetty as the last resort to eliminate the threat.

The Bunt hegemony rules over the political, socio cultural arenas of Tulunadu. They are considered the martial race of Tulu land. The monarchs were depended upon the service of Bunts as soldiers in their army. This also helped the Bunts to hold their influence upon the monarch and there by control and safeguard their interests. They received large amount of grants and lands. It is a matter of prestige for Bunt household to serve in the Army. "If a Bunt household does not volunteer to go to the army, it would be as dishonourable as Delambu Kottari refusing to join the paaneru army and having to forfeit the ritual headship of his family and all the ritual honour that with it" (Chowta 69).

The Billavas are the single largest community in Tulunadu. Traditionally, Billavas were the toddy tappers. Although they are considered as lower caste, the presence of a Poojari, the Billava priest is mandatory during the Bhootha Kola ritual. This implies the inevitable participation of every caste in the cultural construction of Tulunadu. Ammana Poojary, being the closest associate of the rivals of Yamunakka and Mittabail is triggering a new tension through his verdict during the spiritual consultation. The Guttu holds a vast area of land used for cultivating a large variety of crops. Some of these lands were distributed as small plots among the tenants who in return pays the tribute. They were bounded to the household of Mittabail. The colony of Mugera are called dadike. The Bondsmen are mainly belongs to the Untouchable Mugera caste. Mugera and Billava are the largest among the three strata of communities with significant roles in the socio cultural aspect according to Dr, Gururaj Bhat. Dr. Bhat illustrates this in his various works.

> All these are dependent, for their food, clothes and all that go in the name of their live hood, on the and lords' household. They are bound to work for the landlord, and cannot work elsewhere without their lord's permission. Whatever they do, they do only with the permission of the Guttu (Chowta 26-27).

The concept of Varna excludes the Untouchable or the Dalit. They are often like ritual slaves under the Bunt elitist hegemony. They also maintain the cultural and social ties with the Guttu. These Dalit tenets are obliged to observe the pollution due to death after the demise of any member from the Guttu. They are fierce in defending the Guttu and willing to take arms and lives. This is the direct implication of establishing Bunt hegemony over the marginalised.

Apart from these mentioned communities, Other Untouchables like Nalke and Pamabada are also mentioned in the novel. They impersonate the Bhuta deity during the ritualistic Bootha Kola. The dynamics of social upgradation is witnessed with these communities. It is the customary duty, which relies upon these communities to impersonate the Bhuta and perform the Devil dance. The age-old caste restriction applies to every untouchable caste while the ritual is performing. Each community has to maintain their customary distance from the higher castes. The ritual in front of the shrine of Malaraya is attended by all communities but only by adhering to the caste norms.

The concept of pollution barred communities such as untouchables from making any forms of contact with the higher castes. According to Ambedkar, the concept of pollution originates in the priestly ceremonialism and is a particular case of general purity. He also observes that the sole reason for the idea of pollution to be associated with institution of caste is that the high-ranking castes are the priestly castes. Here the unique feature of ritualistic social upgradation and relaxation of norms are to be observed as an exception case. Both the features are only associated with rituals and not in the common life of the society. The origin of the community itself is from the tradition of spirit impersonation and spirit medium, but the social upgradation is temporary. Once the sacred costumes of the Bhuta are removed, the person returned to his old status as an untouchable. During the Nema ritual of Mittabail Guttu, the Untouchables are barred from the common ritualistic grounds for the sake of general purity in the presence of the distinguished Bunt guests and high profiled Brahmin priest, the Tantri of Badaje. "They would not come, anywhere near the route in which the ritual paraphernalia of the deity is taken. Communities like Nalke, Pambada, all the bondsmen and the forest dwellers are still following the old prohibition" (Chowta 24).

Certain communities such as the Jains, Beary, Belchada, and Konkani etc. are also a part of the wider plot of the novel. Jains are traditionally considered as traders. The founder of Mittabail Guttu, Manjanaalva attained his prosperity with the help of the Jain setti of Manjeshwar. The Mittabail produced tons of the precious atikara rice for Jain setti. The relation between the Bunts and Jains were always harmonious in Tulunadu. Due to their status as the high castes, they have been favoring each other. This is proven through the relationship of Manjanaalva and Jaina Setti of Manjeshwar.

The Bearys are the native Muslims of Tulunadu. They share cultural and social ties along with the Mappila Muslims of Malabar. Nevertheless, simultaneously they are also considered a distinct community. According to Prof. B Ichlangod, the Bearys have certain unique features such as the traditions of Illams and Balis when compared to Mappilas. Linguistically Beary speak a tongue of Malayalam lexicon with Tulu phonology and grammar. The Tulu word Beary is a corrupted form of Vyapari meaning trader. Bearys were mainly considred to be the progenies of Arab traders with the native women. Bearys are mainly engaged in trade. They are an integral part of the Tulu society. Several Beary characters appear in the novel like Ullal Sahib.

Every community is described in detail with a strong impression. The Belchda Community became a focus of the story line when Mayila Belchada joins Biranna Banta in his insurgency. These Belchadas belong to the same caste as that of our poojaris. Since they hail from the areas south of the Chandragiri River, they speak Malayalam.....the worship of daivas like Vishnumoorthy and Deities like Bhagavathi, have followed them to our region. (Chowta 142)

The thick description about the single Belchada community indicates the rich ethno linguistic diversity of the region. Their origin to the south of river Chandragiri also points the cultural boundary of Tulunadu. According to traditions, the southern boundaries of Tulunadu are marked along the River Chandragiri in Kasaragod. It marks the boundaries between the Malayalam and Tulu cultural regions. The presence of Belchada community also symbolises the cultural similarities and intakes between Malabar and Tulunadu. The Tradition of Bootharadhane is synonymous to

Theyyam in north Malabar. The practice of matrilineal system of lineage is also some common features. The venerations of local demi gods known as Daiva or Bhuta in Tulu and Theyyam in Malayalam are also common. C Raghavan described the Daivas originated in Tulunadu as Tulu Theyyams in Malayalam. While the Theyyams like Vishnumoorthy, which originated in Malabar are known as Malayala Bhuta in Tulu.

The Konkani presence maintains a strong impression throughout the novel. Konkani characters had vital roles with political as well as social significances. Historical characters of Konkani backgrounds are incorporated into the story line. Subrya Shanbhouge of Koodlu, was the commander in chief in the army of king Ramanatharasu during the Canara Revolt.

Shanubouge is portrayed as a mentor to Manjanaalva. He inducted Manjanaalva into his regiment and trained him in warcraft like swordsmanship, gun shooting, fighting with spears and horsemanship. Subraya Shanbougue grows fond of Manjanaalva. Another historical character is Govinda Pai. Pai was the first Kannada Poet to receive the Rashtra Kavi title. He was also a historian, Writer and Polyglot who contributed to the historical discourses of Tulunadu. Subbayanna have accidently met him at Sabarmathi Ashram. Govinda Pai is depicted in reality while infusing with the fictional character of Subbayanna. The novel holds the historical accounts on the demise of his wife and the return from ashram. Devaya Bhandary of the Banadara Mutt is the closest companion of Manjanaalva. The cordial relationship between Devaya Bhandary and Manjanaalva further grew and solidified with the relations of Bhanadara Mutt and Mittabail Guttu. The Bunt Hegemony was never compromised unless to the Brahmin priest of Badaje. Here the Konkani Saraswat Brahmins forms formal ties with the native Bunt hegemony. "No longer able to put up with the persecution of the Portuguese in Goa, many Konkanis fled the place and some of them reached Manjeshwara. They settled down there and build their houses and developed their business in the town" (Chowta 211).

The projection of Konkani characters could be understood on two ways: one, the historical representation, second hegemonial alliance. Konkani community were always maintained a refugee tag among the native Tuluva community. This alliance should be observed as an initiative in breaking of these tag and establish themselves as a political entity rather than wealthy traders.

In the analepsis, King Ramanatharasu of the Kumble kingdom is summoning a witan to discuss threats of Kalayanappa's attack from the Coorg. The witan is comprised of the representatives from every community in the society. The historical authenticity of this summoning could not be confirmed.

All the heads of the various community groups like Jaina setti of Manjeshwara, the eminent ones of the Konkani community like Bhandary of Bhandara mutt, Shanubouge, Bhakta of Bhakta Mutt, the elders of Maniyani, Bovi, Poojari, Moilaaru of the Beary community...the various groups of Dalit community like

Bakuda, Mugera, Nalke, Koraga, Domba and Panaara were also represented by their leaders at Mujingaavu. (Chowta 167)

Subbayanna, The new anointed head for the Mittabail is also a Gandhian who wish to end the caste practices in front of him. He advocates for the equality of the people and speak against caste discrimination. Despite of his effort to integrate, they are still reluctant to come out of the norm set by the old traditions. "To the yard, in front of the Bhuta shrine at Mittabail, the bondsmen of the household would not step, in spite of the persuasion of the reformist Subbayanna" (Chowta 24).

Social reformation had been complex ever since the independence. The earlier signs of reformations were visible from the middle ages. The complete legal prohibition of caste was only conceived after the adaptation of the constitution. Ambedkar observes "But whether the reform will continue depends upon what scopes the group affords for such individual assertion" (Ambedkar 46). If the group is tolerant enough to receive the message, reformation will live on. If the group is intolerant, the reforms will die out. Here in the post-independence era, the feudal hegemony of Bunt had ended. Subbayanna implements Gandhi's interpretation of freedom. "First there should be freedom for all, irrespective of their castes, to enter temples and shrines in his village. There should be no discrimination between Brahmins, Bakuda, Bunt, Poojary and so on" (Chowta 276). Upon his anointment as the head of Mittabail Guttu, Subbayanna eliminated all forms of discriminations based on Caste. Here the bunt hegemony in society was paving way to a new set of social order. The new socio political climate is devoid of any discrimination on caste but the hegemony continues on the wealth and power. The entry of Subbayanna marks the period of social transition where caste was established as social stratification parameter. The status of caste has become illegitimate, illegal, and no more serves its previous purpose but continues to exist as a cultural identity. The novel is a celebration of the Bunt community and its associating factors such as Guttu culture and traditions during the colonial era. However, the novel is a cross section of the ethnic and linguistic diversity of Tulunadu.

Works Cited

Ambedkar, B R. *Annihilation Of The Caste With A Reply To Mahatma Gandhi*. Bhalchander Mungekar. 1944.

Bhat, Gururaj P. *Studies in Tuluva History and culture.* Kallianpur. P Gururaj Bhat. 1975.

Cancian, Frank. "Social Stratification." *Annual Review of Anthropology*, vol. 5, 1976, pp. 227-248. JSTOR, www.jstor.org/stable/2949312. Accessed 03 June 2020.

Claus, Peter J. *Indo-Iranian Journal*, vol. 16, no. 2, 1974, pp. 158-159. JSTOR, www.jstor.org/stable/24651432. Accessed 21 April 2020.

Claus, Peter J. "Mayndala: A Legend and Possession Cult of Tulunad." *Asian Folklore Studies*, vol. 38, no. 2, 1979, pp. 95-129. JSTOR, www.jstor.org/stable/1177686. Accessed 11 March 2020.

Chowta. D.K. *Mittabail Yamuakka: A Tale of a Landlord's Household.* Translated by B.Surendra Rao and K Cinnappa Gowda. Mangaluru.Aakriti Aashyaya Publications. 2017.

Day, Gary. *Class.* Routledge. 2007.

Devi. B, Meera. "The Billavas And The Socio-Religious Movements In The Colonial South Kanara." *Proceedings of the Indian History Congress*, vol. 77, 2016, pp. 546-553. JSTOR, www.jstor.org/stable/26552682. Accessed 12 February 2020.

Dharampal-Frick, Gita, and Sudha Sitharaman. "Caste." Key Concepts in Modern Indian Studies, edited by Gita Dharampal-Frick et al., NYU Press, 2015, pp. 37-42. JSTOR, www.jstor.org/stable/j.ctt15zc7zj.20. Accessed 05 June 2020.

Ishii, Miho. "Wild Sacredness and the Poiesis of Transactional Networks: Relational Divinity and Spirit Possession in the Būta Ritual of South India." *Asian Ethnology*, vol. 74, no. 1, 2015, pp. 87–109. JSTOR, www.jstor.org/stable/43610653. Accessed 29 March 2020.

Macionis, John J, and Linda M. Gerber. *Sociology*. Prentice Hall, 2002.

Pfautz, Harold W. "The Current Literature on Social Stratification: Critique and Bibliography." *American Journal of Sociology*, vol. 58, no. 4, 1953, pp. 391-418. JSTOR, www.jstor.org/stable/2772361. Accessed 05 June 2020.

Raghavan. *Tulu Nadum Bhasayum Naattarivum*. State Institute of Languages. 2003.

Sharit K. Bhowmik. "Caste and Class in India." *Economic and Political Weekly*, vol. 27, no. 24/25, 1992, pp. 1246-1248. JSTOR, www.jstor.org/stable/4398508. Accessed 12 May 2020.

23

Postcolonial Hangover: Obsession of Fair Skin in Bollywood Songs

Manisha Mishra

Introduction

The term 'colourism' was perhaps first used by Alice Walker in her book *The Color Purple* in the year in 1982. Often colorism and racism are confused. Colourism is the discrimination based on the colour of the skin, whereas racism is the bias based on the virtue of race. Colourism can be seen as a subset of racism. The term might have been used in America, but it is no stranger to India. Sadly, we have all grown up with colorism around us. Shockingly, it begins in most of our homes. From the time that children are born in most Indian homes, the first thing that friends and relatives gauge is their complexion. Surprisingly, even parents start comparing complexions between siblings. Colourism is one hangover that the British left behind in India, even after 71 years of their departure.

Colourism is not limited to India. It was happening and is still happening all over the world. But the scope of my paper limits me to talk about the scenario of India and more specifically Indian films, pointed at Bollywood.

Growing up with Colourism in India

Colourism in India does not stop after children are born. It continues right through teenage years to adolescence. In a subtle and sometimes not-so-subtle way, fair-skinned children are often unfairly favoured by teachers at school, and even preferred more in the Indian marriage market. 'Haldi' is a ritual followed before every Hindu marriage. Turmeric is applied on the bride and the groom to make them 'fair' and beautiful. Indian culture propagates colorism. Let me give you an example from my own state. In an Odia arranged marriage scenario, queries like: "Pila ti safa dekhibaku ta?" ["Is the candidate fair?"] is an oft-quoted one. It is almost implied that next to a properly matched horoscope, skin colour is the only virtue that can make a marriage perfect and prosperous! Dark-skinned girls have to be literally sold off by using heavy dowry in the marriage market; else they are sadly rejected.

Influence of Bollywood in Percolating Colourism

Television and films are one of the chief factors behind propagation of such colourism ideas, apart from deep-rooted colonial hangover. We have all grown up listening to mellifluous Bollywood numbers that use colorism in a seemingly innocent manner. People in India are not black or white per se, but most of them are wheatish, brown or cream-complexioned. No matter what complexion they are born with, they whistle away to the tune of: "Aja piya tohe pyar doon, gori baiyan tumpe vaar doon" [Come dear let me love you, and submit my fair wrists to you] or "Gori tera gaon bada pyaara, mei toh gaya mara" [Your village is very endearing O fair one]. Ironically, the heroine featuring in the song: "Gori tera gaon bada pyara…" is not fair. Stereotypes like Bollywood actors have to be fair is propagated through such misappropriations. Little do they realise how much impact it subconsciously has on its listeners. Everyone wants to be fair. Often people become less worried about a flat nose, big ears or small eyes if their skin is light in colour. But the one with the sharpest facial features lack confidence, if they are dark-complexioned. Skin color becomes an identity marker.

Bollywood Colorism in the 50s

Gori Gori Gori mein pariyon ki chhori (1957) from the film Begunah sung by Lata Mangeshkar seems to indicate that a fair-complexioned girl is born of angel parentage; she is not a mortal. She is an angel. She has been bred in the heavens, and hence the fair looks. *Gori Odhke Malmal Nikli ki Mera Dil* (1959) again talks about a lover being hypnotized by the beauty of his beloved when she opens her silk veil to reveal her fair face. *Nainon mein Gori Kise Basa Liya* (1958) from Naag Champa describes a white young lass trapping her lovers by her eyes. The song seems to imply because she is fair, her eyes weave magic on her lovers. The attractive complexion exudes charm from her eyes.

The 1950 classic song *O Gore Gore Bankhe Chore* from Samadhi is perhaps known to most of us. All of us hum its tune without giving attention to the 'gore chore' and 'gori chori' in the song. *Gori Chupke Se Aaya* (1950) from Meena Bazar, *Kah De Gori Kah De…apno se sharmana kya* (1955) from Chingari and *Naachey re Gori* (1950) from Lajawaab are also popular songs of the 50s that are rhythmic yet colorist in their lyrics.

Bollywood Colourism in the 60s

Gori Ghunghat ko Mukhde pe chupao naa (1960) from Ghunghat talks about the first night of a bride after marriage. The song asks the bride not to be bashful. The idea of a fair bride under the veil is alluring, according to the song. It might also seem to subtly indicate that there is no need for a fair-complexioned bride to hide her face. She should be able to proudly flaunt it. In *Gori Nagin Banke Na* (1960) from Nache Nagin Baje Been, the heroine is compared to a serpent who lures men. The song indicates that a lighter-coloured girl is no less than a seductress. Again, the measure of skin colour as an attractive attribute that cannot be achieved by those with darker complexion.

A song like *Hum Kaale hain toh kya hua dilwale hain* (1965) from Gumnaam makes the underlying assumption that only fair people have good hearts. So, the protagonist tries to woo his lady by trying to convince her that he can be a good-natured man too, even though he is not light-skinned. Here, the song subtly creates a stereotype that only a fair person is good-natured. External appearance becomes the reflection of the inner soul. In a song like *Aaja piya tohe pyaar dun, gori bainyaan tope vaar dun* (1967) from Baharon Ke Sapne, the word 'gori' [fair] seems to have been unnecessarily inserted as a matter of habit to keep up the trend of colorist songs. A girl praising her own wrists as fair and almost using it as an equipment to cure her lover's sadness is phenomenal. The song seems to be indicating that darker-skinned girls cannot make their lover happy because white is the colour of joy, and removal of sadness. The song *Yeh Chaand sa Roshan Chehra* (1964) from Kashmir ki Kali uses the moon as a symbol of whiteness and fair complexion. In this song, the lover heaps tons of praises on the beloved, beginning with the comparison of the lady to the moon. From here on, many lyricists started using the moon in describing the lady protagonist in Hindi films. Again, the comparison with the moon was definitely colorist. *Bol Gori Bol Tera kaun piya* (1967) from Milan is yet another colorist song of the 60s that we cannot forget.

Bollywood Colourism in the 70s

Gora Gora Mukhda yeh tune kahan paya hai, tu hai gori chor tune chaand ko churaya hai (1973) from Bhool Na Jaana is a song by a lover who is praising his beloved's fair skin. It is so fair that he assumes she is a thief as she has stolen the white colour from the moon beams. Again, the adulation of lighter skin! Whiteness is seen as something magical that anyone cannot have; in order to possess it, one has to have some ardour.

In the popular song of K.J Yesudas, *Gori Tera Gaon bada pyaara* (1976) from Chitchor, again the skin colour of the heroine is being discussed, though ironically the girl featuring in the song is not light-skinned. In the second line, the face of the girl is compared to a half-moon. Again, the reference to the moon is a suggestion to white complexion. We see the colourist song tradition again flows into the 70s. A song like *Kaali Palak Teri Gori* (1974) from Do Chor may apparently seem like using the word 'gori' just to provide a contrast to the word 'kaali' [black]; however, the Bollywood song lyricist seems to have internalised the idea that only a fair girl is attractive and beautiful. The actors, director, producer and all people with major stakes in the song and movie seem to buy the idea.

Gore rang pe na itna gumaan kar (1974) from Roti seems to be looking down from the vanity of the young lady-lover because she takes pride in her complexion. He reminds her that skin colour is not a permanent feature; it will be darkened with age. Now again by this statement, it is indirectly implied that lighter complexion is something precious and something to treasure, and it will be lost with the years. This classic song by Lata Mangeswar *Yashumati Maiya Se Puche Nand Laala Radha kyun gori main kyun kaala* (1978) from Satyam Shivam Sundaram deals with an imaginative scene of Krishna complaining to Yashoda about his dark-complexion. He asks her why he is dark, and Radha fair. Now, Bollywood did not have enough reverence of the fair skin that it didn't even spare the gods. The only dark God in Hindu mythology also was made to crib about his colour by comparing it with Radha's fair skin. This also indicates the societal choices in Indian society then. In a marriage, a girl had to be fair, though a darker groom was acceptable. This song kind of explains why this kind of combination of complexion between the genders is okay. Not only does Krishna yearn for Radha, but also her fair skin! And this song won an award! No wonder, colourist songs are popular in Bollywood.

Gori Gori Gaon ki Gori re (1972) from Ye Gulistan Hamara again a melodious song resorts to colorism. 'Gaon ki gori' seems to be a favourite phrase of the Bollywood lyricists. Hence the name of a movie in 1945!

Bollywood Colourism in the 80s

In *Gori Tere Ang Ang Mein* from Tohfa the lover praises his beloved body parts; everything is appealing about her because she is 'gori'. The lyrics seem to point out to the fair complexion being a value addition to her looks. Her looks seem enhanced by her lighter skin tone, and that drives the man crazy. *Jaaoon Kahaan Gori Teri Gali Chhod Ke* (1980) from Qaatil Kaun describes a lover obsessed with his beloved, and cannot even think of leaving the lane in which she lives as she is 'gori'. *O Gori* (1980) from Nishana shows the 'gori' showing 'nakhras' [trantrums] but those are tolerated by the hero because her youth and beauty get more enticing by her fair looks. So, her beloved is crazy about her even if she is 'magroor' [arrogant]. She is also compared to 'Chaand Chakori' and in turn the girl compliments him by calling 'O gore'. *Dhak Dhak Se Dhadakna Bhula De* (1980) from Aasha also uses the colorist term 'gori' in its lyrics that seems to have been used for no special reason, but as if out of a matter of habit by Bollywood lyricists.

In this time period, colorist movies were not also uncommon. Case in point is Naseeb Apna Apna (1986). The protagonist rejects his wife for a fairer lover, and returns only to her after she by some skin treatment appears fairer. The wife is a good-natured one; however, her dark-complexion and rural lifestyle seems to upset the fair hero. The title itself is derogatory in the sense that one's good fate is somehow seemed to be linked to one's complexion.

Bollywood Colourism in the 90s

90s seems to be time in Bollywood when maximum colorist songs came to the forefront: unavoidable fair wrists and fair face! Colorist songs like *Haseena Gori Gori* (1997), *Ye Kaali Kaali aankhen, yeh gore gore gaal* (1993) from Baazigar and *Gori hai*

Kalaaiyan (1990) from Aaj ka Arjun got wide acclaim among the Indian audiences. *Churake dil mera goriya chali* (1994) from Main Khiladi Tu Anadi, *Chori Chori Chal O Gori* (1995) from Ram Jaane, *Aye doston gori kanwari si haseena* (1992) from Deedar,

Gori Gori O Banki Chori (1992) from Shola aur Shabnam, *Goriya re Goriya re mere dil churake le jaa* (1993) from Aaina all followed the colorist trend. Most audiences overlooked the colorism, getting enticed by the music, or better still dance moves if they were watching the song video.

In *Mein hun Gaon ki Gori* (1992) from Bol Radha Bol, the girl addresses herself as a 'gaon ki gori' who wants to be taught by her lover. The vulnerable, fair girl from a village seemed to be a Bollywood prototype since the 60s. The romance between a pardesi babu and a village 'gori' seemed to entice Bollywood audiences and it was a formula in many movies, and the lyrics thus catered to this concept.

Gore Gore mukhde pe kaala kaala chasma (1994) from Suhaag kind of set a new trend for lot of kaala chasma [dark-glasses] songs on white faces. This instantly reminds one of American actors, who often wore dark-glasses. The next line expresses the amazement how God could create such a miracle! Again, the fair complexion is praised. Nothing changed in Hindi songs. The colonial hangover persisted even in the 90s. *Ghoonghat mei Chand hoga* (1999) from Khoobsurat again follows the colorist trend using the moon as a motif for whiteness and fairness.

Bollywood Colourism Post-millenium

Meri Desi look meri desi look meri desi look pe mar gaye gore gore chokre from Ek Paheli Leela establishes the notion that Indian girls also seek fair men, not just vice-versa. The desi girl might opt for 'jhumkas' and 'thumkas' but when it comes to the choice of men, their complexion has to be fair, states the song.

Tenu kaala chasma jachda ae jachda ae gore mukhde te (2016) again reiterates the *Gore Gore mukhde pe kaala kaala chasma* of the 90s in different synonyms of the nearly same lyrics with different beats and Katrina Kaif making sexy moves on the dance floor. Again, everyone forgot the colourist lyrics and danced to the tunes. Chittiyaan kalaaiyan ve (2015) from Roy was again a reiteration of the idea used in the *Gori hai kalaaiyan, tu laade mujhe hari hari chudiyan.* The lady protagonist in Roy requests her lover to bring her golden trinkets ('jhumkes'), take her out for shopping, romantic movie, get her colourful bangles and pink dupatta all because she has fair wrists, and he would ultimately get possession of them. The song includes a refrain: "White kalaiyaan drives me crazy" [white wrists drive me crazy]. That again brings us back to the idea only people (especially women) are appealing when they are fair.

White white face dekhe dilwa beating fast sasura chance maare (2008) from Tashan indicates that innocence is synonymous to a white face ['Bhola chehra jaisa moon']. Lighter skin makes up an innocent look, according to the song.

Gori Gori (2004) from Main Hoon Na and more lately *Mere Mohalle main chand jo aaya hai eid jo laaya hai tu hi toh nahin* (2016) from Dear Zindagi again emphasises colorist attitudes.

Colourism and Gender: Its Repercussions

What we see is maximum colourist songs are based on women, rather than men. Bollywood is obsessed with fair-complexioned women, and so is majority of our Indian society that accepts such songs, and popularises them without any qualms. Such songs have propagated and definitely influenced the great desire of Indian women to be lighter-skinned because the idea of beauty has somehow been linked to fairness. Even after 71 years of independence, the colonial hangover remains; the western standards of beauty are still embraced by the Indian film industry – from the 50s to the present day. Why are Indians not comfortable in all skin colours? The essential question is: should there be a beauty standard?

According to Naomi Woolf in her book 'The Beauty Myth':

> "Beauty is a currency system like the gold standard. Like any economy, it is determined by politics, and in the modern age in the West it is the last, best belief system that keeps male dominance intact. In assigning value to women in a vertical hierarchy according to a culturally imposed physical standard, it is an expression of power relations in which women must unnaturally compete for resources that men have appropriated for themselves." (Woolf 12)

Reasons for Colourist Attitudes in Bollywood Songs and Changes Required

Our Hindi film industry seems to be suffering from colonial hangover. It is somewhere still in the phase of British colonialism. Acculturation, as we know, "is the process of social, psychological and cultural change that stems from the balancing of two cultures while adapting to the prevailing culture of the society." [Wikipedia]. According to a conceptual model of acculturation, there might be four strategies: assimilation, separation, integration and marginalisation. Assimilation is the individual adopting the dominant culture, separation is the individual rejecting the dominant culture, integration is the individual adopting the dominant culture as well as maintaining their own whereas marginalisation is the individual rejecting the dominant culture as well as their own culture.

Bollywood shows assimilation, separation and integration at various stages of its history of making cinema. Post globalisation, Indian films have borrowed many concepts from the West. Perhaps, the only thing quintessentially Indian in Indian movies has been the song and dance sequences. Supposedly, the first full-length Indian film Raja Harischandra included a dance sequence, and the first Indian talkie Alam Ara contained seven songs. But, sadly, many of Bollywood songs display an ardent love for lighter skin complexion that goes into the lyrics of many of our song sequences till today.

The obsession for fairness in Bollywood songs subordinates the typical feature of Indian cinema that makes it peculiarly Indian. This is the paradox. Even when Bollywood is moving towards some original Indian concept films like Dangal, Raazi, Toilet, Padman, Bareily ki Barfi, Badri ki Dulhaniya etc. that reek of Indian soil, culture and tradition, colourism in song sequences are not lessening. In fact, it can be assumed that five out of 10 songs in Bollywood include the word 'Gori' [fair].

Apart from that, Bollywood has also internalised some colonial prejudices up to an extent that a feeling of inferiority complex has developed that is unconsciously reflected in the songs. On the one hand, more and more original patriotic theme movies are emerging. Stories in Hindi films are talking about what happened to Mary Kom, Dhoni, and Sandeep Singh etc. On the other hand, the weakness for the light skin lyrics isn't fading away.

A third reason might be that people in India are receiving, accepting and popularising such colourist songs without any hesitation or questions. No one feels slighted – not even dark-skinned people when white skin is sung with adulations. Majority of the people sway to the melodious music of such songs. Unconsciously, the fair skin obsession percolates the minds of majority people, especially women. Everyone wants to look like a Barbie doll: fair skin, straight tresses and flawless complexion.

A fourth reason might be the excessive love for rhyming scheme in Hindi songs. 'Gori' is often used by lyricists just to rhyme with 'Chori' or just that the phrase 'Gaon ki Gori' appeals to the audience for some reason. It becomes an ultimate fantasy to visualise an innocent village girl – naïve, simple and fair to appease to a town-bred boy. However, such ideas are gradually changing but not our colourist fantasies. An actress like Katrina Kaif is scorned for her non-Hindi accent; however, she is accepted for her fair looks. Kajol does a complete skin treatment to look fair though ironically when she was darker skinned, she was still accepted for her acting. Everyone in the celebrity and succumbs to the peer pressure, and eventually pass on these notions to the society. There has to be more sensitisation for young filmmakers to break away from the trend. Filmmakers and lyricists have to realise the influence that such tendencies have on today's youth. In fact, short films on the subjects can be made and propagated for awareness. This is sadly leading towards an unhealthy "beauty myth" as Woolf would put it. Bollywood seems to be graduating to new levels of Indianness and originality; however, colourist tendencies sadly continue.

Colourism in Ollywood

Colourism is not limited to Bollywood. It has extended to all other film industries, including the Odia film industry. Songs like *Banapur Jhia Lo Tu Haladi Gori, toh pari dekhi nahin ete sundari* reiterates the idea that the yellowish-fair complexion of a girl is the most appealing. A song like *Sabini Gori Kaali Jhia Tinoti kahaku bhala paibi* shows the dilemma of a man who is unable to decide which complexion woman he should fall in love with. Apparently, the song shows the 'kaali' or black girl in a good light; he describes her as a girl with a good heart and the only one who agrees to his proposal willingly; however, it actually shows the hypocrisy of a society that shows the desperation of a dark-complexioned girl to get married. Also, again the 'kaale hain toh kya hua dilwale hain' syndrome comes forth when the guy says that the black girl had a good heart. *Kali gori duhen gadhoi gale* by Akshayay Mohanty again shows the dark girl in a poor light; she is such a disgrace that seeing her, the onlooker's blood pressure increases.

Conclusion

The colourist attitude in India is no longer restricted to aunties advising young dark-complexioned females to apply saffron, besan or haldi to improve their complexion or beauticians suggesting they go for a bleach or tan removal. Yes, 80 per cent newspaper matrimonials advertisements in India still emphasise on the 'fair' complexion, especially in case of a bride. But lately, the situation has become more dangerous because we are showing our hostility openly by violence. A case in point is the attack and harassment of the African students living in Greater Noida. 24-year-old Imran Uba was attacked because a school boy Manish Khari had gone missing and the Khari community supposedly thought it was an act of cannibalism by his Nigerian neighbours. Three other Africans men were attacked inside Ansal Plaza. Africans in India are stereotyped as 'cannibals', 'rapists' and 'untrustworthy'. What seems alarming is we are doing exactly the thing that the British did to us some 100 years ago. We are repeating the mistakes that made us suffer. Our colourist attitudes are not fading away. Though Bollywood cannot be the sole reason; it is definitely one subtle reason, apart from fairness cream advertisements and matrimonial advertisements that is percolating the 'obsessive fairness syndrome'.

Works Cited

Abraham, Mary-Rose. 2017. "Skin lightening: India's obsession that is becoming a medical problem." September 10, 2017. *scroll.in* <https://scroll.in/pulse/850030/skin-lightening-indias-obsession-that-is-becoming-a-medical-problem> (12.17.2019)

Alleyne, Mervyn C. 2002. *The Construction and Representation of Race and Ethnicity in the Caribbean and the World*. Kingston: University of the West Indies Press.

Ayyar, Varsha & Lalit Khandare. 2013. "Mapping Color and Caste Discrimination in Indian Society." In: Ronald E. Hall (ed.). *The Melanin Millenium: Skin Color in 21st Century International Discourse*. New York: Springer. 71-96.

Banks, Taunya Lovell. 2015. *Colorism Among South Asians: Title VII and Skin Tone Discrimination*. Research Paper. University of Maryland. 1-18.

Beatty, Muna. 2018. "Colour me right: It's time to end colourism in India." *Aljazeera News*. September 10, 2018. <https://www.aljazeera.com/indepth/opinion/colour-time-colourism-india-180906101053056.html> (12.29.2019)

Beeman, Angie and Anjana Narayan. 2011. "If You're White, You're Alright: The Reproduction of Racial Hierarchies in Bollywood Films." In: Rodney D. Coates (ed.). *Covert Racism: Theories, Institutions, and Experiences*. Leiden: Brill. 155-174.

Bell, Lee Anne, Michael S. Funk, Khyati Y. Joshi, & Marjorie Valdivia. 2016. "Racism and White Privilege." In: Maurianne Adams, and Lee Anne Bell with Diane J. Goodman and Khyati Y. Joshi (eds.) *Teaching for Diversity and Social Justice.* 3rd ed. New York: Routledge. 133-182.

Chakraborty, Juhi. 2019. "Nora Fatehi on her Bollywood Struggles." *Hindustan Times.*

<https://www.hindustantimes.com/bollywood/nora-fatehi-on-her-bollywood-struggles- it-gets-complicated-when-you-don-t-belong-to-india-there-are-a-lot-of-barriers/story-N0CuJ3RF3JnATNBCRFqc5K.html> (10.23.2019)

Chatterjee, Suprateek. 2015. "That Viral Story of Kangana Ranaut Rejecting A Fairness Cream Ad Is Nearly Two Years Old." *Huffington Post India*. May 25, 2015. <https://www.huffingtonpost.in/2015/05/25/kangana-ranaut-fairnessc_n_7434944.html> (11.10.2019)

Chaudry, Lakshmi. 2013. "Miss America Nina Davuluri: Too 'Indian' to ever be Miss India." *First Post*. September 16, 2013. <https://www.firstpost.com/living/miss-america- nina-davuluri-too-indian-to-ever-be-miss-india-1111477.html> (11.16.2019)

Desai, Rajvi. 2019. "Brownface in 'Super 30' Reveals Bollywood's Structural Racism." *The Swaddle*. July 2, 2019. <https://theswaddle.com/brownface-in-super-30-reveals-bollywoods-structural-racism/> (11.06.2019)

Dhillon-Jamerson, Komal K. 2019. "Marketing Marriage and Colorism in India." In: Guillaume D. Johnson, Kevin D. Thomas, Anthony Kwame Harrison & Sonya A. Grier (eds.) *Race in the Marketplace: Crossing Critical Boundaries*. Palgrave. 121-136.

DiGioia, Amanda. 2018. "Love Breed or Hate Haven? Localised Narratives of Identitiy in Heavy Metal Scene of New Haven, Connecticut." In: Toni-Matti Karjalainen (ed.). *Sounds of Origin in Heavy Metal Music*. Newcastle: Cambridge Scholars Publishing. 169-190.

Fanon, Frantz. 2008. *Black Skin, White Masks*. London: Pluto Press.

Feldman, Jamie. 2018. Fighting India's 'Specific and Narrow' Beauty Standards, One Photo At A Time." *HuffPost*. June 15, 2018. <https://www.huffpost.com/entry/indian-beauty-standards-photo_n_5b228d39e4b0adfb8271dc35> (01.14.2020)

Ganti, Tejaswini. 2004. *Bollywood: A Guidebook to Popular Hindi Cinema*. New York: Routledge.

Glenn, Evelyn Nakano. 2009. "Consuming Lightness." In: Evelyn Nakano Glenn (ed.). *Shades of Difference: Why Skin Color Matters*. Stanford: Stanford University Press. 166-187.

Harrison, Matthew S., Wendy Reynolds-Dobbs, & Kecia M. Thomas. 2008. "Skin Color Bias in the Workplace: The Media's Role and Implications Toward Preference." In: Ronald E. Hall (ed.). *Racism in the 21st Century: An Empirical Analysis of Skin Color.* Michigan: Springer. 46-62.

Harvey, Richard D., Kira Hudson Banks, & Rachel E. Tennial. 2014. "A New Way Forward: The Development and Preliminary Validation of Two Colorism Scales." In: Kimberly Jade Norwood (ed.). *Color Matters: Skin Tone Bias and the Myth of a Postracial America*. New York: Routledge. 198-217.

24

Investigating Issues of Identity Politics and Space Negotiation in *The Namesake* by Jhumpa Lahiri

Mouna Benhaddou

Introduction

One of the most problematic and thorny issues in diaspora and migration studies are the ideas of identity and space negotiation. Diasporic narratives are replete with dilemmas of identity, where subjects delve in a complex and often an ambivalent journey in search of their identity as a way to solve the intricate issue of belonging to a certain place. Stuart Hall relates the complex construction of identity to the idea of hybridity when applied to diaspora. He states that: "The diaspora experience as I intend it here is defined, not by essence or purity, but by the recognition of a necessary heterogeneity and diversity; by a conception of "identity" which lives with and through, not despite, difference; by hybridity. Diaspora identities are those which are constantly producing and reproducing themselves anew, through transformation and difference". Thus diaspora in its full form is a sheer terrain for ambivalence and hybridity, where aspects of cultural mixing come into display, for example diasporic subjects could confront features of the host culture that could be appropriated and hence bringing about, reconfiguring and eventually reproducing new hybrid entities

The novel under study *The Namesake* by Jhumpa Lahiri attempts to profoundly accentuate, though in different ways, the characters' deep quest of self-realisation which is an inherent experience among diasporas. The analysis will offer additional and expanding dimensions to conceptualising identity which bring along dynamic modes of self-discovery through the different articulations of the characters' identities.

Reconfiguring the Politics of Identity and Space in *The Namesake* by Jhumpa Lahiri

Jhumpa Lahiri in *The Namesake* traces the characters' transformation throughout the novel and introduces us to the multiple phases that they engage in towards the construction of their identity. She also presents the process of identity construction in an intergenerational milieu, the first generation tries hard to cling to their roots along with trying to adopt different strategies of survival to seep into the host culture smoothly, whereas the second generation feels entangled in both cultures, with their hyphenated identity hence culturally displaced in either sides.

Ashima and Ashoke are typical examples of first generation diasporas, they tightly cling to their diasporic community, though a small one but they keep in touch on a regular basis, as a way to revive and remind themselves of their Bengali identity that may have been lost in case of cultural dispersal. When they are present in one of the Bengali gathering they tend to speak solely Indian and relish the Bengali food. Besides, Ashima struggles to teach her children the Indian deities in order to familiarise them with the religious or cultural aspects of their homeland. Nevertheless, she is quite aware of the different nuisances at the same time of identity that her children go through hence she tries to make them reconcile their complex identity by joggling both at the same time. Ashima tells Gogol when he is a child to watch American TV shows and programs such as Sesame Street so as to make them acquire the language quickly so as to face no problem at school just because their parents speak Bengali.

Gogol witnesses various phases of identity construction since his childhood. he floats simultaneously between two sides, he is caught in two worlds. Sometimes he drifts away from the shore and feels totally disoriented unable to cope with his hyphen or ambivalent situation of sticking to one's root in favor of assimilation and total integration in the united states, a country that he often considers his real home. Or, at other times he resorts to the culture of his ancestors.

The initial stages of Gogol's self-realisation of identity begins in his childhood ; at first he accepts things concerned with culture with passivity since he was not mature enough to take sides or decides for himself. However as he gets older he starts having funny feelings about both the word 'home' that his parents keep insisting on and his name. what explains Gogol's confusion about the "home" is his family's frequent visits to India, since both Gogol and his sister feel alien in Calcutta they do not have any affective attachment or fondness for their country of origin since they have been bred and raised in the states, hence they think of it as any other American might think of it. Their lack of attachment to India extent to his scope of friends, Gogol befriends only American boys and avoids making contacts with Bengali fellows, ah he meets them only in case his parents make communal gatherings in their house. Gogol' reluctance to hang out with Bengali boys could result from his inner wish to detach himself from his land of origin and embarks in various kinds of relationship that would not make him recall that country that his parents venerates with great awe.

The second issue which makes Gogol wonder about his identity is the name he was given by his parents. He lives in a constant bewilderment because of this name, when his father relishes and feels pride in the fact that his son is named after the savior of his life, Gogol is oblivious of this fact which causes a severe identity crisis. Gogol feels appalled to be connected with a name which is neither American nor Indian especially that this mere name causes him lots of embarrassment and led him to awkward situations during his scholar life, so we find him occasionally grumbling that his name "sounds ludicrous to his ears, lacking dignity of gravity."

Gogol at some point of his adolescence, not knowing the emotional load of his name; is overwhelmed with feeling of repulsion and antipathy towards his name, when his father gives him the novel by the Russian writer Nikolai Gogol, he tossed it with negligence, being strongly unwilling to read it or to have a closer look at it since he assumed that the act of reading repugnance.

Moreover, the incident of the trip to a graveyard which was mentioned previously in the other section, proves Gogol's torn identity he strongly wishes to identify with American culture, through having a certain admiration towards the American names carved in the marbles above each grave, he wants to be part of that culture and have similar names at the same time. Nevertheless the peculiarity of his name stands against the fulfillment of his wish. As a consequence, Gogol steps into another phase of identity quest where he tries to withdraw from the culture of his ancestors and immerses himself instead suddenly in the American one, hoping to strip himself off from his past and be occupied merely with the present. Gogol conceals his real name from the girls he meets in order to facilitate his complete access to the American culture as demonstrated in this passage

> It's the first time he's kissed anyone, the first time he's felt a girl's face and body and breath so close to his own. "I can't believe you kissed her, Gogol". His friends exclaim as they drive home from the party. He shakes his head in a daze, as astonished as they are, elation still welling inside him. "It wasn't me", he nearly says. But he doesn't tell them that it hadn't been Gogol who'd kissed Kim. That Gogol had had nothing to do with it.

Gogol's monologues shows clearly his unsettling dual identity he associates the name Gogol with social marginalisation and isolation which according to him could deny him the right to fully assimilate or know people from the same age as he is. Thus, when graduates from high school and gets admitted to Yale university he tells his father about the decision to change his name officially to Nikhil along with his upcoming departure to the university claiming that he does not want to see his former name Gogol on the certificate of his graduation since it sounds peculiar to the hearers. Even if at first he did not acquaint himself with it completely as the narrator explains: "After eighteen years of Gogol, two months of Nikhil feels scant, inconsequential." But gradually after the renaming that he feels a huge relief and comfort to get away from the culture that bound his freedom and curbed his acculturation since his childhood, also the name Nikhil estranged him from his parents, "... in that instant that he is not related to them, not their child". Since when they called Gogol they had certain memories embedded in the name which could have been the reason for their existence and which brought them to this country, however Gogol shuns this fact and delves into living on his own, traveling from place to place as if going after his split identity. In addition he takes up different activities freely that would not have been possible with his previous name, such as going clubbing, drinking alcohol, or having successive sexual relationships with young women as a way to articulate his independence.

The event succeeding Gogol''s appointment as an architect brings along the most the significant transformation for his identity where he really confronts the burden of a double identity that does not seem to let go of him despite his attempt to change his name. his cultural confrontation occurs when he becomes seriously engaged in a relationship with an American girl named Maxine, he moves in to her house where her parents live and becomes tremendously infatuated with their life style that is stamped by indulgence and an overly sense of independence, hence he immerses himself in his girlfriend's life:

> She has the gift of accepting life;... he realises that she never wished she were anyone other than herself, raised in any other place, in any other way. This, in his opinion, is the biggest difference between them, a thing by far more foreign to him than the beautiful house she'd grown up in, her education at private schools.

He starts discovering the enormous disparity between the way he was raised and the way she did, somehow he wishes he was in her shoes relishing the same amount of individualism and liberty when he was a child as she did. This huge contrast that exists between their lives is the same reason which makes him realise where exactly their cultural paths diverge and are unlike to converge in any ways. He adds on while gathering piles of difference which differentiates between both cultures:

> He is continuously amazed by how much Maxine emulates her parents, how much she respects their tastes and their ways.... There is none of the exasperation he feels with his own parents. No sense of obligation. Unlike his parents, they give her pressure to do nothing, and yet she lives faithfully by their side.

Consequently, the main reason that drove Gogol to settle down with an American family and avoid sticking to his ancestral roots, is his wish to claim another space that is less restrictive to him and which grants him the choice to venture doing things that could not have been possible in his communal or familial sphere specifically. His relationship with Maxine and her family gives him access to the American life style that he always wished to attain during his schooling years.

What is more perplexing perhaps about the second generation of diaspora is their constant shifting of spaces. Despite Gogol's complete immersion with the American, the thing which might have temporarily spared him from feeling confused about his hyphen, his mother's calls bring him back to his former state of feeling the urge to joggle two identities at once. When paying visits to his family he assumes that "Nikhil evaporates and Gogol claims him again". This exemplifies Gogol's sense of acute hybridity and cultural ambivalence; he is forced to revert back to his old self where he must be fluctuating back forth between his past as Gogol Ganguli with the name that attaches to his family and the same time not forgetting his present as Nikhil the rebellious adult.

As noticed, from the examples above, Gogol lives in a constant psychological turmoil, feeling split between two different cultures. Thus he has no choice but to straddle both spaces all together in the midst of this puzzling cultural situation that generates difference and leaves no room for homogeneity. a condition that is inherent with transnational individual who are left with the necessity to be suspended in an" in-between space" as Bhabha asserts and negotiate multiple identities instead of one pure essentialist one, which is in the case of Gogol neither Indian nor American but a hybrid identity.

Moshoumi, Gogol's ex-wife, is also another striking character who represents the identity crisis of diasporas. Being a hyphenated individual dealing American identity meshed with an Indian descent, she chooses to get married to Gogol knowing that they have the same dilemma of belonging which might be more acute to that of Gogol. Moushoumi is continuously haunted by a strong sense of both physical and psychological displacement, since her childhood she has been on the moved, because she spent part of her early life in Britain then moving to United States with her parents then again traveling to France. As a consequently, she basically feels no sense of belonging to any place despite her parents her parents claim to cling to their Bengali roots. After a couple of years being marriage to Gogol, she indulges with an adulterous relationship with Dimitri Desjardins the thing that ended her marital life. Her unexpected sexual engagement could be a sign of her rebellious personality to ward off any kind of cultural manifestation which might bind her long lasting independent nature.

At last Moshoumi travels back to France as a way to escape any nuisance that are related to identity and solace in a country that is neither a place of her birth nor the place that her parents claim roots in, so it is a place that has no cultural connotation to claim over her. She is trying to assert her sense of rootlessness through adopting a third culture that does not remind her of any claimed origin. Hence she chooses to occupy a neutral space that defies attaching identity to any place and as her name Moushoumi means 'a season that keeps changing' she opts for a position that is intrinsically fluid and which claims to no cultural or physical context. Benzi Zang explains the idea perfectly by stating that diasporic identities are not built through ready-made concepts, paradigms or theories, but "through re-imagining, re-describing, and re-denying our national or rather post-national liminalities'.

From the beginning she does not belong either to the place of her birth, i.e. America, or to the place of her parents' origin i.e. Bengal. Moushumi's suffering is due to her hedonistic life style. In order to cash every moment of her life, she transcends the Rubicon of morality even in her conjugal life. Her dissoluteness is analogous to the meaning of her name because Moushumi is a season that keeps changing.

Conclusion

Diasporic identity is undoubtedly a controversial and highly a paradoxical concept in its nature, it makes the individuals who are part of its circle to engage in several discourses that clash, intermingle and reconstruct each other in a non-linear process. Diasporic subjects often delineate a perplexing hankering of belonging to somewhere and be rooted to an imaginary homeland or a space where they could externalise their feelings of catharsis. At the same time diasporas seek ways even if implicitly to be admitted to the host culture, hence the need to assimilate and be integrated in the host land comes in contrast with their internal feelings of belonging, in light of these explanations the diasporic experience thus, proves to be certainly problematic and ambiguous.

Works Cited

Bhabha, H.K. *The Location of Culture*. New York, NY: 1994

Lahiri, Jhumpa. *The Namesake*. Boston: Houghton Mifflin, 2003.

Hall, Stuart. "Cultural Identity and Diaspora" *Identity: Community, Culture, Difference*. Ed. Jonathan. London: Lawrence & Wishart, 1990. 222-37.

Virinder S. Kalra et al. *Diaspora and Hybridity*. London :SAGE, 2005.pp. 21-4.

Zhang, Benzi. "Identity.in Diaspora and Diaspora in Writing: the poetics of cultural trans relation." *Journal of Intercultural Studies*, Vol. 21, No. 2, 2000.

25

Postcolonial Literature and Subaltern Cultural Context

JS Anantha Krishnan

Introduction

Marxism and Postmodern thought moulded the significant streams of literary criticism and theory in the final decades of 20th century. The inclusion of subaltern studies as a major focus of post-colonial theoretical practices owes its development primarily to the establishment of Subaltern Studies Group at The University of Sussex. Ranajit Guha and Eric Stokes established this school of thought though their extensive lectures and discussions on developing an alternative popular perspective of history unlike the regular streams of historiography focussing on the lives of the elite classes. The foundational essays of this influential group were compiled as *Select Subaltern Studies* (1988) edited by Ranajit Guha and Gayatri Spivak. The book also carried a foreword from Edward Said.

Classical use of 'subaltern'

The term 'subaltern' was first used by Antonio Gramsci by referring to the proletariats subjected to the hegemony of the ruling class of the Soviet Union. All of those who do not wield the hegemonic power gets classified as the subaltern according to Gramsci. He further developed this concept in his *Notes on Italian History* where he defends the necessity of the study of the subaltern:

> The history of subaltern social groups is necessarily fragmented and episodic. There undoubtedly does exist a tendency to at least provisional stages of unification in the historical activity of these groups, but this tendency is continually interrupted by the activity of the ruling groups; it therefore can only be demonstrated when an historical cycle is completed and this cycle culminates in a success. (132)

Development of Subaltern in Post-colonial Studies

The publication of the monograph entitled *A Rule of Property for Bengal* in 1963 by Ranajith Guha marks the beginning of a subaltern approach to the historiographical and cultural narratives of the erstwhile colonies. After a decade, Dipesh

Chakrabarty's *Rethinking Working-Class History* (1989) illustrated the inefficiency of Marxist class analysis in the study of the marginalised in post-colonial analysis. Even before Gramsci, anticipation about this approach can be observed in *The First War of Indian Independence* (1911) of Karl Marx and Friedrich Engels. In the book, Marx exposes the narrative of the British Raj to degrade the popular revolution of 1857 into sepoy mutiny. Refuting the contentions of the ruling class, which forms the backbone of subaltern studies, thus gets portrayed primarily in Marx.

The study of subaltern was simultaneously political and intellectual. By the time of the establishment of Subaltern Studies Group, Eric Hobsbawm, George Rude, Christopher Hill and E.P. Thompson had already ventured into the study of the 'people from below' in the UK. These scholars had a profound impact upon the academicians of the group including Gyanendra Pandey David Arnold, David Hardiman, Deepesh Chakrabarthy, Shahid Amin and Partha Chatterjee. By the time, these writers were in their academic pursuits, there was a schism in the social theory into diverse paths that separated the political economy from the cultural economy. The scholars in subaltern studies were much concerned with what Guha refers to as the "Politics of the people" instead of fantasising the ideal state narrative moulded primarily by the intention to stabilise the state machinery.

In *Homo Hierarchicus: The Caste System and its Implications* (1966), a very early attempt, Louis Dumont gives how a subaltern perspective is pursued to analyse social conditioning. The book explores how the conditions of caste system in India prevent the solidarity among the masses to manifest and thereby avoiding a chance of popular revolution. Rather than following the regular pattern of generalising the national trends, the author focuses on localised hierarchies. The analysis also explored how the subaltern, the lower castes, follow the habits of the upper castes. The tendency was later referred to as Sanskritisation by MN Srinivas This is one of the key features of subaltern studies.

Gayatri Spivak's *Can the subaltern Speak* (1985) was an iconic publication in the history of subaltern studies. The book raised arguments with much scepticism about the practicality of restoring the voices of the subaltern. She also had her objections about the romanticising of the subaltern classes. Her book though had a critical impact upon the academia, received mixed responses. Critics like Benita Parry questioned her "silencing of the subaltern", "homogenisation" and attributing absolute authority to the hegemonic discourse, especially in Spivak's reading of *Wide Sargasso Sea*. Spivak herself had later questioned the subaltern studies in her *A Critique of Post-Colonial Reason* (1999).

Altogether the scholars of the subaltern studies group, were concerned with the deconstruction grand narratives that the colonial era left behind, later to be celebrated by the political classes in their attempt to secure power in modern democracies.it is in this context that Dipesh Chakrabarthy refers to India not as a discovery but as an invention. The school later fathered many critical traditions including Transnational Feminism propunded by Chandra Mohanty and Jacqui Alexander.

Subaltern in Literature

The legacy of the colonial rule often gets celebrated in the domination of the 'British tongue' in the erstwhile colonies. Though the argument is much contented, Sapir-Whorf hypothesis maintains the argument that language determines cognition. The literary production of the post-colonial world written in English exceeding maintains the notions of the western canon. The Euro centric Hegemony never ceased to exist though comparatively in smaller proportions. Such a portrayal would always resist the representation of the subaltern, oppressed and marginalised classes and thereby establishing a homogenous identity for the populace.

The tryst of the subaltern studies with literature served two primary functions. Primarily this critical engaged with the need of representing the indigenous, otherwise marginalised communities. Such an attempt of find the voice for the voiceless was observed in the writings of the postcolonial world. The new literatures tried to explore the indigenous landscape and life. Exceptional examples of the same can be observed in African literature. The writings of Chinua Achebe and Wole Soyinka explored the life of the Igbos and Kikuyus in all its magnificence.

Another academic function of the scholars concerning subaltern studies was to identify the power structures of silencing and marginalisation. Marxists maintain the notion that literature is the register of superstructures. Therefore it is essential to maintain the judicial and democratic representation of the social classes without any bias. Failure in any such attempt would eventually lead to the creation of false ideologies followed by interpellation of the consumer of the literary text into the dominant hegemonic narrative. The writings of the iconic Bengali writer, Mahaswetha Devi do this function of representing the subaltern. Her works were studied and analysed in detail by Spivak herself in the development of the subaltern studies. Spivak herself translated her *Breast Stories* and in the introduction to the book she hints on how the book becomes elemental in the representation of the subaltern representing "the economically affluent socially emerging nouveau-riche, petit-bourgeoisie class of Indians".

The subaltern approach in literature was also critiqued heavily for its bias towards the representation of a pro-oriental narrative. Bell Hooks argued about the necessity of the post-colonial critic to decenter himself from the discourse to listen to the native voice in her *Marginality as a Site of Resistance* (1990)

> "There is no need to hear your native voice, when I can talk about you better than you can speak about yourself. No need to hear your voice. Only tell me about your pain. I want to know your story. And then I will tell it back to you in a new way. Tell it back to you in such a way that it has become mine, my own. Re-writing you, I

write myself anew. I am still author, authority. I am still [the] coloniser, the speaking subject, and you are now at the center of my talk." (87)

Though critiqued heavily, the attempt at analysing the social classes in the confines of imperial narratives and conventional cultural norms brought forth a revolutionary change in perspectives of postcolonial studies. There will always be a risk for the critic to be dominant while analysing the lives of the subaltern. This is yet another form of discrimination. To be one with the subaltern is the only way to study the lives of the oppressed by transcending the intellectual constraints that deny the critics to listen to their voices.

Works Cited

Devi Mahasweta. *Breast Stories.* Seagull Books, 2014.

Dumont, Louis. *Homo Hierarchius.* Gallimard, 1966.

Gramsci, Antonio. *Prison Notebooks.* Columbia University Press, 2011.

Guha, Ranajit. *A Subaltern Studies Reader: 1986-1995.* University of Minnesota Press, 1997.

Khare, R. S. *Caste, Hierarchy, and Individualism: Indian Critiques of Louis Dumonts Contributions.* Oxford University Press, 2006.

Krishnan, JS Anantha. *Beyond the Island.* Dream Books Bindery, 2020.

Mambrol, Nasrullah. "Subaltern (Postcolonialism)." *Literary Theory and Criticism,* 15 Dec. 2018, literariness.org/2016/04/08/subaltern-postcolonialism/.

Spivak, Gayathri Chakravorthy. *Can The Subaltern Speak?* Turia and Kant, 2014.

Srinivas, Mysore Narasimhachar. *Caste in Modern India: and Other Essays.* Asia Pub. House, 1962.

Weng, JM. "Becoming the Other." *Postcolonial Voices,* 29 Sept. 2019, postcolonialvoices.wordpress.com/2018/04/15/becoming-the-other/.

26

The Loss of Native Language: Towards a Modern Post-Imperial Writing (Yeats and Joyce)

Fedya Daas

Appeals to the native language in colonial and post-colonial contexts are among the commonest of strategies to recover one's indigenous identity. What animates such appeals is actually not only the consciousness that one's language is perishing and along it one's culture but that patterns of power become dependent upon the learning, speaking and writing in the imperial language. And therefore the native language is associated with narratives of loss and disablement. Hence, the retrieval of the language becomes a positioning and re-positioning of the colonial subject on the map of power. This problem raises automatically the discussion about what language should be deployed by the subject people and especially in national literature.

Ngugi wa Thiong'o in his *Decolonising the Mind* stresses the importance of using one's native language in the process of independence and post-independence to secure a fully African identity. He explains the workings of language in the politics of cultural identity:

> Language carries culture, and culture carries, particularly through orature and literature, the entire body of values by which we come to perceive ourselves and our place in the world. How people perceive themselves and affects how they look at their culture, at their politics and at the social production of wealth, at their entire relationship to nature and to other beings. Language is thus inseparable from ourselves as a community of human beings with a specific form and character, a specific history, a specific relationship to the world. (16)

Here language overwhelms its communicative function: not only our personal, historical and social specificities are mapped in language and through language but the entirety of our being is determined by our linguistic faculty. Excluding all other modes of self-perception, Thiong'o posits language as the sole mode of perceiving ourselves, others and our inter-relations, theorising for an organic relationship between language and the self.

Thiong'o's view is shared by David Diop who sees that relinquishing the native language is an enslaving modern strategy from the part of the coloniser and an uprooting of the natives, a neo-classical project par excellence:

> The African creator, deprived of the use of his language and cut off from his people, might turn out to be only the representative of a literary trend (and that not necessarily the least gratuitous) of the conquering nation. His works, having become a perfect illustration of the assimilationist policy through imagination and style, will doubtless rouse the warm applause of a certain group of critics. In fact, these praises will go mostly to colonialism which, when it can no longer keep its subjects in slavery, transforms them into docile intellectuals patterned after Western literary fashions which besides, is another more subtle form of bastardisation.

The quote exposes the politics of an essentialist identity that is formed around opposites, coloniser versus colonised, a "conquering nation" versus a conquered one, masters versus slaves, originals versus imitation, and agents versus passives and nobles versus bastards.

Obi Wali joins the chorus of the exponents of nativist languages linking nativism to advancement: "the whole uncritical acceptance of English and French as the inevitable medium for educated African writing is misdirected, and has no chance of advancing African literature and culture" (qtd in *Decolonising the Mind* 24).

In the Irish context, Douglas Hyde in his lecture "The Necessity of De-Anglicising Ireland"[3] "delivered to the Irish Literary Society in November 1892" which "led within a year to the foundation of the Gaelic league, a movement for the preservation of Irish" (Kiberd, *Inventing Ireland* 140) voices his fears of losing the Irish language. According to him, such a loss will shatter all hopes of the restoration of the "Irish race" and the "Gaelic nation" as the Irish will find themselves "despoiled of the bricks of nationality" namely their "language, traditions, music, genius, and ideas".

Though the nativists' calls are benevolent in their intentions, the fanatic clinging to the pure language of the natives in a now-hybridised community is very intricate if not impossible. The danger is that the nativists will always seek a pure past, a pristine language and heritage that existed so to speak in the pre-colonial times, reducing the polyvocality of the moment back into the too-familiar, too-reassuring fictions of the old days. Besides, in these calls, the all-too-omnipresent danger is the imitation of the coloniser's logic of binarism and therefore the embracing of what they claim to refute. Ania Loomba brilliantly captures the idea that in "the process of exposing the ideological and historical functioning of such binaries, we are in danger of reproducing them" (104).

The practice of writing in the language of the coloniser, however, is deemed justifiable and even national for writers who believe in the inevitable reciprocity by which the experience of the colonised is bound to that of the coloniser. No matter how ironically Thiong'o refers to this idea as "the fatalistic logic", the share of the coloniser in the making of the present of the colonised is undeniable. Chinua Achebe, for example, points to the possibility of writing about African experience in English: "I feel that the English language will be able to carry the weight of my African experience. But it will have to be new English, still in full communion with its ancestral home but altered to suit new African surroundings".[4] Gabriel Okra speaks about varieties of English: "There are American, West Indian, Australian, Canadian and New Zealand versions of English. All of them add life and vigour to the language while reflecting their own respective cultures. Why shouldn't there be a Nigerian or West African English which we can use to express our own ideas, thinking and philosophy in our own way?" (qtd in *Decolonising the Mind* 9).

Back to the Irish context, the situation is complex for "the Irish writer [who] has always been confronted with a choice. This is the dilemma of whether to write for the native audience – a risky, often thankless task – or to produce texts for consumption in Britain and North America" (Kiberd, *Inventing Ireland* 136). For Yeats, the situation seems the most complicated of all because of his Anglo-Irish background. He confesses: "the English language in which I think, speak and write...everything I love has come to me through English; my harted tortures me with love, my love with hate. I am like the Tibetan monk who dreams at his initiation that he is eaten by a wild beast and learns on working that he himself is eater and eaten" (SCP 263).

Yeats, though aware of the Anglo-Irish crisis of identity does not believe that English as a language prevents the articulation of a national identity. Although he sees eye to eye with Hyde on what makes up a genuine nationality, namely the restoration of Gaelic games, music, traditions and heroes mentioned in the latter's lecture, he wonders whether placing the Irish language at the centre of Irishness makes of English-speaking Ireland "a nation of imitators" without "the power of native initiative and alive only to second-hand assimilation":

> Is there, then, no hope for the de-anglicising of our people? Can we not build up a national literature, which shall be none the less Irish in spirit from being English in language? Can we not keep the continuity of the nation's life, not by trying to do what Dr. Hyde has practically pronounced impossible, but by translating and retelling in English, which shall have an indefinable Irish quality of rhythm and style, all that is best in the ancient literature? Can we not write and persuade others to write histories and romances of the great Gaelic men of the past, from the son of Nessa to Owen Roe, until there has been made a golden bridge between the old and the new. (Yeats, UPI 255)

O' Brien discusses Yeats's peculiar notion of deanglicisation that consists of writing about Irish themes in English and believes that "Yeats is offering a way out of the closed system of essentialist Irishness" (130). This leads to his encompassing description of Yeats as "the Anglo-Irish, English-speaking deangliciser of Ireland" (135).

Yeats's project of deanglicisation, then, consists of endowing his English verse with an Irish spirit, imbuing it with Irish rhythm and style and introducing great Gaelic men of the past. It becomes, therefore, clear that Yeats employs English to carry what he used to call the "Irish subject", Yeats succeeds not in reversing the hierarchy English/Gaelic but in asserting that "a self could only awaken by an act of hybridisation" (Kiberd, *Inventing Ireland* 165). Yeats's intense engagement with Irish old spirits by reporting, narrating, composing, unearthing, rediscovering and reviving the heritage of his people within the confines of the English language helps the emergence of a new "mode of expression" which "was nothing other than the search for a national style" (Kiberd, *Inventing Ireland* 116) and an intelligent exploitation of the creative possibilities of the language. The word *style* for Yeats is highly connotative both aesthetically and politically; their very fusion is what enables "the idea of a nation" (Yeats, *Autobiographies* 364).

Yeats's practices amount to what is described by Ashçroft in *The Empire Writes Back* as "abrogation or denial of the privilege of 'English' [which] involves a rejection of the metropolitan power over the means of communication [and] appropriation and reconstitution of the language of the centre, the process of capturing and remoulding the language to new usages, marks a separation from the site of colonial privilege" (37). He continues: "Appropriation is the process by which the language is taken and made to 'bear the burden' of one's own cultural experience, or, as Raja Rao puts it, to 'convey in a language that is not one's own the spirit that is one's own.' (Rao 1938: vii)" (38).

The late Yeats moves a step forward from the simplistic form of appropriation and starts an enterprise of shattering old forms of dramaturgy by incorporating Japanese Noh techniques in an English-speaking Irish national theatre allowing the breakthrough of a new context, a post-imperial writing.

The enterprise is carried on extraordinarily by James Joyce who founds new narrative modes that use international English rather than English English or Irish English permitting the emergence of a cosmopolitan identity. If the national literature is but a conflict between English/ the language of the coloniser and the native language of the colonised, then Joyce's literature affords an open and free space in which the relation between the two is simultaneously enacted in the text and absent from the text jumping not only from the traditional narratives that conceive the encounter of the coloniser and colonised as antagonistic but from the more tolerant approach that sees the coloniser and the colonised as mutually constitutive to a revolutionary stance that positions the coloniser and the colonised in a universal and cosmological system.

The issue of language is directly addressed in *A Portrait* where Stephen ponders over his ambivalence towards the English and native language alike. When conversing with the English dean of studies at his university in English, he ponders:

> The language in which we are speaking is his before it is mine. How different are the words *home*, *Christ*, *ale*, *master*, on his lips and on mine! I cannot speak or write these words without unrest of spirit. His language, so familiar and so foreign, will always be for me an acquired speech. I have not made or accepted its words. My voice holds them at bay. My soul frets in the shadow of his language. (Joyce, *Portrait* 146)

Stephen's soul that "frets in the shadow of" English is akin to Yeats's being "eaten" by the English language. Both writers as colonised subjects acknowledge a deep-seated unrest with the use of a language that is not theirs, yet at the same time working within that language to invent a tradition. Stephen in an attempt to fight the hegemony of the English dean, "this courteous and vigilant foe" (Joyce, *Portrait* 146), uses the word "tundish" that the latter has "never heard of" instead of "funnel" which is common in the imperial English (Joyce, *Portrait* 145). As a matter of fact, "Irish was for [Joyce] no longer a feasible literary medium, but a means whereby his people had managed to reshape English, to a point where their artists could know the exhilaration of feeling estranged from *all* official languages" (Kiberd, *Inventing Ireland* 331). Joyce celebrates hybridity in language and culture because it reflects the hybrid reality of modern Ireland.

Language besides religion and nationality "are nets flung at [the soul of a man born in Ireland] to hold it back from flight" (Joyce, *Portrait* 157). Joyce, like Stephen, his autobiographical character, "shall try to fly by those nets" (*Portrait* 157) "using for [his] defence the only arms [he] allow[s] [him] self to use –silence, exile and cunning" (*Portrait* 191). Silence invokes observation and contemplation but above all it is an abstention from speech, from a specific language per se. Exile in the Joycean philosophy is particularly interesting. His novel *Ulysses*, for example, when about Dublin is written in exile, namely in Trieste, Zurich and Paris. Linguistically speaking, Fritz Senn coins the word "Lexile" to refer to "displacement or foreigness or salient oddity… on the lexical aspect" (137). Senn details multiple techniques that Joyce uses to exile language such as deviant terms, traces of origin, aberrant catalogues, textual transfers, black holes and others.[5] Chief among lexiles, however, is the juxtaposition of different world languages undermining the centrality of the English language but also of other languages. Senn writes:

> Stephen Dedalus is fond of recondite or foreign words, in "Proteus" particularly: German (nacheinander, nebeneinander), Latin (iniuria patiens), Italian, Greek (adiaphane, euge), French (Zut, nom de Dieu), Gipsy, cant, etc. They are plug-ins

> from alien, often remote, areas. In groping for the most appropriate verb, Stephen tries out a series in English, German/Yiddish, French and Italian: "She trudges, schlepps, trains, trascines her load" (U 3.392), aiming for the best effect. (141)

Cunning in a linguistic context may be equated with Senn's notion of lexile because tampering with language is a dexterous skill that Joyce masters very well. Eugene O'Brien points to Joyce's transformation of "William Shakespeare" into "Patrick W. Shakespeare" in *Ulysses*, which he sees as "name ... transformed into trope, with a 'turning away' ... from colonial associations into those of the post-colonial" (7) and which "is symbolic of Joyce's project, namely the redefinition and pluralisation of Irish identity" (7). O'Brien later concludes that "Joyce sees the nominal troping of Patrick W. Shakespeare as a liberation from that sterile Irish-English binarism, and as a displacement of the language of empire into the empire of language" (8). Of course, Joyce's literature is abundant of lexiles and cunning, which services as a testimony to Joyce's cosmopolitanism.

The loss of the native language, therefore, is not a fact to be lamented, it rather demonstrates the capacity to profit from the loss in producing new narrative modes, in allowing traditionally-competing narratives to some degree to mingle and to even a greater degree to annul each other and be part of a universal and cosmopolitan system. It has granted post-colonial writers the possibility of experimenting with the language of the other, an experimentation whose multifarious techniques can invest the post-imperial language with extraordinary aesthetic and political power. Paradoxically, losing the native tongue marks a new departure for post-colonial literature that cuts with colonialist form of discourse catapulting its writers into the forefront of the modernist movements, into the modern age, into the age of globalisation.

Works Cited

Achebe, Chinua. 'The African Writer and the English Language', *Morning Yet on Creation Day*, London: 1975.

Ashcroft, Bill, Gareth Griffiths and Helen Tiffin, *The Empire Writes Back: Theory and Practice in Post-colonial Literatures.* London and New York: Routledge, 2002.

Diop, David. "Contribution to the Debate on National Poetry," *Présence Africaine* 6, 1956.

Fanon, Frantz. *The Wretched of the Earth*, translated from the French by Richard Philcox. New York: Grove Press, 2004.

Hyde, Douglas. "The Necessity of De-Anglicizing Ireland", *The Revival of Irish Literature: Addresses by Sr Charles Gavan Duffy, KCMG, Dr. George Sigerson, and Dr Douglas Hyde.* London: T. Fisher Unwin, 1904, 117-161, Web, 27 Aug. 2015.

Joyce, James. *A Portrait of the Artist as a Young Man.* GB: Wordsworth Classics, 1992.

Kiberd, Declan. *Inventing Ireland: The Literature of the Modern Nation.* London: Vintage Books, 1996.

Loomba, Ania. *Colonialism/Postcolonialism, New Critical Idiom Series.* Ed. John Drakakis. London: Routledge, 1998.

O'Brien, Eugene. "The Language of Empire and the Empire of Language: Joyce and the Return of the Postcolonial Repressed", *Enemies of Empire: New Perspectives on Imperialism, Literature and History*, Ed. Eoin Flannery and Angus Mitchell. Dublin: Four Courts Press, pages 160-171.

Senn, Fritz. "Joyce in Terms of Lexile", *James Joyce: The Joys of Exile*, Joyce's Studies in Italy, Ed. Franca Ruggieri, 2018.

Thiong'o, Ngugi. *Decolonising the Mind: The Politics of Language in African Literature.* Great Britain: Pen to Print, 1986.

Yeats, W. B *Yeats: Selected Criticism and Prose*, first published 1964 (London: Pan Classics, 1980).

......., *Autobiographies*, ed. William H. O'Donnell and Douglas N. Archibald (New York: Scribner, 1999).

27

The Subaltern in Sara Suleri's *Meatless Days*

Nilim Mohan

Women narratives have created a revolution throughout the world. In the literary canon they too have managed to earn a dominant position. Through their narratives they protest against the assigned roles and beliefs of the society towards women. Throughout history men are considered superior and women inferior. The postcolonial era did not usher any change in the attitudes of the society towards women. They were given the same treatment as they were treated during the colonial period. In the minds of men women can only be housewives, mother or some inferior roles. So a kind of response was needed. This response came in the form of feminists in literature. Women are not victims, they are warriors – this is the motto of every feminist writer in literature. These feminist writers with the progress of time have been able to create a space for women in literature. They have always tried to depict a positive sketch of women in literature. Apart from keeping women confined only within the restricted spheres of society, these feminists have elevated a women's position beyond that and have shown them as admirable and praiseworthy persons. Some of the notable feminists are Mary Wollstonecraft, Jane Austen, Aphra Behn, Mary Astell etc. Literature serves as one of their best ways to resist and defend their rights against such patriarchal and chauvinistic dominion. In *The Empire Writes Back,* one of the popular works by Bill Ashcroft, Gareth Griffiths and Helen Tiffin which shows the problematic relationship between first world and third world nations. It also shows how the third world writers through their works revolt against the corrupted and manipulative side of the first world nations. Feminist writers too with the help of their writings strike back against the patriarchal violence and retake their identities from which they have been stripped and deprived of. As one of Maya Angelou's popular saying goes "I am no bird and no net ensnares me. I am a free human being with an independent will."

Sara Suleri one of the remarkable writers hailing from a Pakistani background has well depicted the traumas of identity, immigration and the aftermaths of colonialism in her works. Her works very well reflects the fact that though the colonial period is over, its evils are still inherent in the minds of people. Her most notable works are *Meatless Days, The rhetoric of English India* and *Boys will be Boys: A Daughter's Elegy.* Her works are interesting in the sense that they are a intermingling of public and private life. Her works can be called as a critical insight into the minds of people. The characters in her works are not ordinary people, each of them are unique and represents a certain virtue. *Meatless Days* (1989), which can be called as one of Suleri's memorable works is an exploration of vivid minds and different periods of history. The autobiography contains striking parallels of Suleri's personal life with some major historical events such as The Shimla Agreement of 1972, the rise and downfall of Zulfikar Ali Bhutto (the fourth President of Pakistan) and some religious upheavals such as the islamisation of Pakistan. The autobiography too portrays the life of Pakistani women during the postcolonial times. It presents a perfect critique of the patriarchal mindset that is still present in the life of a modern day Pakistan. Suleri's autobiography deals with the life of Suleri and her family members – her grandmother, father, mother, and her sister Ifat and her little brother Irfan. The autobiography begins with a chapter entitled "Excellent Things in Women" in which the first sentence is "Leaving Pakistan was of course, tantamount to giving up the company of women" (Suleri 1). Through this sentence Suleri expresses a sense of displacement and longing for her motherland. As we all know, Suleri was a diasporic writer who was born in Pakistan and had her education in both London and Lahore, she is well aware of the traumas of immigrants. This trauma is well expressed through the character of her mother suffered a cultural turmoil in her personal relationship. As she was of a welsh background she felt the lack of social space with her husband and her eldest son. Her husband, Suleri's father too neglected her and didn't give any prime importance to her. Suleri's father in the early part of her autobiography is shown as an obedient patriarch of the household. But as the story progresses, the reality comes to the forefront that he actually considers every woman as an afterthought. The relationship between Suleri's father and mother is shown as the coloniser and colonised. Suleri's sister Ifat too becomes a pathetic character. Ifat initially revolted against the patriarchal opinions of Pakistan but ultimately she had to submit to her husband. As Suleri I one of her line quotes "There is no women in the third world" (Suleri 45). The narrow mindset of society towards women is also well reflected in Suleri,s lines how her sisters "conceived at the drop of a hut and kept popping babies out of delight" (Suleri 67). The character of Halima, the cleaning woman paid a heavy price of losing her son. It can be said that the society of that time only views the role of woman only as a mother, house wife or a submissive character. This aspect can be related to the subaltern in Gayatri Chakravarti Spivak's one of famous essays *Can the Subaltern Speak?* According to Spivak a subaltern refers to an inferior class or person judged on the basis of race, class, gender. Suleri's father almost degrades her mother to the class of a subaltern. Suleri's mother never spoke any word against her father's views. She remains as a subaltern. The same can be said in regard to Suleri's grandmother, Dadi. She was a woman who despite having all lost everything. After doing everything she didn't receive the care and love she expected. She is shown as a pure, religious, devoted woman about whom nobody cares a bit. Spivak in her essay also puts forward the concept of other. According to Spivak the notion of other always remains; there's no pure or true another, the other always exists in relation to the discourse that would name it as other. Suleri's mother, sister and her grandmother becomes the other in the household. Also we can relate these dichotomies in Frederic Jameson's essay *Third World Literature in the era of Mutinational Capitalism.* This essay offers a critical enquiry into the relations between first world and third world nations. As the first world nations exploit the third world nations, similarly patriarchy expoits the relationship between man and women. Man is first world and women are third world as per the rules of society. Also the lines "My reference to a place where the concept of woman was not really part of an available vocabulary" (Suleri 34) shows the role of a nation in framing identities. Suleri also laments over the fact that even though the colonial period is over, its imprints are still felt. However Suleri too offers resistance against such manipulative beliefs through her autobiography. For example Dadi's comments on the attitude of Suleri's father towards his family members "Men! There is more goodness in a women's little finger than in the benighted minds of men" (Suleri 120) sarcastically mocks the corrupted system of patriarchy. Also Suleri through her own character in her autobiography recreates the image of independent women. Suleri despite suffering all such traumas manages to break such shackles of confinment and emerge successful. She praises her mother who "was prepared to extend the courtesy of change to her daughters" giving them a chance to reform and progress. Though Dadi is shown as a pitiable character, Suleri admires her nature and whose presence is felt by Suleri throughout her life, even after Dadi's death. As Dadi's death coincided with the death of Zulfikar Ali Bhutto, it symbolised the change in Suleri's life. On one side Suleri portrays her characters as subaltern and on the other side she presents them as fighting subalterns. Suleri through her autobiography deconstructs the whole notion of the word subaltern. There is no subaltern, these are merely constructs or manmade structures.

True to the title Meatless the identity of women has become like a piece of meat which has been mashed and gnawed upon by the jaws of patriarchy. Sara Suleri reconstructs and frames the identity of post-colonial women through her work which indeed makes her a notable feminist. Her autobiography is a wonderful narration of history, self-exploration and response. As in the opening lyrics of Home, a wonderful song by artists Jordan Schor and Harley Bird sings "These roads intersect, on each one I reflect. These lines ride my story. These places change me, each one replacing like night into morning." Suleri through her glimpses and experiences has become strong in her decision to choose the course of life. She has managed to create a home for the marginalised, victimed and the subaltern. Her autobiography *Meatless Days* is a voice for the subaltern.

Works Cited

Suleri, Sara. *Meatless Days*. Penguin Books. 1989

Spivak, Gayatri. "Can the subaltern speak?"'. Cary Nelson and Lawrence Grossberg: 1988

Jameson, Frederic "Third World Literature in the Era of Mutinational Capitalism". Duke University Press. 1986

28

Trails Back to the Past: an Assessment of Women's Past in Pre and Post-independence Era with Special Reference to Bengal

Angana Bose

The issues of women are always centrifugal to the core issues of human society. Rather, the issue has some lurid aspects that only provides embargo towards their progression into different spheres of life. This paper encompasses and also analyses their status during the colonial era and their evolving roles in different dimensions in the post-colonial period. If we start with the British – India, the status of women was no better than a subject to His Master. The very word 'subservience', 'subdue', sub-ordinate', could only relate their circumstances with what they went through in the colonial India. The deep-laid belief of 'Sati', that plagued the whole women society, had to be ironed out anyhow. It is very interesting point to note that Burdwan had a long tradition of Sati. Except for Hughly, amongst all British districts in India Burdwan had the highest instance of satis recorded.

The nineteenth century social reform mainly found on the problems like Sati, female infanticide, child marriage, female illiteracy and no sanction to widow remarriage. The British served as beacon of hope through social reforms who tried to root out all the evils and they were successful in their attempt. Widow Remarriage Act 1856, Age of Consent Act 1891, and Abolition of Sati 1929, were passed on that time to serve out as a nostrum. "It took Raja Ram Mohan Roy nine years to convince the colonial authorities that there was no mention of Sati in the Hindu Scriptures. Ishwar Chandra Vidyasagar dedicated his life to widows' remarriage and was able to get 60 widows remarried at a time when such marriages had to be solemnised under police protection and when such no couples used to be ostracised by society." (Panjini 28)

Colebrooke's essay in *Asiatic Researches*, on the duties of a Faithful Hindu Widow, here, Colebrooke quotes from a Sanskrit source as the ritual preparation: "Having first bathed, the widow dressed in clean garments, and holding some cusa grass, sips water from the palm of her hand. Bearing cusa and tila (seasame), she looks toward the east or north, while the Brahmana utters the mystic word Om". (Colebrooke 206)

Colebrooke ends with a description by an unidentified witness, from quoting various Sanskrit texts: "Adorned with all jewels, decked with minimum and other customary ornaments, with the box of minimum in her hand, having made puja, or adoration to the Devatas (gods), thus reflecting that this life is nought: my lord and master to be was all, – she walks round the burning pile; she bestows jewels on the Brahmanas, comforts her relations, and shows her friends the attention of civility, while calling the Sun and the elements to witness, she distributes minimum at pleasure; and having repeated the Sancalpa (Samkalpa). (Samkalpa, meaning in this context, a vow or declaration of the widow to burn herself with her deceased husband.) Proceeds into her flames; these embracing the corpse, she abandons herself to the fire, calling Satya! Satya! Satya!" (Colebrooke 214-15)

The status of women in Bengal was rather low, lower than that of their sisters in Europe and America. Almost all women within the age of 10 years were either married off or widowed and majority of the women were illiterate and worked in the fields. Women from higher strata of society lived most of their lives in segregated antapurs (inner-houses). They had no formal education with few exceptions that they formed part in the public life. In urban areas, poor women from lower echelon of society engaged as domestic or as prostitutes, more fortunate ones worked as dancing girls or singers.

The history of most gender relevant law reform in India during the colonial period has been a tussle for determining the contours of the public and the private. On one hand, national politics centred round the private sphere as a sphere of autonomy for the Indian male, which itself was a product of the colonial construction of the Indian space. On the other hand, reformist interventions through legislations scrutinised all the problems of the private. Most of the reforms took place in India and were expressed through legislation and concerned with the lives of the women in the private sphere but had little impact on the amelioration of the women's actual lives. Moreover, internal conflict within England over the issues of women's rights to make family and reproductive decisions spilled over into Indian reforms because of the India's consolidated presence in the British imagination of the pre and post-colonial periods.

There were tussles over the gaining of power between colonial authorities, native elites British feminists in order to define an authentic Indian tradition and culture as well as the proper parameters of gender within England and India. What is most notable, however, is that while British feminists and the colonial authorities were running to the defence of the Indian women to protect her from Indian men, they could not see her as an autonomous individual. The entire colonial mission embarked upon the righting the wrongs of Indian women, a group never consulted and never viewed as able to construct its own identity.

There can be no doubt that The Maiden Tribute played a role in the reform movement in India in order to make alteration in the Age of Consent Act. In 1891, an Age of Consent Bill was introduced to raise the age of consent from ten to twelve. The bill raised a controversy over the death of a child – bride of ten or eleven who was killed by a brutal sexual encounter with her thirty-five year old husband. However, the Age of Consent Bill had been opposed vehemently by the natives, because it directly interfered with the rights of native male over their wife.

While the Age of Consent mostly centred over the issue of marriage, in England, there was a debate on prostitution that had been formed by it. And vividly, it was not concerning over the welfare of the child-bride in India as legislation against child marriage was not passed until 1929, nearly forty years later. The issue was with the English aristocratic male license, while the issue in India was with the Colonial interference in the sexual relations, of a husband and his child-bride.

Abortion was not regulated in India during the pre-colonial period. But, induced abortion became illegal in India, in the nineteenth century, unless "medically indicated to save the life of a pregnant woman", (Jesani and Iyer 2591) as governed by the Indian Penal Code and the Code for Criminal Procedure. Performing miscarriage with an intent to terminate the pregnancy and without taking note to save the life of the pregnant woman would lead to punishment, including the mother herself. Although, illegal abortions were routinely conducted, as in England, which had an adverse effect on maternal mortality. Abortion, was legalised in India by the Medical Termination Pregnancy (MTP) Act of 1971. This Act was virtually a copy of 1967 English law, giving the same therapeutic and eugenic grounds for an abortion. And the law passed with essentially no dissent.

There was significant progress in the sphere of female education pioneered by Begum Rokeya, from behind the purdah. Founder of the Anjuman-e-Khawateen-e-Islam (Islamic Women's Association), she believed that, reform is much needed, particularly for women, and had also of the view that parochialism and excessive Conservatism were principally responsible for the relatively slow development of Muslims in British India. The ardent supporter of female education, Begum Rokeya established a girls' school in Kolkata, Sakhawat Memorial Girls' High School after the name of her husband, Sakhawat Hussain, after his death.

The organisation Anjuman-e-Khawateen-e-Islam, worked at the forefront of the fight for women's education and employment. Its members vouched for women's legal and political rights, backed women's attendance at school, gave shelter to orphans, offered legal and financial assistance to widows. It was the cornerstone of the feminist movement in Bengal, and paved the way for vibrant and political progressive feminist movement.

If we move forward to post-independence era, the status of women was about to reach to its culmination due to its manifold dimensional character. The facet of progression can vividly be expressed through the landmark judgment of Supreme

Court in Shah Bano case (1985), where a Muslim Woman named shah Bano fought for his maintainance after her divorce with her husband. Taking refuge to Muslim Personal Law, her husband refers to Iddat period (waiting period for a woman must observe after the death of her husband or divorce before she can marry another man. The period is usually for three months after either of the two instances. In case the women are pregnant, the period carries on until the childbirth.) That only provides for maintainance after divorce. However, she filed a petition u/s 123 of the Code of Criminal Procedure, 1973 which brought a man under obligation to provide for his wife during the marriage and after divorce too if she isn't able to fend for herself. Supreme Court, with taking all under its consideration, gave orders for Shah Bano under Criminal Procedure Code. For its part, the apex court increased the maintainance amount. Later on, shah Bano withdraw the maintainance claim she had filed.

In another landmark judgment, Supreme Court acquired praise from different corners to its distinction for its verdict on Sabarimala issue (2018). The age-old custom of Sabarimala temple bars the women within the age bracket of 10-50 from entry into the temple due to their menstrual hygiene which directly conflicts with the sancity of the temple and also with practice of Hindu religion. A petition was filed before Supreme Court which mentioned that it was fully in violation of the Fundamental Rights of women that bans entry of women to the temple. Later on, Supreme Court, in its verdict, said that temple gate should be thrown open for all the ages of women. But now, the verdict is still under review before Supreme Court.

Supreme Court, again, in its verdict spoke volume of the daughters that they have equal birth-right to property. It will have a retrospective effect as the amended Hindu Succession Act, gives daughters equal rights to ancestral property. The substituted Section 6 of the Hindu Succession Act, 1956 bestowed the status of 'Coparcener' upon a daughter born before or after the amendment in the same manner as a son. (Coparcener is a person who has a birth right to parental property). The Supreme Court overruled its earlier 2015 decision as the right to coparcenary of a daughter is by birth, it is not necessary that the father should be alive as on Sept.9, 2005.

Works Cited

Mukherjee, A. "Sati as a social institution in Bengal, in *Bengal Past and Present*". (1975).

Paanjini, Manoj. "Ideological Progression of the Women's question in Colonial India" (1820-1947).

Colebrooke, *Asiatic Researches.*

Colebrooke, Asiatic Researches, pp. 214-15.

Chakrabarty, U. *Condition of Bengali women, around the second half of the nineteenth century*, Calcutta, 1963.

Kapur, Ratna. *Erotic Justice: Law and the new politics of post colonialism* (2005).

Borthwick, Meredith. *The changing role of Women in Bengal:* 1849-1905. (1984).

Kosambi, Meera. "Gender Reform and Competing State Controls over Women: The Rakhmabai Case" (1884-1888), in *Social Reform, Sexuality and the State*, Patricia Uberoi ed. 1996.

Rajan, Nalini. "Personal Laws and Public Memory," *Economical and Political weekly*, pp. 2653, 2654-55 (2005).

Mukherjee, Susmita. *Using Legistative Assembly for Social Reform: The Sarada Act of* 1929. (2006)

Hirve, Siddhi. *Policy and Practice*, Dec. 2003.

Jesani, Amar & Iyer, Aditi. "Women and Abortion, Economical and Political Weekly", pp. 2591 (1993).

Menon, Nivedita. The Impossibility of "Justice". Female Foeticide and the Feminist Discourse on Abortion, in *Social Reform, Sexuality and the State.*

Jahan, Mitali. "Begum Rokeya: A trailblazer in Women's Rights", www.dailystar.net., 16.04.2021

Notes on the Contributors

1. **Dr. Shraddha Dhal** is working as a Faculty Associate in the School of Humanities, KIIT Deemed to be University (Institute of Eminence), India.
2. **Dr. Swagata Bhattacharya** is a Post-Doctoral Fellow in the Department of Comparative Literature, Jadavpur University, India.
3. **Jalendra Phukan** is a current Research Scholar in the Department of English at Sikkim University, Gangtok.
4. **Yacine Mohamed** BELGUENDOUZ is a translator/ interpreter (English, French, and Arabic), journalist and poet from Algeria.
5. **Dr. Amandeep Rana** is working as Head of Post Graduate Department of English at JC DAV College Dasuya (Hoshiarpur) in Punjab (affiliated to Punjab University, Chandigarh).
6. **Abhijit Maity** is a lecturer in the Department of English and Cultural Studies at Mahishadal Girls' College affiliated to Vidyasagar University.
7. **Manidip Chakraborty** is an Assistant Professor in the Department of English of Bhairab Ganguly College, West Bengal State University.
8. **Shreyosee Chattopadhyay** is a U.G. student of English Literature in Presidency University, W.B.
9. **Manik Mandal** is working as a State Aided College Teacher at Egra S. S. B. College, Egra, Purba Medinipur, West Bengal.
10. **Abhilasha Phukan** is working as an Assistant Professor in the department of English (Head) in BRM Govt Model College, Assam.
11. **P.K. Smitha** is an Assistant Professor at MGGAC Mahe.
12. **Shivani Sharma** is pursuing her PhD from Sharda University.
13. **Giangthuiliu Gonmei** is a final year student at Christ (Deemed to be University) doing her Masters in English with Communication Studies.
14. **Bame Jude Thaddeus Tomnyuy** is a PhD research candidate in the Department of English at the Faculty of Arts, The University of Bamenda, Cameroon.

15. **Mohonlal Patra** is currently working as a State Aided College Teacher (SACT I) in the Dept. English at K.D College of Commerce & General Studies, Midnapore.
16. **Dr. Rafraf Shakil** is an Assistant Professor at Sharda University. **Mehak Fayaz** is a Ph.D. scholar at Sharda University.
17. **Amitava Das** is an English teacher at Kachimuha junior high school.
18. **Manashi Singh** is a second-year MA in English student from Christ University's Humanities and Cultural Studies Department.
19. **Kalyan Pattanayak** is a Research Scholar in Department of English, Seacom Skills University, West Bengal, India and a Lecturer in Department of English, Ghatal Rabindra Satabarsiki Mahavidyalaya, Vidyasagar University, West Bengal, India.
20. **Animesh Biswas** is a State Aided College Teacher (Category-I) at Dumdum Motijheel College.
21. **Priya Samni** is a Masters student at Christ University, Bangalore.
22. **Mridul C Mrinal** is an Assistant Professor, PG Department of English, MES KEVEEYAM College, Valanachery, Malappuram, Kerala.
23. **Dr. Manisha Mishra** works as Assistant Professor of English, Rama Devi Women's University, Bhubaneswar.
24. **Mouna Benhaddou** is a PhD researcher and a teacher of English.
25. **J S Anantha Krishnan** is a poet, critic, translator, and orator and has authored eight books. He is currently Junior Research Fellow at the Department of English, Sri Sankaracharya University of Sanskrit, Kalady, Kerala.
26. **Dr. Fedya Daas** holds a Ph.D. from the University of Letters, Arts and Humanities, Manouba, Tunis.
27. **Nilim Mohan** is a Research Scholar at Dibrugarh University.
28. **Angana Bose** is a Research Scholar in English literature in Basic Sciences and Humanities, Rajiv Gandhi Institute of Petroleum Technology, Jais, Amethi, Uttar Pradesh.

Index